Charles Foster Kent, Frank Knight Sanders

The Messages of the Later Prophets

Charles Foster Kent, Frank Knight Sanders

The Messages of the Later Prophets

ISBN/EAN: 9783337813475

Printed in Europe, USA, Canada, Australia, Japan

Cover: Foto ©Lupo / pixelio.de

More available books at **www.hansebooks.com**

The Messages of the Bible

THE MESSAGES OF THE LATER PROPHETS

ARRANGED IN THE ORDER OF
TIME, ANALYZED, AND FREELY
RENDERED IN PARAPHRASE

BY

FRANK KNIGHT SANDERS, PH.D.
Woolsey Professor of Biblical Literature in Yale University

AND

CHARLES FOSTER KENT, PH.D.
Professor of Biblical History and Literature in Brown University

LONDON
JAMES CLARKE AND COMPANY
13 AND 14 FLEET STREET, E. C.
1899

Copyright, 1899, by Charles Scribner's Sons
for the United States of America

Printed by The Caxton Press
New York, U. S. A.

PREFACE

This volume completes the arrangement and analytical paraphrase of the prophetic writings of the Old Testament begun in the *Messages of the Earlier Prophets*. The hearty response of the public to that volume has encouraged the authors to continue and finish their task.

We cannot expect in a work like this to avoid criticism. Opinions differ widely regarding the exact dates to be assigned to particular prophetic addresses. Many will be led, for reasons that seem fair and convincing, to differ from the authors in regard to the proper setting of certain passages. Such candid criticism is only helpful and contributory to the desired result of establishing the true history of prophecy. This is the goal of modern scholarship. It is not of supreme importance to determine whether Isaiah, the son of Amoz, or one of his spiritual disciples, wrote chapters 24 to 27 of the book that bears his name; the one needful task is to ascertain the proper position of their contents in the development of Old Testament revelation. The authors have adopted the conclusions embodied in this volume after repeated and minute consideration of the data. While not infallible, it

Preface

may be said that conclusions which in the main agree with those of such careful scholars as George Adam Smith, Kirkpatrick, Driver and Nowack cannot be regarded as without a reasonable foundation.

Three remarks may help to prepare the reader to appreciate the point of view of the authors in a rearrangement of the prophetic material which otherwise might impress some readers as unduly radical and even reckless. In the first place, as was intimated in Vol. I. (pp. 12, 84), the principle of arrangement is strictly historical. Every passage is arranged chronologically according to the period to which it refers. In no other way can the student of prophecy be enabled to estimate the progress of revealed truth. The fragmentary condition (see Vol. I., pp. 11-14) of the majority of the prophetic books and the absence of dates or clear chronological data compel the scholar to rest his final judgment on the authority of tradition and mere juxtaposition, or else upon a careful analysis and comparison of the subject-matter of a passage. The latter seems to be the only sure criterion. It is open to revision, but not to rejection.

Again the prophetic writings, historically studied, gain wonderfully in clearness, force, significance, and spiritual impression. The reader puts himself into the situation of the prophets, catches the glow of their convictions, and climbs the sublime heights of their hopes. He forgets the writers in their messages and comes face to face, not

Preface

with the mouthpiece of Jehovah, but with his living word. The messages of the prophets thus become communications for to-day and for all times.

We may be permitted to add that a paraphrase knows no partisanship. It should be without color. This volume may prove useful even to those who hesitate to accept the historical conclusions of its authors. Their chief aim has been to render into expressive English the exact thought of each prophetic paragraph. The explanatory headings indicate the interpretation which is deemed to be on the whole the truest and most helpful.

To the Reverend Samuel B. Sherrill, who has reviewed this volume in manuscript, we are indebted for valuable suggestions.   F. K. S.
                                                                           C. F. K.

CONTENTS

INTRODUCTION

PAGE
I. THE CHARACTERISTICS OF EXILIC AND POST-EXILIC PROPHECY 3
II. THE DECADE BEFORE THE FINAL FALL OF JERUSALEM AND ITS TWO GREAT PROPHETS 11

EZEKIEL, THE PRIEST-PROPHET OF THE EXILES

I. THE PROPHET AND HIS PROPHECIES 19
II. THE IMAGINATIVE ELEMENT IN EZEKIEL'S PROPHESYING 23
III. THE PROPHET'S CALL AND COMMISSION (1 : 1 to 3 : 21)
   1. The Vision of the Divine Presence (1 : 1-28) . . . 28
   2. Jehovah's Message of Mingled Discouragement and Cheer (2 : 1 to 3 : 11) 29
   3. The Prophet Appointed as a Watchman 30

PREDICTIONS OF EZEKIEL CONCERNING THE CERTAIN FATE OF JERUSALEM AND JUDAH

I. SYMBOLIC PROPHECIES OF THE COMING OVERTHROW OF CITY AND LAND (3 : 22 to 7 : 27)
   1. The New Method of Prophetic Work (3 : 22-27) . . 35
   2. Symbolic Representations of the Fate About to Overtake Jerusalem (4 : 1 to 5 : 17) 35
   3. The Certain Devastation of the Land of Israel (6) . 38
   4. The Doom of the Nation (7) 39

ix

Contents

                                                             PAGE

II. THE VISION OF THE SIN OF JERUSALEM AND ITS CONSEQUENCES (8 : 1 to 12 : 20)
   1. The Shameless Idolatry of Jerusalem (8) 40
   2. Its Inevitable Consequences: Destruction of the People by Sword and Fire and the Departure of Jehovah (9 to 11) 42
      (1) A Slaughter of the Idolatrous Inhabitants Decreed (9 : 1-11)
      (2) The City to Be Set on Fire (10 : 1-7)
      (3) The Identification of the Cherubim with the Living Creatures (10 : 8-22)
      (4) The Departure of Jehovah from the Deluded City (11)
   3. The Certain Exile of King and People (12 : 1-20) . 45

III. THE MORAL NECESSITY OF JUDAH'S DESTRUCTION (12 : 21 to 19 : 14)
   1. The Popular Scepticism Supported by False Prophets (12 : 21 to 13 : 23) 46
   2. The People Idolatrous beyond Pardon (14) . . . 47
      (1) Jehovah cannot Answer Stubborn Idolators (14 : 1-11)
      (2) The Nation Not to Be Saved by a Few Good Men (14 : 12-23)
   3. Jehovah's People a Worthless Vine (15) 48
   4. The Moral History of the Israelitish Race (16) . . 49
   5. The Consequences of Zedekiah's Breach of Faith (17) 51
   6. The Principles in Accordance with which God Exercises Judgment (18) 52
   7. The Sad Fate of Judah's Rulers (19) 53

IV. FINAL PROPHECIES OF JUDGMENT (20 to 24)
   1. The Secret of Jehovah's Past Dealings with His People (20 : 1-44) 54
   2. Jehovah's Avenging Sword (20 : 45 to 21 : 32) . . 55
   3. The Indictment of Jerusalem (22) 57
   4. The Two Unfaithful Wives of Jehovah (23) . . . 58
   5. The Tidings of the Siege of Jerusalem (24) . . . 59

Contents

PAGE

PROPHECIES OF OBADIAH AND EZEKIEL AGAINST FOREIGN NATIONS

I. THE LONG-EXPECTED CATASTROPHE 63

II. OBADIAH'S DIATRIBE AGAINST EDOM
   1. Edom's Hereditary Relations with Judah 67
   2. Edom's Apparent Triumph to be Reversed (Obadiah 1-21) 69

III. THE STAND-POINT OF EZEKIEL'S FOREIGN PROPHECIES 72

IV. THE PREDICTIONS OF EZEKIEL AGAINST FOREIGN NATIONS (25 to 32)
   1. Prophecies against Judah's Immediate Neighbors (25) 74
   2. Prophecies against Phœnicia (26 to 28) 75
     (1) The Coming Destruction of Tyre (26)
     (2) A Dirge over her Downfall (27)
     (3) Tyre's Opportunity and Well-deserved Fate (28: 1-19)
     (4) The Fate of Sidon (28: 20-26)

   3. Prophecies against Egypt (29 to 32) 79
     (1) Egypt to be Humbled to the Dust (29: 1-16; 30: 1-19)
     (2) The Pharaoh to be Crippled (30: 20-26)
     (3) Egypt the Fallen Cedar (31)
     (4) Egypt's Coming Desolation (32: 1-16)
     (5) The Dirge for the Dead (32: 17-32)
     (6) Egypt to be Nebuchadrezzar's Reward (29: 17-21)

JEREMIAH'S MESSAGE TO THE JEWISH FUGITIVES IN EGYPT

I. THE REMNANTS OF THE JEWISH NATION IN THE LAND OF EGYPT 87

Contents

	PAGE
II. PREDICTIONS AND SOLEMN WARNINGS (43 : 8 to 44 : 30)	
1. The Coming Conquest of Egypt by Nebuchadrezzar (43 : 8-13)	91
2. The Certain Fate of Those Unfaithful to God (44 : 1-30)	92

EZEKIEL'S MESSAGES OF COMFORT TO THE EXILES IN BABYLONIA

I. THE SUPREME NEED OF PROPHETIC MINISTRATION . 97

II. PROPHECIES OF PROMISE AND CHEER (33 to 39)
  1. The Prophet Appointed to Announce Israel's Possible Future (33) 99
  2. The True Ruler of Israel (34) 101
  3. The Certain Restoration of Israel's Land (35 to 36) 102
     (1) Edom's Usurpation to be Severely Punished by Desolation (35)
     (2) Judah to be again a Fertile and Populous Land (36 : 1-15)
     (3) Jehovah's Motive for Restoration (36 : 16-38)
  4. The Revivified and United People (37) 104
     (1) The Vision of the Nation's Resurrection (37 : 1-14)
     (2) The Symbol of its Unification (37 : 15-28)
  5. Jehovah's Final Triumph (38 : 1 to 39 : 24) . . . 106
  6. Restored and Purified Israel (39 : 25-29) 108

EZEKIEL'S VISION OF THE RESTORED HEBREW STATE

I. THE CHARACTER AND IMPORTANCE OF THE VISION . 111

II. THE DETAILS OF THE VISION
  1. The New Sanctuary on Mount Zion (40 to 43) . . 115
     (1) Its Gateways and Outer Court (40 : 1-27)

Contents

PAGE

  (2) The Inner Court (40 : 28-47)
  (3) The Temple and its Adjuncts (40 : 48 to 41 : 26)
  (4) Other Buildings of the Inner Court (42 : 1-14 ; 46 : 19-24)
  (5) The Whole Temple Area (42 : 15-20)
  (6) The Return of Jehovah to His Abode (43 : 1-12)
  (7) The Great Altar and its Consecration (43 : 13-27)

2. Ordinances Regarding the Temple (44 to 46) . . 121
  (1) The Use of the Outer Eastern Gateway (44 : 1-3)
  (2) The Functions of the Levites and the Priests (44 : 4-31)
  (3) The Apportionment of their Land (45 : 1-7)
  (4) The Rights and Duties of the Prince (45 : 8-17; 46 : 16-18)
  (5) The Stated Offerings (45 : 18 to 46 : 15)

3. The Renewing and Allotment of the Land (47 ; 48) 126
  (1) The Fertilizing Stream from the Temple (47 : 1-12)
  (2) The Boundaries of the Land (47 : 13-20)
  (3) The Allotment of the Land (47 : 21 to 48 : 29)
  (4) The Holy City (48 : 30-35)

SONGS OF EXULTATION OVER BABYLON'S APPROACHING FALL

I. THE RISE OF CYRUS 131

II. THE DATE AND AUTHORSHIP OF ISAIAH 13 : 2 to 14 : 23 ; 21 : 1b-10 ; JEREMIAH 50 : 1 to 51 : 58 134

III. PREDICTIONS OF THE FALL OF BABYLON (ISA. 21 : 1b-10 ; 13 : 2 to 14 : 23 ; JER. 50 : 2 to 51 : 58)
  1. The Vision of Coming Overthrow (Isa. 21 : 1b-10) . 137
  2. Jehovah's Judgment upon Babylon (Isa. 13 : 2 to 14 : 23) 138
  3. Retribution for Babylon and Restoration for Israel (Jer. 50 : 2 to 51 : 58) 140

Contents

PAGE

THE MESSAGE OF THE GREAT PROPHET OF THE EXILE (Isaiah 40 to 55)

I. The Authorship, Unity, and Date of Isaiah 40 to 55 149

II. The Ideal of Service Presented in the Portraits of the True Servant of Jehovah . . . 155

III. The Certainty and the Reason of the Release of Jehovah's People (Isa. 40 to 48)

1. The Proclamation that Deliverance is at Hand (40 : 1-11) 160
2. Deliverance Certain because the Deliverer is Omnipotent (40 : 12-31) 161
3. Jehovah's Irresistible Purpose to be Realized through Cyrus (41 : 1-7, 21-29) 163
4. A Personal Message of Encouragement to Jehovah's Servant Israel (41 : 8-20) 164
5. The Contrast between the Ideal Servant whom Jehovah Seeks and the Actual Israel (42) 166
6. The Preparation and Mission of the True Israel (43 : 1 to 44 : 5) 169
7. Jehovah's Incomparable Superiority to the Gods of the Heathen (44 : 6-23) 171
8. The Real Purpose and Significance of the Conquests of Cyrus (44 : 24 to 45 : 25) 173
9. The Contrast between the Deities of Babylon and Jehovah of Israel (46) 175
10. A Taunt Song Commemorating the Impending Fall of Babylon (47) 176
11. A Recapitulation of Preceding Arguments, Culminating in an Exhortation to Flee from Babylon (48) 178

Contents

PAGE

IV. THE REDEMPTION OF ISRAEL AND OF MANKIND TO BE SECURED THROUGH SELF-SACRIFICING SERVICE (49 to 55)
  1. The Preparation and Mission of the True Servant of Jehovah (49 : 1-13) 180
  2. Jehovah's Assurances that he will Surely Restore his People (49 : 14 to 50 : 3) 181
  3. The Experiences of the True Servant of Jehovah and their Lesson (50 : 4-11) 183
  4. Words of Exhortation and Encouragement in View of the Coming Restoration (51 : 1 to 52 : 12) . . . 184
  5. The Mission and Future Vindication of Jehovah's Martyr Servant (52 : 13 to 53 : 12) 187
  6. Renewed Promises of Restoration (54) 189
  7. A General Invitation to Participate in the Blessings of the Coming Restoration (55) 191

THE MESSAGES OF HAGGAI AND ZECHARIAH TO THE TEMPLE BUILDERS

I. THE FIRST TWO DECADES OF THE PERSIAN PERIOD 197
II. THE PERSONALITY OF HAGGAI AND ZECHARIAH . . 204
III. THE OPENING ADDRESSES OF THE PROPHETS (HAG. 1 : 1 to 2 : 9 ; ZECH. 1 : 1-6)
  1. Haggai's Call to Begin Building the Temple (1 : 1-11) 206
  2. Haggai's Encouragement to the People to Persevere (2 : 1-9) 207
  3. Zechariah's Lessons from the Past (1 : 1-6) . . . 209
IV. HAGGAI'S SERMONS IN CONNECTION WITH THE LAYING OF THE FOUNDATION OF THE TEMPLE (2 : 10-23)
  1. The Former Uncleanness of the Community and the New Promise of Blessings (2 : 10-19) 210
  2. The Revival of the Natural Hopes of Israel (2 : 20-23) 211

Contents

	PAGE
V. ZECHARIAH'S VISIONS OF COMFORT AND PROMISE (1 : 7 to 6 : 8)	

    1. The Prophet's Use of the Vision as a Form of Teaching 212

    2. The First Vision—The Report of the Angelic Horsemen (1 : 8-17) 216

    3. The Second Vision—The Destroyers of the Four Horns (1 : 18-21) 217

    4. The Third Vision—A Picture of Restored Jerusalem (2) 218

    5. The Fourth Vision—The Vindication of the Community and Re-establishment of the Priesthood and Nation (3) 219

    6. The Fifth Vision—The Temple Candlestick and its Sources of Supply (4) 221

    7. The Sixth Vision—The Winged Volume (5 : 1-4) . 223

    8. The Seventh Vision—The Woman within the Ephah (5 : 5-11) 223

    9. The Eighth Vision—The War-Chariots of Jehovah (6 : 1-8) 223

VI. THE SYMBOLIC RE-ESTABLISHMENT OF THE HEBREW MONARCHY (6 : 9-15)

    1. The Messianic Hopes Centring Upon the Prince of the House of David 224

    2. The Crown Prepared for the Head of Zerubbabel (6 : 9-15) 226

VII. ZECHARIAH'S PRACTICAL EXHORTATION AND ENCOURAGING PROMISES (7, 8)

    1. The Judean Community at the Close of 518 B. C. . 227

    2. The Mistakes of the Past and the Glorious Possibilities Awaiting Jehovah's People (7, 8) 230

Contents

PAGE

ANONYMOUS REFORM SERMONS

I. CONDITIONS WITHIN THE JUDEAN COMMUNITY BEFORE THE INSTITUTION OF THE PRIESTLY LAW OF EZRA 237

II. THE MESSAGE OF THE BOOK OF MALACHI
1. The Date and Authorship of the Prophecy 240
2. The Evidence of Jehovah's Love and his People's Shameful Ingratitude (1 : 2 to 2 : 16) 244
3. The Judgment which Jehovah will Speedily Institute (2 : 17 to 4 : 6) 249

III. MESSAGES OF DENUNCIATION AND EXHORTATION (ISAIAH 56 to 59)
1. The Date and Authorship of Isaiah 56 to 59 . . . 252
2. The Selfishness and Incapacity of the Leaders of the Community (56 : 9 to 57 : 2) 255
3. The Shameful Heathen Practices of the Samaritans (57 : 3-13ª) 256
4. False and True Worship (58 : 1-12) 257
5. The Social Crimes of the Community its Undoing (59 : 1-15ª) 258
6. Jehovah's Impending Judgment (59 : 15ᵇ-21) . . . 260
7. Promises to the Faithful (57 : 13ᵇ-21 ; 58 : 13, 14) . 260
8. Promises to Proselytes and Eunuchs (56 : 1-8) . . 262

PROPHETIC MESSAGES OF ENCOURAGEMENT IN CONNECTION WITH THE WORK OF · NEHEMIAH AND EZRA

I. THE HISTORICAL BACKGROUND OF ISAIAH 34; 35; 60 : 1 to 63 : 6 ; 65 ; 66
1. The Rebuilding of the Walls of Jerusalem and the Institution of the Priestly Law 265
2. The Date of the Individual Prophecies 272

Contents

	PAGE
II. THE GOSPEL PROCLAMATION TO THE JEWISH RACE (Isa. 60 to 62)	
1. The Song of Glorified Zion (60)	275
2. Jehovah's Promise of Salvation and Restoration (61 : 62)	277
III. VENGEANCE UPON THEIR GUILTY FOES AND DELIVERANCE AND HONOR FOR JEHOVAH'S PEOPLE (Isa. 34; 35; 65; 66)	
1. The Opposite Fates Awaiting the Samaritans and Jews (65 : 1 to 66 : 5, 17, 18a)	279
2. Jehovah's Judgment upon the Hostile Nations and Especially upon Edom (63 : 1-6 ; 34)	281
3. The Glorious Era to Follow Jehovah's Judgment (35)	283
4. The Establishment of Jehovah's Universal Kingdom (66 : 6-16, 18b-24)	283

THE MESSAGE OF JOEL

I. THE DATE AND THEME OF JOEL'S PROPHECY	289
II. THE COMING OF THE LOCUSTS AND JEHOVAH'S JUDGMENT (1 : 1 to 2 : 17)	
1. The Locust Devastation a Summons to National Repentance (1)	293
2. Only Repentance will Avert the Terrors of Jehovah's Day (2 : 1-17)	296
III. THE PROSPERITY, INSPIRATION AND DELIVERANCE FROM ENEMIES IN STORE FOR JEHOVAH'S PEOPLE (2 : 18 to 3 : 21)	
1. The Return of Prosperity (2 : 18-27)	298
2. The Inspiration and Deliverance of all true Israelites (2 : 28-32)	299
3. The Judgment of the Heathen Nations (3)	300

Contents

MESSAGES OF DOUBT AND HOPE FROM THE CLOSE OF THE PERSIAN PERIOD

PAGE

I. THE LAST HALF-CENTURY OF PERSIAN RULE . . . 305

II. THE LITERATURE OF THE PERIOD 308

III. THE WAILS AND PETITIONS OF THE DISTRESSED JUDEAN COMMUNITY (ISA 63 : 7 to 64 : 12)
   1. Jehovah's Past Acts of Deliverance (63 : 7-14) . . 310
   2. A Cry for Deliverance from Present Calamities (63 : 15 to 64 : 12) 311

IV. THE FINAL JUDGMENT AND THE ESTABLISHMENT OF JEHOVAH'S KINGDOM (ISA. 24 : 1-23 ; 25 : 6-8 ; 26 : 20 to 27 : 13)
   1. The Overthrow of Existing Conditions (24 : 1-23) . 313
   2. The Nature of Jehovah's Universal Rule (25 : 6-8) . 315
   3. Jehovah's Unceasing Care for His People (26 : 20 to 27 : 13) 316

V. SONGS OF THANKSGIVING TO JEHOVAH (ISA. 25 : 1-5 ; 25 : 9 to 26 : 19) 317

MESSAGES OF PROMISE TO THE JEWS IN THE GREEK PERIOD

I. THE AUTHORSHIP AND HISTORICAL BACKGROUND OF ZECHARIAH 9-14 323

II. THE COMING OF ALEXANDER AND THE PRINCE OF PEACE (9)
   1. The Advance of the Conqueror (9 : 1-8) 326
   2. The Conflict with the Greeks (9 : 13-17) 327
   3. The Promised Prince of Peace (9 : 9-12) 328

Contents

	PAGE
III. THE FORTUNES OF THE JEWS UNDER THEIR GREEK MASTERS (10-13)	
1. Jehovah's Indignation against Their Tyrants and His Restoration of His People (10)	328
2. The Rejection and Murder of the Good Shepherd (11 : 4-17 ; 13 : 7-9)	330
3. The Certain Deliverance of Imperilled Jerusalem (12 : 1 to 13 : 6)	332
IV. THE JUDGMENT OF THE HEATHEN AND EXALTATION OF JERUSALEM (14)	334

THE MESSAGE OF THE BOOK OF JONAH

I. THE DATE OF THE BOOK OF JONAH	339
II. THE PURPOSE AND METHOD OF THE AUTHOR OF THE BOOK	341
III. THE STORY OF JONAH AND ITS MORAL	
1. The Prophet's Refusal to Proclaim Jehovah's Message to the Heathen (1 : 1-3)	348
2. The Discipline, Conversion and Deliverance of Jehovah's Rebellious Messenger (1 : 4 to 2 : 10)	349
3. The Repentance and Pardon of the Ninevites (3)	352
4. The Contemptible Jealousy of his Prophet Contrasted with Jehovah's Infinite Compassion (4)	353

APPENDIX

I. THE MESSIANIC ELEMENT IN PROPHECY	357
II. THE RELATION BETWEEN THE MESSAGES OF THE PROPHETS AND THAT OF JESUS	367
III. BOOKS OF REFERENCE	374
INDEX OF BIBLICAL PASSAGES	381

INTRODUCTION

INTRODUCTION

I

THE CHARACTERISTICS OF EXILIC AND POST EXILIC PROPHECY

The beginning of the Babylonian exile marks a turning point in both Hebrew prophecy and history. The changed conditions and the new point of view gradually developed a new type of prophet. Although the distinctions between the earlier or pre-exilic and the later or exilic and post-exilic prophets must be interpreted broadly, they are clearly defined. The aims of the two groups of teachers were the same, but the earlier spoke to a nation and dealt with the problems of an independent state, while the latter addressed the scattered, discouraged, often oppressed remnants of their race. For a time the Jews were a people with only a past and a future; and, during all the period represented by the later prophets, they were subject to foreign masters, so that they had little or no political life of their own. Hence the prophets ceased to be active statesmen who de-

Introduction   *Messages of the*

voted much of their time and thought, as did Isaiah and Jeremiah, to political questions. Instead, they reviewed the past history of their race to learn the lessons which it taught, or else devoted themselves to drawing up, as did Ezekiel, the constitution of an ideal state.

The practical problems of social life, also, were no longer as important and insistent as they had been before the exile, so that, although they are not ignored, they are only treated incidentally. In the writings of the later prophets—as Professor George Adam Smith has well said—"political and social righteousness largely gives way to divine righteousness." A people with few or no responsibilities could not by them be taught of God. Consequently great social teachers like Amos and Micah found few successors in the later period.

The prophets also began to study intently the writings of their predecessors and to draw from them most of their conceptions of Jehovah, so that they brought to their race no startlingly new theological ideas, as did Amos and Hosea.

If the later prophets were not great statesmen nor social teachers nor original theologians, they were true to the prophetic ideal, and devoted themselves to the vital questions of their age. In so doing they attained their real greatness, and performed for their race and mankind an inestimable service.

When the Hebrew state fell in ruins, the prophets

turned from the nation to the individual. Hitherto they had addressed him only as an integral part of the commonwealth; henceforth he possessed an importance in himself, apart from the community to which he belonged. Thus the very circumstances which limited the activity of the prophets opened to them an unlimited field, which only the great prophet of Nazareth fully occupied. The daily interests and achievements of the people whom they addressed were personal, not national. If they were to meet the practical needs of their contemporaries they were obliged to a certain extent to turn pastors, and to deal more with religious and ethical than with political and social questions. In so doing they touched the hearts of the masses more closely than did the earlier prophets. They were also more intimately acquainted with the interests and problems of the individual. Consequently, like the sages and psalmists, they speak more directly to the heart of mankind, and their messages have an obvious and perennial application independently of their historical setting.

Since the life of Judaism constantly centred more and more about the temple at Jerusalem and its ritual, the later prophets, instead of denouncing mere ceremonialism as meaningless, as did the earlier, held up the hands of the priests. They devoted much of their attention to emphasizing the importance of the temple and its service. In this they were doubtless influenced by the irresistible tendency of their age. They also recognized that conditions had radically changed since the days of Amos and Isaiah, and that a ritualistic type of religion was essential to the preservation of the integrity and faith of their race amid the terrible trials and temptations to which it was being subjected.

Sacerdotalism and legalism also supplied more and more the religious needs of the people, so that the demand for the work of the prophets became less and less. In the law the teachings and principles presented by the earlier prophets were preserved and enforced upon the minds of the people in a form which even the most obtuse could appreciate. Before the exile that process had begun, and at the great reformation of Josiah the Book of Deuteronomy was publicly adopted as the law book of the nation. This continued to be the constitution of the community in Palestine until Nehemiah and Ezra introduced at the great assembly a still more detailed and expanded code. Until that time, questions not settled by the Book of Deuteronomy were referred, in accordance with its injunctions, not to the prophets, but to the priests, for an authoritative decision (Hag. 2:11-13; Mal. 2:7).

Although the prophetic order continued to exist, and apparently to count a considerable number of prophets and prophetesses among its ranks (Ezra 5:1; Neh. 6:12, 14; Zech. 7:3; 13:4), it no longer enjoyed the prestige of earlier times. The prophets were ever conscious of the sceptical attitude of their hearers and recognized

Later Prophets Introduction

that their predictions would not be fully believed until they had been at least partially fulfilled (compare for example Zech. 2:11^b; 4:9^b; 6:15^b). To the pernicious influence of the false prophets, who in the name of Jehovah had often misled the people, undoubtedly is largely due the destruction of the old popular confidence in the word of the man of God.

No prophetic bishops appear, like Isaiah and Jeremiah, to have maintained for a long period over the community a growing influence. The personalities of the later prophets were also less prominent and distinct. The names of only five or six of them have been preserved. Of the private life of the prophets we know practically nothing. Ezekiel alone gives us a few details respecting himself.

The date of a large part of the prophecies can be determined only by a study of the internal evidence. They represent bursts of prophetic eloquence evoked by great crises or problems. After their messages had been sent forth, the prophets quickly retired to the seclusion of private life. In all probability many of the prophecies were originally issued anonymously. A large proportion of them are clearly the product of study rather than the spontaneous expressions of the public orator. Haggai alone is an exception. The simple directness of his sermons is in striking contrast to the carefully developed, elaborate style of most of the later prophetic writings.

The weird apocalyptic symbolism which in general characterized the exilic and post-exilic prophecies is evidence that their authors had ample time to develop the form as well as the content of their messages.

The fact that they were anonymous undoubtedly explains why later editors appended them to older prophecies, in the language or thought of which they detected certain points of likeness. The same tendency that led them to associate the entire proverbial literature with the name of Solomon (Prov. 1 : 1) influenced them to join many of these anonymous fragments to the original sermons of Isaiah, the prince of prophets.

The task of assigning the different sections of such a book as that which bears the name of Isaiah to their original historical setting is difficult; but the resulting gain in vividness, clearness, and reality abundantly rewards the trouble. Then the historical allusions which the different prophecies contain contribute, not to the confusion, but to the lucid interpretation of their meaning. They also in turn throw much light upon the development of that life and thought which was the background of the New Testament.

The writings of the later prophets group themselves about certain critical epochs in the history of their race, such as the beginning and the close of the Babylonian exile, the rebuilding of the temple, and the reforms of Nehemiah and Ezra, with long intervening periods of

Later Prophets — Introduction

silence. Although the names of only five or six prophets are known, the work of at least twelve can be distinguished. The impartation of their divinely given message, not the enhancing their own fame, was their first and sole aim. The names of the earlier prophets were preserved because the performance of their mission brought them prominently into public life and their acts and words became a part of their nation's history. The later prophets spoke more privately to their race. Fortunately men preserved the message long after the man who delivered it had been forgotten. The history of exilic and post-exilic prophecy emphasizes the great fact that it is acquaintance with the truth itself, not with the one who imparts it, that is essential.

The later prophecies are more general and contain less local and nationalistic elements than do the earlier. The experiences of the exile also forced the prophets to recognize the existence of other nations as a part of Jehovah's creation and as objects of his love. Gradually the missionary ideal found expression in their writings, and there rose before their enlightened vision the outlines of a universal kingdom in which all nations were to join in the worship of Jehovah. In the moments of their darkest distress this vision cheered and inspired them. The realization that their race was to be herald of that kingdom impelled them to spare no effort to prepare their countrymen for the exalted service.

Saddened and discouraged by the sins of mankind, they frequently proclaimed the necessity of a great world-judgment, in which the wicked would be condemned and the righteous vindicated. As they recognized the pitiable weakness and incapacity of the living representatives of the chosen people, they did not lose hope in the coming kingdom of God on earth; but they looked more and more for its realization through supernatural intervention. Thus the prophetic horizon was extended far beyond the boundaries of Palestine, of the ancient Semitic world, and of the earth itself. Dimly certain prophets also began to see the kingdom, not of flesh, but of spirit, which lay beyond the gates of death.

By their broad outlook, by their regard for the individual, by their lofty ideal of service, by their universalism, and by their firm belief that Jehovah would surely establish his kingdom on earth, the later prophets completed the otherwise incomplete work of the earlier. Their messages are all the more precious and luminous because they come from the night of their nation's humiliation and distress, and voice mankind's inspired faith, not in the seen, but in the unseen.

II

THE DECADE BEFORE THE FINAL FALL OF JERUSALEM AND ITS TWO GREAT PROPHETS

The year 597 B. C. was of great significance to the Hebrew people politically and religiously. The obstinate, unreasoning confidence of his people Israel in Jehovah's protection which had blinded the eyes of the majority in Judah to the ruin toward which the state was drifting, and made them deaf to the earnest appeals of Jeremiah, began to be shaken, when the flower of the nation was transported to Babylon. Instead despair and a passionate desire to see the vengeance of God upon their bold, even contemptuous, oppressors took possession of their minds. The times seemed to them to be completely out of joint and Jehovah the one at fault. They failed to realize that their misfortunes were wholly due to their own shortsightedness, disloyalty, and corruption, and that nothing but a thorough-going national reformation could restore them to divine favor. They counted themselves rather the victims of adverse political and religious conditions. They considered their triumphant restoration to Judah the only possible way in which Jehovah's character could be vindicated and their own great wrongs righted.

The prospect of an immediate deliverance, however, was

anything but bright. They were completely and helplessly in the power of Nebuchadrezzar, because of the insensate folly and perversity of their late King Jehoiakim and his nobles. Placed on the throne of Judah about 608 B. C. by Pharaoh Necho, he became, by virtue of the crushing defeat which that sovereign suffered at the hands of Nebuchadrezzar two years later, a vassal of the Babylonian king. Under Jehoiakim's sway the kingdom of Judah became a nursery of insurrection and corruption. The young king was thoroughly selfish and incompetent. He dreamed of impossibilities; he was impatient of criticism; he was superstitious and vain. Swayed completely by his likeminded counsellors and resisting the disinterested warnings of Jeremiah, he trusted the promises of the king of Egypt and revolted from Nebuchadrezzar. Such an open defiance of his power could not be overlooked by one who aimed at the absolute sway of the western world. The great king in 597 B. C. marched westward to subdue his rebellious vassal. Before his army had effected the capture of the city of Jerusalem King Jehoiakim died, thus escaping the bitter consequences of his blunder. These were inevitable. In accord with the military policy of the Assyrians and Babylonians, Nebuchadrezzar not only took due vengeance upon the rebellious people and their leaders, but also made another formidable rebellion impossible by removing those who would naturally instigate and give it strength. As soon

Later Prophets Introduction

as the hapless young King Jehoiakin, three months a nominal sovereign, was forced to surrender, he, his attendants, officials, warriors, and thousands of his substantial subjects, among others the young priest Ezekiel and probably the youthful Daniel, were transported to Babylonia. The king was placed in confinement; a few were drafted into the service of the great king; the great majority were settled by themselves, not far from the city of Babylon. Here they were free, apparently, to live, undisturbed, a community-life of their own, to engage in industrial occupations, and to make the most of their opportunities. They even held intercourse with those who were left behind in Judah, but any word or act which tended to arouse discontent among those at home was sure to incur severe punishment.

In Judah Nebuchadrezzar had appointed Zedekiah, another prince of the royal Davidic house, to the throne, and had left the kingdom once more to itself, content with having crippled its power for mischief.

For the remaining decade of Judah's history its people were living in these two widely separated and contrasting communities. The Jews in Babylon represented the strongest elements of the race and were compared by the prophet Jeremiah to good figs fit for use (Jer. 24). On them he based all his hopes for the future. The people left in Judah he likened to rotten figs, fit only for destruction. Well might he despair of them, for they gave little heed to his warnings and subjected him to constant persecution. They had no desire to confess, much less to repent of their evil ways, but defiantly persisted in the idolatry which he denounced.

The heart and hopes of Jeremiah were with the other portion of the nation, far away beyond the trackless desert. He saw that the real future of his nation must be achieved through them. He counselled patience and submission, urging them to settle down in quiet and to pursue their normal life (Jer. 29), asserting that the exile would continue at least more than a generation (29:10). That his words were read with respect is indicated by the indignant protest of Shemaiah, a man of standing among the exiles, who wrote to Jerusalem (Jer. 29) urging that his action be rebuked by the ecclesiastical authorities in Judah.

But God had raised up for these lonely and homesick exiles—unhappy in the midst of plenty, impatient under the slight restrictions laid upon them, haunted by the hateful thought that they dwelt in an unclean land—a faithful shepherd in the person of the prophet Ezekiel. He was one of themselves, dwelling in their midst, sharing their experiences, entering into their needs. It was he who held them together, kept alive a spirit of hope, fought their idolatrous tendencies and taught them broader views of the purposes and methods of Jehovah. During the decade between the first captivity and the destruction of Jerusalem, however, his most prominent task was to throw a clear light upon the attitude of Jehovah toward Israel and to assert the absolute certainty of the downfall of the city and state.

For some years Ezekiel uttered no word of which we have record. So far as we know, his ministry began in 592 B. C., five years after the deportation itself. For the latter half of the decade he labored earnestly to prepare his fellow-captives to understand the approaching catastrophe. They still believed that the holy city was inviolable, for there was located Jehovah's holy temple, which he could not allow to be destroyed. Hence Ezekiel's God-given task was to set in a clearer light the true character of the city and land, to indicate that, because of the sins of the inhabitants, Jehovah had abandoned his once-loved sanctuary, and to predict in unmistakable ways the speedy end of city, state, and temple. Every such plain utterance, unpalatable though it was, helped to save some Judean patriots from despair and infidelity when the crushing blow descended. It helped them to understand the great principles of the kingdom of God more clearly, and thus—even at the period when the true prophets had only denunciations and warnings for their hearers—prepared them to appreciate the future work of Israel among the nations.

EZEKIEL, THE PRIEST-PROPHET OF THE EXILES

EZEKIEL, THE PRIEST-PROPHET OF THE EXILES

I

THE PROPHET AND HIS PROPHECIES

A recent writer has said that the prophet Ezekiel has "the most interesting personality in the great group of prophets." He certainly deserves the place among the prophets of highest rank which has been given him. Yet this is not due to our intimate knowledge of his personal history. As in the case of his predecessors, Isaiah and Jeremiah, we do not know the circumstances of his early career nor of his death; it is from the events and utterances of his active life that we must form our conception of the man.

His ministry opened in the fifth year of Jehoiakin's exile (592-3) and continued over twenty years, until the middle of the period of captivity. He describes himself as the son of Buzi (1:3) and a member of the aristocratic priestly caste in Judah. According to Josephus he was carried away from the home-land while only a youth; but many incidental facts indicate that this was mere conjecture on the part of the Jewish historian. The elders in the Babylonian community came to him at his own house for counsel; he even refers to the period of youth (4:14) as somewhat distant. Adding to these the indications of broad culture and of a careful mastery of civil and ritual law and of the historical and prophetic writings of his people, we are led to the conclusion that he was a man of considerable maturity, and that it was partially for that reason that his words carried great weight in the exiled society.

In one important characteristic Ezekiel was more prophet than priest; he was a growing man, a student of life as it unfolded before him. His published sermons are a rich storehouse of the ideas of the age—geographical, historical, legal, ethical, and religious. He even learned much from his Babylonian surroundings of which he made use in planning for the future development of his own people. In many ways, however, he differed from the prophets who preceded him. During the first five years of his ministry he seems, at first glance, to direct his gaze almost wholly toward his native land and its approaching fate, ignoring the community of which he was a part, and failing to exercise the leadership characteristic of the true prophet. But we note, on closer inspection, that he was a prophet in order that he might be a pastor. His declarations regarding guilty Israel were intended to affect the thought and the action of his own community even more than of the men of Judah. His faithful presentations of God's attitude toward Israel was the true enlightening cause of the passive submission of the exiles to their lot and of their gradual participation in the opportunities afforded by Babylonia.

Ezekiel's early training as a member of the order of the priesthood is indicated, not only by the breadth of his culture and by his personal refinement, but also by his respect for priests as a class in the community and particularly by the prominent place which he assigns to them in the future development of his nation (Ezek. 44). His training also suggests the reason why he promptly recognized the necessity of a more exact and far-reaching legal organization of the future state which was so well wrought out by him in the closing chapters of the book. Hence in many ways he was rarely fitted for the much-needed task of anchoring the old ethical standards by new ritual requirements.

The strength and depth of Ezekiel's nature are best revealed, however, by a detailed study of his writings. While his wide acquaintance with the earlier prophets and his particular indebtedness to his immediate predecessor and teacher Jeremiah are very apparent, he was his own master in every way. There is a distinct individuality in his methods as well as in his words. When he sought to make a deep impression upon his neighbors, his messages of judgment against guilty Israel were often prefaced and supported by acted parables of the most impressive sort (4; 5; 12). His surveys of past history were effectively presented in elaborate allegories, which could not be forgotten. His hopes for the future took the form of striking visions (37-48), which served as standing texts for stirring descriptions of the life that was to be.

The book of Ezekiel is readily divided into two great sections, the first twenty-four chapters being devoted to the teachings and actions of the prophet prior to the destruction of Jerusalem. These two divisions of the book have been happily characterized as respectively destructive and constructive. In the latter half of the book a threefold arrangement is noticeable: chapters 25-32, a collection of predictions against various nations; chapters 33-39, a collection of comforting messages to Ezekiel's fellow exiles; and chapters 40-48, the vision of the reconstructed city and sanctuary. This regularity of arrangement exhibits the elaboration, symmetry, and artistic character of the book as a whole. The arrangement, as in the case of other prophetic collections, appears to have been made primarily on a topical rather than chronological basis. This is particularly obvious in the last half of the book. In general, however, the order is also that of original production. The prophetic book of Ezekiel has, without much doubt, come down to us substantially as Ezekiel or some one of his disciples arranged it. Its literary defects, no less than its merits, are of a kind which a man of priestly training would produce. The style, though stately and polished, is often prosaic and full of mannerisms. Ezekiel has no such poetic soul as Isaiah, although he makes frequent use of figures of speech (15; 19; 26, etc.), is fond of plays upon words, and revels in imagery of every description. There is, nevertheless, an element of formalism in the prophet's attitude which is fatal to the choicest lyric productiveness. The book of Ezekiel is to be judged, not by its artistic arrangement, nor by its beauty of detail, but by its breadth of outlook, by its grasp of the true relation between the divine and the human, by its presentation of the possibilities of the future to his disheartened countrymen, and by its inspiring assurances that the times, far from being out of joint, were being directed by Jehovah, and that the Jewish race, by its very misfortunes, was making progress toward the goal ever present to the divine mind.

II

THE IMAGINATIVE ELEMENT IN EZEKIEL'S PROPHESYING

A very characteristic element in the predictions of Ezekiel is his free but careful use of imagery and symbolism. Both are employed by other prophets. Abijah, for example, gives point to his assertion that Jeroboam had been chosen to lead the revolt of the northern kingdom by rending his new mantle into twelve pieces, ten of which he gave to the incredulous overseer (1 Kgs. 11). Isaiah, by walking thinly clad and barefoot (Isa. 20), made a vivid prediction of the threatened captivity of Judah. When Jeremiah wished to impress upon his sceptical audience the destruction which Jehovah was about to visit upon the city of Jerusalem, he dashed an earthen jar to fragments in their presence. By such actions these incomparable preachers enforced their messages. Teaching by symbols not only insured the attention of their hearers and added to the impressiveness of their words, but often conveyed an idea the open expression of which might have been dangerous or inexpedient. Even more constantly do the prophets make use of various forms of imagery to illumine and beautify their addresses. Isaiah's parable which likened Judah to an unfruitful vineyard (5), or Micah's bold series of paronomasias (1: 10–15), by which he announced the approach of danger, illustrate in strikingly different ways this tendency. All other prophets, however, are surpassed by Ezekiel in the use of figurative language. He rarely puts forward an idea without some embellishment. Sometimes he proposes a riddle to his hearers (17), or utters a parable which he also illustrates by a symbolic action (24), or he unfolds an elaborate allegory (16), in each case making the figure of speech a mere means to the end of expressing his message more effectively. But he stands peculiar in his remarkable use of symbolism, especially of the vision, which is a higher form of the same mental tendency. He passes readily from the simpler forms of symbolism, like the metaphor, the parable, and some form of objective action, to the most complex, such as the allegory and the vision.

Ezekiel's visions appear to be carefully worked-out products of his own creative imagination. This is one difference between the inaugural vision of Isaiah and that of Ezekiel. Isaiah conveys effectively his sense of the majesty and holiness of Jehovah, but furnishes little else, while Ezekiel describes with minuteness of detail the appearance of the Divine. Isaiah, in connection with his prophetic activity, makes no further reference to his one vision, but Ezekiel repeatedly describes the divine glory in this form. Thus, whatever may have been the objective impression made upon Ezekiel at the time of his call and at other times, he seems to have leisurely thought out and expressed in literary form what seemed to him an adequate description of the details of the vision. Hence Ezekiel's use of the vision in prophecy is intended to be significant. Every detail must be scrutinized for its meaning.

It is of interest to note the probable sources of the details which enter into such a composite vision as, for example, that of the first chapter of his prophecy. It is a vision of God. The cherubim, wheels, arch, and throne are mere accessories. Some of them are furnished, no doubt, by the current symbolism of Hebrew poetry (Isa. 19: 1; Ps. 18: 9, 10). Others seem to be an elaboration of details already employed by Isaiah in his inaugural vision. Some were probably suggested by the symbolism of Babylonian temples and palaces. Ezekiel freely used suggestions from every available source.

So clear is the literary stamp upon the prophecies of Ezekiel that it is often difficult to determine what the prophet actually did or saw. Did he really lie for months upon his left side to represent the duration of the captivity of the northern kingdom (4)? Was it, on the other hand, a mere parable, not acted at all? Did he, on another occasion, remove all the hair of his head and face (5), and dispose of it by burning and in the other ways prescribed? It is possible, as Professor Moulton suggests, that the real action was very slight, serving as an introduction and illustration of the discourse that followed. Yet we may deem it probable that the prophet, for many years, acted as well as proclaimed his message, even symbolizing in various ways the great thoughts uppermost in his mind.

The finest example of a detailed vision, never meant to be understood as other than ideal, is found in the closing chapters of his book. The prophet fitly crowns his work of consoling and cheering the discouraged exiles and his additional task of creating a new social and religious system by formulating what is at once a bold and brilliant prediction of a return to Judah and of the re-establishment of the state and a notable scheme of organization. This vision is a masterpiece of literary skill and of imaginative power and yet affords clear evidence of being something more.

No careful reader can fail to appreciate the force of Ezekiel's frequent declaration that Jehovah spoke to and through him, when he realizes that through these seemingly prosaic details of organization the prophet formulated a working ideal of religious and social life for the generations yet unborn. Ezekiel was an exceedingly important factor in influencing his people to adopt the new religious point of view, which developed in course of time into Judaistic legalism. For the last results of this development he is not responsible; its helpful and useful features he strongly advocated.

The prophet Ezekiel is thus a connecting link between the old and the new. He loved and understood his nation, but as a close student of her history he saw that her work under the old forms was done. The exile he looked on as a period of transition, a time of preparation for the larger future of which he was fully confident. He believed that Jehovah had revealed to him what the proper development of that future should be, in order to realize the unchanging plans of God, and he gave himself wholly to its ex-

Ezekiel 1:1   *Messages of the*

pression. No prophet had a greater task; none fulfilled it with greater fidelity and success.

III

THE PROPHET'S CALL AND COMMISSION (1:1 to 3:21)

1. *The Vision of the Divine Presence* (1:1-28)

The time and place of the prophet's call (1:1-3)
It was the fifth year of the sorrowful exile of Jehoiakin and his people in far-off Babylonia, when I was dwelling in the Hebrew settlement on the banks of the stream known as the Chebar¹, that Jehovah revealed himself to me and called me to be his prophet. I seemed to see a

The fiery storm-cloud from the north, Jehovah's abode (1:4)
great cloud approaching swiftly from the north, driven by a furious wind. A luminous splendor, which was produced by an inward fire that glowed with the brilliance of polished metal, surrounded the cloud. As I gazed I saw

The four living creatures which support and guard his throne (1:5-14)
within it the forms of four creatures. Each had four faces, that of a man in front, of a lion on the right, of a bull on the left, and of an eagle behind. Each had four wings, two being extended above the heads, the tips touching those of its neighbors on either side, while the other two covered the body. Their limbs, which glistened like burnished brass, were straight and jointless, their feet shaped

¹ A canal in the vicinity of Nippur, running west toward Babylon, mentioned in the cuneiform tablets recently discovered by the University of Pennsylvania expedition.

like the hoofs of a calf. Each had four hands concealed from view by the wings. Since a similar human face was looking outward toward each quarter, they seemed to be always moving straight ahead. In the midst of these creatures glowed the flame, emitting flashes like the lightning[1].

I looked again and saw four similar wheels of the color of topaz, one beside each creature. Each wheel seemed to be double, consisting of two wheels cutting each other at right angles, so that in whatever direction the chariot moved four wheels appeared to be moving thither. The wheels, like the creatures, seemed alive. They were covered with eyes and moved whenever the creatures moved, responding to the same impulse. The wheels which symbolize his constant movement (1 : 15-21) The eyes, symbolizing divine omniscience (1 : 18)

Supported by the heads and outstretched wings of the four creatures was an arch, transparent as crystal. Resting upon this was a throne resembling a sapphire, on which sat a human-like form, bright and radiant as the rainbow. I saw that I was in the very presence of Jehovah himself and fell upon my face in reverence. The throne and its divine occupant (1 : 22-28)

2. *Jehovah's Message of Mingled Discouragement and Cheer* (2 : 1 to 3 : 11)

"Finite mortal," said a voice," arise and hear my message to you." A power divine pervaded my being ; I arose in obedience to the divine summons, and received this com- The prophet sent to disobedient Israel (2 : 1-7)

---
[1] Verse 14 is generally regarded as a gloss.

Ezekiel 2:3 — *Messages of the*

mission: "I am about to send you to disobedient Israel to declare my will. Whether the people listen to you or not, they will eventually recognize your office. In whatever ways they threaten you by word or action making your life a burden, have no fear, but declare unflinchingly the truth.

Assured of divine instruction (2:8 to 3:3)
"Let no sense of weakness or unworthiness lead you to imitate this rebellious people in refusing to do my will. Lo, I will put into your mouth the messages you are to utter. To symbolize this commission, eat this scroll, which represents the oft-repeated messages of distress and woe which you must declare in Jehovah's name." I obeyed, but the bitter words seemed sweeter than honey, symbolizing that in the performance of the task allotted by Jehovah I would find true joy.

Encouraged to be fearless and faithful (3:4-11)
My mission was then made more clear. "You are to have an arduous struggle with unfaithful Israel. Your difficulties will not result from an inability to make your message understood, but from their stubborn unwillingness to obey. Jehovah will help you to be bold and steadfast, and to declare, without fear or favor, your God-given message to the Israelites in Babylonia."

3. *The Prophet Appointed as a Watchman*

The prophet removed to Tel-Abib (3:12-15)
At once I seemed to be lifted up and borne away toward the scene of my prophetic work. A mysterious sound as of rustling wings and moving wheels behind me comforted me by the indication of the ever-active power of Je-

Later Prophets Ezekiel 3:21

hovah¹. I departed, stirred to the heart by indignation at my unrepentant people, and strengthened by a sense of divine guidance. Arriving at Tel-Abib, where I was to begin my work, I sat seven days in silence, reflecting on the work before me. Then Jehovah made known to me that I was to be a watchman to give warning to my people of the crisis now at hand, to turn the wicked from the evil of his way, and to keep the righteous from falling into sin. His function to be that of a watchman (3 : 16-21)

¹ By the change of one letter verse 12 is made to read "when the glory of Jehovah rose."

PREDICTIONS OF EZEKIEL CONCERNING THE CERTAIN FATE OF JERUSALEM AND JUDAH

PREDICTIONS OF EZEKIEL CONCERNING THE CERTAIN FATE OF JERUSALEM AND JUDAH

I

SYMBOLIC PROPHECIES OF THE COMING OVERTHROW OF CITY AND LAND (3 : 22 to 7 : 27)

1. *The New Method of Prophetic Work* (3 : 22-27)

For some time I performed with but little success my ministry of warning and exhortation among the exiles at Tel-Abib. But one day, being bidden to go to a secluded valley, I again seemed to come into the very presence of Jehovah, who had laid his commands upon me. "Depart to your house and abandon this useless preaching. You shall not be permitted in public to utter your warnings to this incorrigible people until I again give you permission. The second vision of the Heavenly Presence (3 : 22, 23) His public preaching to give way to private teaching (3 : 24-27)

2. *Symbolic Representations of the Fate About to Overtake Jerusalem* (4 : 1 to 5 : 17)

Unable to preach with freedom or success, I was encouraged to portray by symbolic actions the sad and certain

Ezekiel 4 : 1

fate which was to come to my beloved city. In these ways I forced the people to give unwilling heed to the messages which they had refused to consider.

The representation of the siege of Jerusalem (4 : 1-3, 7)

On a tablet of clay I drew a sketch of Jerusalem besieged by active enemies. Between me and this pictured city I set up an iron plate, in token of the barrier between Jehovah and his people, and to signify that he was no longer their protector, dwelling in their midst, but their foe.

The symbol of the captivity to endure for a generation (4 : 4-6, 8)

Then I represented in expressive symbol the sore punishment that awaited guilty Israel. For one hundred and ninety[1] days, a day for every year of exile, I laid myself down, as if bound and helpless, on my left side, in token of the penalty visited upon the northern kingdom, and for forty days, representing a generation, on my right side, in token of the fate of Judah.

The prediction of famine and of pollution (4 : 9-17)

While carrying out this symbolic action I was led to portray the extremities to which my people would be reduced. Making an unaccustomed mixture of all available grains with vegetables, and grinding them together into a coarse kind of flour, I prepared a food of which I ate sparingly, taking only a small measure of water.[2] Even this distasteful food I was told to bake publicly with loathsome fuel, in order to drive home to the hearts of all who saw

[1] The reading of this number by the Septuagint in place of three hundred and ninety is very generally accepted as probable.
[2] Half a pound of food, about a pint and a half of water.

me the awful deprivations of the coming siege, and the pollutions of a foreign captivity.

But the fourth symbol was yet more significant. With a sword of keen edge I was to remove my hair and beard, dividing the severed hair into three portions. One third I burned in the fire, representing the inhabitants of Jerusalem about to die of pestilence and hunger during the siege. Another third I cut in pieces with the sword to indicate that as many would perish in battle. The last third I scattered to the winds, since my people were to be dispersed among the heathen. Not all were to perish, but some, after being subjected to purifying judgments, were to be preserved. *The prediction of the threefold disaster impending (5: 1-4, 12)*

And this was the explanation [1] of these symbolic actions. Since Jerusalem, the favored city, the very centre of the earth, has surpassed all nations in deliberate wickedness, not even recognizing and living up to such standards as they maintain, she must be visited with exemplary punishment, so severe that the whole world will be impressed. The horrors of the siege, the distant exile, are but modes of punishment which give expression to Jehovah's righteous indignation because his people have polluted his very sanctuary with idolatrous rites. Jerusalem shall become a laughing stock to hostile nations, a desolation ravaged by *The meaning of the four symbols (5: 5-17)*

---

[1] Most scholars regard, "Therefore shall a fire come forth" (v. 4,) as a gloss, and read, with the Septuagint, "and say to the whole house of Israel."

wild beasts and robbers, an example of the just vengeance of the Almighty.

3. *The Certain Devastation of the Land of Israel* (6)

<small>The land with its guilty inhabitants deserving of devastation (6 : 1-7)</small>

Jehovah also bade me denounce the land of Israel and its idolatries. " O land of mountains, ravines, and villages, whose hill-tops are dotted with altars, obelisks, and idols,[1] wholly unable to protect you in the day of danger, Jehovah's message to you is one of menace. Only a demolition and devastation will cause you to recognize me and give me obedience. In the years to come, when a petty remnant of your people has survived the horrors of invasion and exile, they at least will remember me, and with breaking hearts will sincerely repent.

<small>The remnant shall repent (6 : 8-10)</small>

<small>The present corruption not to be condoned (6 : 11-14)</small>

" But Jehovah can only cherish the utmost horror and detestation of the present wickedness. As the champion of justice he bids me rejoice over the well-merited calamities which are impending. Not one sinner shall escape his wrath. By a judgment which will desolate the land from south to north,[2] defiling every idolatrous shrine, he will manifest his power."

[1] An unknown word, meaning an object of worship.
[2] Properly, " from the Wilderness to Riblah."

4. The Doom of the Nation [1] (7)

Again came the necessity of proclaiming the dread message of approaching doom. "O land of Israel, for your abominations a requital is near at hand. Jehovah can show no pity, for you have shown no inclination to repent. Alas! only calamities are in prospect. The catastrophe draws near.[2] There will be shouting on the hills, but it is the tumult of hostile invasion, not of a vintage festival. For the coming day of doom the avenging rod has blossomed, since those who once were merely violent had become defiantly corrupt. In the day of retribution they shall be stripped of all they hold most dear.[3] All social security will be lost. None will be able to claim his rightful property nor to secure a livelihood by fair means or foul.

"Preparations for defence will be wholly useless; no one will have the courage to resist Jehovah's will. Those who do not perish by sword and famine and disease will be as helpless doves, paralyzed with terror. They shall fling away their treasures of gold and silver as something unclean and unserviceable. Since they have used these as an instrument of idolatry, they shall become the spoil of

The day of requital for the land and its inhabitants approaches (7 : 1-9)

No security for life or property (7 : 10-13)

Defence impossible (7 : 14-18)

Their wealth a spoil (7 : 19-21)

The temple profaned (7 : 22-24)

---
[1] The text of verses 1-9 is in confusion, or else verses 3, 4 and 8, 9 are refrains. Bertholet (*Ezekiel*) regards the original poem as a lyric of eighteen strophes of four lines each.
[2] The Hebrew consists of a play on words, not easily imitated.
[3] Very obscure.

the cruel Babylonians, who shall profane at will the very sanctuary,[1] since it is no longer a fitting abode for God.

<small>Despair because Jehovah has ceased to reveal his will (7 : 25-27)</small>
"Alas! it will be a time of anguish. Repeatedly will calamities overwhelm the land. Every source of revelation—prophet, priest, and sage—will be dumb. Israel's ruler will be utterly dismayed, the people will give themselves up to despair. According to their deeds will it be rendered unto them, that they may learn that Jehovah is their God."

II

THE VISION OF THE SIN OF JERUSALEM AND ITS CONSEQUENCES (8 : 1 to 12 : 20)

1. *The Shameless Idolatry of Jerusalem* (8)

<small>The prophet carried in a vision to Jerusalem (8 : 1-4)</small>
More than a year had passed away after my summons to the prophetic work, and I was receiving in my own house certain rulers of the Jewish community who had come to inquire concerning Jehovah's word regarding Israel, when I suddenly fell into a trance and seemed to see before me a human [2] form, radiant as fire or glistening brass. He took me in a moment's time to Jerusalem and set me down by the northern gate of the inner temple

---

[1] "Make the chain" seems unintelligible.
[2] For the first word "fire" in verse 2 the Septuagint substitutes "a man," improving the sense.

Later Prophets   Ezekiel 8 : 18

court and, lo! I was once more in the presence of Jehovah's glory.

My guide exhibited to me the various idolatries and abominations which were being practised in the very temple itself, the supposed abode of Jehovah. At the entrance I saw an image of Astarte, so defiling his sanctuary that Jehovah could no longer dwell therein. The image insulting to Jehovah within his temple (8: 5, 6)

Passing through the gateway of the court, I found a secret door which opened into a chamber whose walls were covered with symbolic pictures of every kind of creature. Within the room were the principal men of the nation offering incense to these pictures, as if they thought that Jehovah, the true God of their race, had abandoned the land. At one of the outer gateways were women celebrating the rites of the Syrian god, Tammuz. I even saw in the inner court, near the great altar itself, a company of men, their faces turned eastward, adoring the rising sun. Idolatrous rites practised in secret by leading citizens (8: 7-13) Women bewailing Tammuz (8: 14, 15) Sun worshippers (8: 16)

"Mortal one," demanded my divine guide, "can I overlook such abominations as these which flourish unrestrained throughout the land? My people are but mocking me.¹ I must unsparingly chastise them." The certain penalty (8: 17, 18)

¹ A possible meaning of "they put the branch to their nose." The text and interpretation of the passage are very uncertain.

2. *Its Inevitable Consequences: Destruction of the People by Sword and Fire and the Departure of Jehovah* (9 to 11)

(1) *A Slaughter of the Idolatrous Inhabitants Decreed* (9: 1-11)

<small>Executioners summoned to the presence of Jehovah (9: 1-3)</small>

While I was listening he uttered a summons, and six heavenly beings in human form appeared, equipped for the work of slaughter. With them was an officer, who carried in his girdle materials for writing. They halted by the brazen altar, and a voice from the cloud which surrounded

<small>An officer ordered to mark true wo shippers on the forehead (9: 4)</small>

Jehovah's glory ordered the officer to pass through the city and mark the foreheads of all who grieved over its idolatries and bade the others to follow him, and slay without mercy all who failed to receive the mark. They began in my very presence by slaying the idolatrous citi-

<small>All others to be slain (9: 5-7)</small>

zens whom I had seen, but soon passed out into the city, leaving the heaps of corpses to defile the sacred courts. Appalled by the terrible judgment, I cried out, "O Jeho-

<small>All appeals for pardon in vain '9: 8-11)</small>

vah, surely the nation will not be completely destroyed;" but I received the answer, "The people are given over to violence and wrong-doing, because they think I cannot punish them. I will be inexorable."

(2) *The City to Be Set on Fire* (10: 1-7)

This announcement was followed by one no less startling. The officer, who had completed his former task, was commanded to scatter throughout the city glowing coals, taken from the fire within the chariot of God. When he advanced to obey, the whole court seemed aglow with a radiance from Jehovah's presence.¹ A cherub handed him some of the coals and he departed on his mission.

<small>The officer also ordered to burn the city (10: 1-7)</small>

(3) *The Identification of the Cherubim with the Living Creatures* (10: 8-22)

Meanwhile I observed more carefully the supernatural glory before me. I noted the wheels of topaz color, symbolizing the constant activity of God, covered with eyes significant of his all-seeing power.

<small>The wheels, symbolic of activity and insight (10 : 8-13)</small>

While I was gazing the glory departed from the temple and hovered over the eastern gate. The living creatures, which I had formerly seen supporting Jehovah's throne, I now perceived to be the cherubim which guard the very presence of God and uphold his throne.² I realized with increased certainty that Jehovah himself had uttered the message of doom and was about to depart from his polluted sanctuary.

<small>The living creatures seen to be cherubim (10 : 14-22)</small>

(4) *The Departure of Jehovah from the Deluded City* (11)

At the eastern gateway of the temple I saw a throng of men, among whom were two well-known princes, busily

---

¹ Verses 1 and 5 are purposely left without paraphrase because of their uncertainty.
² Cherubim in the Old Testament seem to have these two distinct functions. Compare Ezekiel 28: 14 and Ps. 18: 11.

Ezekiel 11 : 2 *Messages of the*

The band of conspirators at the eastern gate (11 : 1-3) — plotting revolt against Nebuchadrezzar and discouraging peaceful occupations, urging that the city was still strong enough to protect its inhabitants against all invaders. Obeying a prophetic impulse from Jehovah, I said, "O men of Judah, your reliance upon Jehovah's protection and upon the strength of your defences is futile. Your plots

The certain consequences of their folly (11 : 4-13) — only result in filling the city with corpses. But you who hope to escape the consequences of your folly will bear them to the uttermost in the camp of the great king whom you defy." While I was speaking one of the princes died. Horror-stricken by the earnest of what was to be, I humbly prayed that my nation might not be completely destroyed, and I received a message of comfort and hope.

Jehovah's purposes hold good wherever his people are dwelling (11 : 14-21) — "These men of Jerusalem consider that your fellow exiles,[1] scattered far and wide among foreign peoples, are out of reach of my power and cut off from their own land and sanctuary. Great is their mistake, for the faithful exiles can still worship me in their new homes and their punishment shall not always continue. I will gather them and bring them back to Judah. They shall cleanse the land of all abominations, draw close to me and become a docile, obedient people. But those who have given themselves up to idolatry shall receive their just deserts."

With this mingled threat and promise the divine presence seemed to move away from his temple until it rested

---

[1] "The men of thy kindred" (R. V. margin "redemption") probably should be read "thy fellow exiles."

Later Prophets   Ezekiel 12 : 16

on the Mount of Olives. Jehovah had abandoned his beloved city to its doom. My vision ended, and I related what I had seen to the elders. Jehovah compelled to abandon the once holy city (11 : 22-25)

3. *The Certain Exile of King and People* (12 : 1-20)

Despite these plain declarations of Jehovah's purposes, the members of the exiled community stubbornly refused to give them credence. I therefore felt impelled to impress my message regarding Jerusalem upon their minds in a more striking way. Arousing the attention of all by publicly packing such articles as I would need in a hasty flight, I placed the bundle near the city wall. In the night I dug through the wall, and then, in the presence of the wondering bystanders, having blinded my eyes with a bandage, I groped my way through the tunnel, bearing the bundle on my back. When my neighbors inquired the meaning of these strange actions I replied, "Jehovah has appointed me to represent symbolically the certain exile of prince and people. King Zedekiah will prepare for secret flight, but he shall be captured, blinded, and brought in triumph to a city which his eyes shall never behold. His supporters shall be scattered and slain. The few whom Jehovah spares will be an evidence to the world of his righteous character and of the horrible guilt of his people." The need of renewed symbolic preaching (12 : 1-2)
The pantomime of escaping through the wall by night (12 : 3-7)
Its explanation (12 : 8-16)

Again I manifested every sign of terror as I ate my food,

III

THE MORAL NECESSITY OF JUDAH'S DESTRUCTION
(12 : 21 to 19 : 14)

1. *The Popular Scepticism Supported by False Prophets*
(12 : 21 to 13 : 23)

<small>The sceptical attitude of Ezekiel's contemporaries (12 : 21-28)</small>   The unwelcome truth came home to me that, in spite of my repeated warnings, the people were sceptical concerning the realization of the prophecies and careless regarding the future, saying to one another that none of the many predictions of past years were being fulfilled. Accordingly I warned them that the time appointed was at hand and that the sceptics themselves should see the execution of Jehovah's word.

<small>The baneful influence of the false prophets (13 : 1-7, 10)</small>   "Do not wonder that the people are losing their confidence in the prophetic word, for they have been deceived by uninspired prophets, unable to comprehend or proclaim the thoughts of God. Lacking moral insight and convictions, these often predict peace instead of judgment. Like jackals, they can only undermine; they do not help the nation to be strong. While not always intentional deceivers, their words cannot be trusted. Whatever wild

scheme of deliverance is proposed they approve; but their sanction is as valuable as a coat of whitewash on a tottering wall.

"These false religious leaders Jehovah will visit in judgment, for he cannot abide them. He will wholly cut them off from Judah; they shall never again see their native land. To make manifest to all their entire lack of wisdom and foresight, Jehovah will lay prostrate the walls which they pretend to strengthen.   *Jehovah's judgment against them (13: 8, 9, 11-16)*

"Jehovah's righteous indignation is also against the women who follow prophesying as a profession, freely practising divination, thereby dragging his sacred name into disrepute and creating moral confusion. Since they discourage the righteous and embolden the wicked to be defiant, he will put an end to their activity, that all may come to know him as Jehovah."   *A judgment equally necessary against the women who practise divination (13: 17-23)*

2. *The People Idolatrous beyond Pardon* (14)

(1) *Jehovah cannot Answer Stubborn Idolaters* (14 : 1-11)

One day when the elders came to consult me concerning Jehovah's purposes, I saw that they were not honoring him by their lives, but, like the rest of the people, were really idolaters at heart. I therefore told them plainly that no persistent idolater would get an answer from Jehovah except in vigorous acts of judgment.   *The request of the elders refused (14 : 1-8)*

Moreover, if a so-called prophet should respond to the

The fate of a subservient prophet (14 : 9-11) request of idolaters and give them a pretended answer from Jehovah, both they and the prophet would be destroyed together in order that the survivors might thus be influenced to cease from such wickedness and to become in reality his people.

(2) *The Nation Not to Be Saved by a Few Good Men* (14 : 12-23)

The occasion of the utterance In response to the oft-expressed opinion that Jehovah would not destroy his people despite their wickedness, because of the many good men among them, I received the declaration from Jehovah, "If a land deliberately acted so *A wicked land not to be delivered by the virtue of a few of its citizens (14 : 12-20)* as to deserve any one of my great judgments—famine, wild beasts, armed invasion, or pestilence—although there lived in that land such noble and perfectly righteous men as Noah or Daniel or Job, they would not even deliver their own families from my just vengeance; they would save themselves alone.

Jerusalem, least of all (14 : 21-23) "Since Jerusalem has sinned so deeply as to deserve these four judgments at once, how impossible is it for her thus to be delivered. Those who are preserved, however, shall serve to prove the reasonableness of my action."

3. *Jehovah's People a Worthless Vine* (15)

The people often urged, "Are we not Jehovah's vine, planted and nourished by him. Will he destroy his own possession!" To which Jehovah bade me reply, "When

a vine is unfruitful, has it any value in comparison with a | Judah is Jehovah's vine, but unfruitful and hence worthless (15 : 1-5)
tree? If already half consumed by fire, can it be put to
any use? Judah is such a vine, so utterly useless as a
nation that Jehovah can only destroy the fragment which
still remains."

4. *The Moral History of the Israelitish Race* (16)

To bring home to the people the necessity of Israel's | How Jehovah adopted Israel and brought her up in Egypt (16 : 1-7)
destruction, I pictured the continued unfaithfulness of the
nation to Jehovah from the beginning of its history in the
familiar figure of a faithless and ungrateful wife.

Israel was a foundling child of heathenish parentage, | The covenant at Sinai and gift of the treasures of Canaan (16 : 8-14)
uncared for and exposed in a public field to perish. But
Jehovah pitied her and supplied her needs and watched
over her until she grew to womanhood. Then he took
her to himself in lawful marriage, bestowed upon her
costly attire and jewels and gave her delicate fare. All that
wealth could buy was hers, and she became celebrated for
her beauty.

But she soon became unfaithful to her husband, and | Israel's rapid adoption of idolatry (16 : 15-22) Her alliances with other nations and adoption of their religious rites (16 : 23-34)
made use of the gifts with which he had loaded her to attract her lovers. She even sacrificed her children to their
desires, entirely disregarding him who had redeemed her
from her disgraceful fate. Finally, in her shameless and
unbridled license, she allied herself with foreigners, the
Egyptians, the Assyrians, and the Babylonians, enticing
them with gifts to come to her.

Ezekiel 16 : 35

Her appropriate punishment inevitable (16 : 35-43)

What will Jehovah do to a spouse so persistently faithless? He will expose her to shame in the very presence of her lovers; he will take away her ornaments and costly garments of which she is proud, will cause her to undergo painful punishment in the sight of all the people, and thus bring her adulterous career to an end.

Her sins more heinous than those of Sodom or Samaria (16 : 44-52)

"Had you, O Israel," Jehovah declares, "merely followed the example of your Canaanitish mother and your sisters, Samaria and Sodom, you would deserve to suffer their merited fate. Sodom was made to prosper, but in her self-satisfied pride, she forgot her duties to man and God. Samaria, your older sister, deliberately neglected her obligations. Nevertheless, both nations were righteous in comparison with you, for they had less reason to be faithful to me. Hence your punishment must be the greater.

After suitable punishment Jehovah will restore her to Canaan and intrust to her instruction other nations (16 : 53-63)

"In the distant future I will restore the people of Samaria and Sodom as well as you to Palestine, but conditions will then have altered. After having paid the penalty of your own wickedness you will no longer be able to speak of Sodom or Samaria with contempt. Stirred to sincere repentance by the proof of my faithfulness, you will make an everlasting covenant with me, and will become a guardian over these nations which I will place under your protection. Because of my goodness and grace you will then be overwhelmed by mingled regret and gratitude."

5. The Consequences of Zedekiah's Breach of Faith (17)

Word came to the exiled community that Judah had again broken out into open revolt against Nebuchadrezzar. Then the prophet related a parable to show Jehovah's view of this disloyalty. A great eagle of splendid appearance flew to Lebanon, and, plucking the topmost twig of a stately cedar, carried it to Babylon. At the same time he took a cutting which he found in Canaan and planted it under favorable conditions, hoping that it would flourish and become a fruitful vine. The vine, however, instead of contentedly bearing fruit for the eagle who planted it, put forth its runners longingly toward a rival eagle, seeking nourishment from him. What does such a disloyal vine deserve except to be blasted by a wind from the east? *The parable of the great eagle which carried off the cedar twig to Babylon (17 : 1-4) The parable of the two eagles and the dissatisfied vine (17 : 5-10)*

The meaning of the parable is plain. King Nebuchadrezzar carried off to Babylon King Jehoiakin and the princes. He placed Zedekiah on the throne of Judah, taking from him a pledge to be a loyal vassal. Zedekiah has foolishly broken his oath, relying on the support of King Hoph'a of Egypt. When Nebuchadrezzar attacks him the Pharaoh will give no protection. He will be brought a captive to Babylon and his warriors will be scattered as exiles, because he has defied, not only his political chief, but also Jehovah. *The explanation of the first parable (17 : 11, 12) The explanation of the second (17 : 13-19) Zedekiah's punishment (17 : 20-21)*

"Although Nebuchadrezzar's experiment was not a success, the time will come," saith Jehovah, " when I will plant

51

Ezekiel 17 ; 23 — *Messages of the*

Jehovah's purpose for the future (17 : 22-24)
a twig from the cedar on Jerusalem's mountain, where it will become a stately tree, giving shelter to all creatures, towering over all trees. Then shall I be known as the creator and governor of the world."

6. *The Principles in Accordance with which God Exercises Judgment* (18)

The popular discouragement as proverbially expressed (18 : 1, 2)
An oft-repeated proverb, "The fathers have eaten sour grapes and the children's teeth are set on edge," pithily expressed the popular feeling of my countrymen that their calamities were an inheritance from the past and that they were powerless to avert them. I urged that the time had

The prophetic announcement of the moral freedom and responsibility of the individual (18 : 3, 4)
come to give up this despairing attitude, since every man stands in a direct relation to God and is responsible for himself alone. For instance, if a man lives a pure and upright life, observing faithfully his religious and social obligations, taking no advantage of others' weakness or need, he shall live. If such a man has a son who does the

The threefold illustration (18 : 5-20)
reverse, breaking every law of God, that son shall die as he deserves. If, in turn, that wicked son shall have a son who sees his father's wickedness and determines to live a righteous life, he shall not die for the sin of his father, but shall live because of his righteousness.

A man's past will not of itself condemn or save him (18 : 21-29)
Another principle must also be kept in mind. A man's past will not of itself condemn or save him. If a wicked man sincerely repents and lives a righteous life, his transgression will be forgiven and he shall live. If a man who

has been righteous deliberately does evil, his previous goodness shall not avail. Thus men's deeds determine their own fate. Is not this a sound principle of life? Let this thought of the moral freedom and responsibility of man inspire within you, O Israelites, renewed earnestness and obedience. Jehovah takes no pleasure in judgment, but is only striving to lead you into a purer and more normal life.

The reasonableness of Jehovah's ways (18 : 30-32)

7. The Sad Fate of Judah's Rulers (19)

Well may you sing, fellow captives, over the rulers of Judah this song of lamentation [1]:

Judah, the lioness and her two unfortunate whelps, Jehoahaz and Jehoiakin (19 : 1-9)

>How was your mother a lioness,
>   Among the lions,—
>Amid young lions she couched,
>   She reared her whelps.
>And one of her whelps she brought up,
>   He became a young lion.
>And he learned to catch prey,
>   He devoured men.
>Against him the nations cried out,
>   In their pit they took him.
>Away they led him with hooks,
>   To the land of Egypt.

---

[1] The peculiarity of the elegiac line is that it consists of two clauses, the second the shorter of the two, and finishing the line with a mournful, falling cadence. The whole chapter is a poem of which the last few verses are in some confusion.

When the mother lioness saw that her whelp was lost to her she took another young lion and sought to make him the defender of her lair. In time men heard his roaring and captured him and carried him into captivity.

<small>Judah, the vine, consumed by fire from its own branch, Zedekiah (19: 10-14)</small> Judah may be also likened to a vine which has put forth many branches and spread its foliage toward the clouds. But when the hot wind from the far East withers the vine, breaks down its branches, and sets them on fire, the branch which seemed so promising will but aid in consuming the vine.

IV

FINAL PROPHECIES OF JUDGMENT (20 to 24)

1. *The Secret of Jehovah's Past Dealings with His People* (20 : 1-44)

<small>The occasion of the utterance (20 : 1-4)</small> About two years after my first vision of God, some of the elders came one day to inquire Jehovah's will. I was at first impelled to refuse to receive them, for I knew how superficial was their devotion ; but Jehovah bade me unfold to them the lessons of their history.

<small>The idolatry of the Hebrews in Egypt forgiven (20 : 5-9)</small> " When I chose Israel as my own people, making myself known to them in Egypt and promising them the delightful land of Canaan, I bade them forsake their primitive idolatry. This they would not do; yet for my name's sake, I spared them. They were delivered from Egyptian

thraldom, and in the wilderness I set before them laws and precepts of righteousness. These they ignored or broke, but again I could not bring myself to destroy them entirely. Their children, however, were as rebellious as their fathers. I threatened to scatter them among the nations and I allowed them to injure themselves with heathenish follies, but for my name's sake I still spared them. But when they came to Canaan, they forthwith adopted the Canaanitish rites.[1] *(Their refusal to obey the commands given in the wilderness (20: 10-17). Their gross and repeated idolatries thereafter (20: 18-29))*

" Now, O Israelites, do you think that I will countenance your persistence in idolatry? Must I look on passively while you worship manufactured gods? Nay! I will assert my sovereign rights and bring you again under my dominance. Idolators I will not tolerate in my land, but only those of you who serve me on Mount Zion. Thus will I be honored in the sight of the world. Then my goodness will cause you to repent of your evil ways and you will realize that I have dealt with you as befits the all-powerful and just Ruler of the universe." *(Jehovah will now assert his sovereign rights (20: 30-44))*

2. *Jehovah's Avenging Sword* (20 : 45 to 21 : 32)

The news came to our community at Tel-Abib that the great king had started westward to inflict an adequate punishment upon his faithless vassals in Syria. I felt that

---

[1] Verse 29 contains a curious play on the word for "high place," not easily paraphrased. "What (mā) is the high place (bāmā) to which you go (bā)."

Ezekiel 20 : 45

The fire about to devour Judah (20 : 45-48)	Judah's days were numbered and predicted that Jehovah was about to kindle in Judah an unquenchable, consuming fire, which would devour green and dry trees alike, scorching all onlookers because of its fierceness.
	The people laughed at my parable and failed to give sober heed to my warning. So Jehovah inspired me to present another, much more distinct and plain. "Je-
The avenging sword about to slay (21 : 1-5)	hovah is about to draw from the scabbard his avenging sword, which will slay all in the land—righteous and wicked alike. It shall not be replaced until it has done its work." I was bidden to show signs of great emotion, as a suggestion of the paralyzing tidings soon to be heard.
The prophet's expressions of grief (21 : 6-17)	My passionate grief found expression in a wild sword song [1] concerning the keen and gleaming blade ready for use by the executioner. With horror I seemed to see the slaughter of the leaders and of the people of Judah. It flashed like the lightning, here and there, bringing universal destruction, according to Jehovah's decree.
Nebuchadrezzar's indecision settled in favor of Jerusalem (21 : 18-27)	By a symbolic action I pointed out who was to be the wielder of this sword. Marking out a road, which finally forked, I set up a sign-post, which indicated that one branch led to Jerusalem and the other to Rabbah of Ammon. At this parting of the ways stood Nebuchadrezzar, uncertain as to which city he should go. Consulting the omens, he selected Jerusalem. Alas, what sad results! a king discrowned, a city in ruins, everything in hopeless

[1] Verse 9b-11 is probably a poem of two stanzas of four lines each.

confusion! There can be no alteration for the better until the true Davidic king comes.

Another sword of vengeance—that of Ammon—seems to be unsheathed. Their diviners urge a raid against the helpless people of Jerusalem. "These visions of conquest, O Ammon, are vain. Put back the sword. In your own land Jehovah will administer the chastisement you deserve."

<small>The avenging sword of Ammon (21 : 28-32)</small>

3. *The Indictment of Jerusalem* (22)

Realizing how false an idea of Jerusalem's value men had, I held the mirror to her face. "O, bloody and idolatrous city, you deserve the doom which is coming upon you. Injustice, irreverence, oppression of the stranger and of the weak, profanation, lewdness, bribery, extortion —all these social crimes are practised and God is forgotten. With grief and horror Jehovah witnesses these enormities. He will deal justly and firmly with you, even though he seems to put himself to shame in the eyes of the world.

<small>Jerusalem's social crimes (22 : 1-12)</small>

<small>Its certain punishment (22 : 13-16)</small>

"Jerusalem to-day is like a melting pot and Judah is like mixed metals, fit only to be tested in the fervent heat, that the pure silver may be made manifest. So will Jehovah purify his people.

<small>It can serve only as a melting-pot (22 : 17-22)</small>

"For the nation is full of wickedness. It is unfruitful like a land without rain. All classes do evil—the princes are rapacious and violent; the priests are careless in per-

<small>Its inhabitants wholly corrupt (22 : 23-31)</small>

forming their duties, the nobles are cheats, the prophets apologize for them all and give them support, while the people rob, oppress, and deceive. Not a man can be found who can really protect them. Jehovah has no option but to destroy the nation.

4. *The Two Unfaithful Wives of Jehovah* (23)

The two sisters (23 : 1-4)   To set forth more clearly the long continued infidelity of Samaria and Jerusalem to Jehovah, in their constant appeal to strangers for protection instead of to him, the prophet used again an allegory concerning two beautiful sisters, Oholah and Oholibah, who were, in their youth, wedded to Jehovah.

Samaria's alliances with Assyria and Egypt, which ended in captivity (23 : 5-10)   Oholah, attracted after a while by the sturdy and warlike character of the Assyrians, deserted her husband and gave herself to them and to the Egyptians. At length he left her in their hands to insult and abuse according to their brutal disposition,

Judah's alliances with Assyria, Babylon and Egypt (23 : 11-21)   Oholibah, her sister, did far worse. She, too, intrigued with Assyrians; but, in addition, had dealings with Babylonians, of whom she quickly wearied. When her husband would not receive her back again she turned to Egypt.

Her severe punishment (23 : 22-35)   " Now, O Oholibah, your husband Jehovah will stir up against you those with whom you have had criminal dealings. They shall encompass and capture you, and expose your folly and shame. You have brought this calamity upon yourself. As your sister suffered, so shall you, for you have forgotten him to whom your loyal allegiance was due.

"Does anyone question the justice of this punishment? These sisters have been guilty of nameless abominations. They have broken every covenant. Their punishment shall be that of faithless women, for such wickedness must cease." Additional details of their sin and punishment (23 : 36-49)

5. *The Tidings of the Siege of Jerusalem* (24)

For four years and a half I had been quietly conveying to my countrymen these messages of Jerusalem's sure destruction, when, on the very day that Nebuchadrezzar began the siege of Jerusalem, Jehovah bade me announce to them the imminent catastrophe. Remembering how the conspirators within Jerusalem[1] had likened their stronghold to a kettle, which would keep its contents from the fire, I too adopted the symbol, but I indicated that the kettle, although full of choice portions of meat, was unfit for use, because it was covered, within and without, with rust. Jerusalem a rusted kettle to be cleansed by fire (24 : 1-14)

"What will Jehovah do," I urged, "with a rusted kettle, whose foulness all can see? He will remove its contents, heap fuel on the fire and heat the empty kettle until it is cleansed from its impurity. Only judgment can purge the city of its blood guiltiness."

No sooner had I delivered this message than a more difficult burden was laid upon me. "Mortal one," said

---
[1] See page 44.

Ezekiel 24 : 16-27

Ezekiel's manner of mourning for his wife a symbol of the effect of the coming news upon his fellow captives (24 : 15-24)

Jehovah, "I will suddenly bereave you of your beloved wife, but show no signs of grief, and mourn not in public." That very night she died, and, with bursting heart, I obeyed the strange command. When my friends inquired the meaning of my unwonted action, I declared that the city and temple, so endeared by many associations to their hearts, were to be profaned, and their relatives, whom they loved, were to perish. So crushing would be the news that they would be incapable of expressing their grief.

Ezekiel at last recognized as Jehovah's prophet (24 : 25-27)

At that time Jehovah's servant, Ezekiel, would again be permitted to preach in public, and all would be convinced that he had truly spoken the mind of Israel's God.

PROPHECIES OF OBADIAH AND EZEKIEL AGAINST FOREIGN NATIONS

PROPHECIES OF OBADIAH AND EZEKIEL AGAINST FOREIGN NATIONS

I

THE LONG-EXPECTED CATASTROPHE

The destruction of Jerusalem was an event of signal importance in Hebrew history. As a catastrophe it was appalling, for it marked the end, not only of a reign and a dynasty, but also of a nation. It was even more notable as a turning point in history. It closed one era and opened another. It inaugurated more than a period of exile, since it furnished convincing proof that the new national life, should that ever be renewed, must be wholly reorganized.

The historical narrative preserved in 2 Kings throws but little light upon the political, social and religious conditions which hastened the disaster. It is rather concerned with the event itself. From the impassioned predictions of Jeremiah, however, and from the impressive visions and symbols of Ezekiel, may be discovered the various factors which co-operated in bringing about the downfall of the old national life. These were a well-meaning, but inefficient king (Jer. 37 : 15-21 ; 38 : 5), under strong obligation to maintain his political fealty (Ezek. 17) to Nebuchadrezzar ; turbulent and reactionary advisers, who had great confidence in themselves (Ezek. 11 : 1-3) and were hostile to Jeremiah and his party; a number of false prophets who encouraged their schemes (Ezek. 13 : 1-16 ; 22 : 28); and a people blindly confident that Jehovah, their God, would put forth his power, so grandly manifested in the past (Isa. 37), to save his city and temple; a nation restless under the heavy Babylonian yoke and willing to try the experiment of revolt, if opportunity offered. Thus disposed, the Jews were easily stirred by quiet proffers of aid from Egypt. The spirit of rebellion spread like a forest fire. Even the lofty cedar, as Ezekiel, perhaps with a touch of irony, calls King Zedekiah, yielded to its fury. About 588 B. C., Judah, in coalition with one or two petty principalities of Palestine, renounced allegiance to Babylonia.

Nebuchadrezzar did not, apparently, hasten to crush this revolt, yet his policy in regard to it could have been anticipated. Upon the tranquillization of the territory bordering the Great Sea depended both the continuance, unharassed, of the overland trade, which vitally affected the prosperity of great sections of his empire, and the achievement of his future schemes of Egyptian conquest. Judah's restless and ambitious population, protected by a fortress of unusual strength, constituted a never ending source of uneasiness to the overlord. According to the standards of the day, he had acted, ten years before, with reasonableness and moderation, when he had merely deported the politically dangerous elements of the population to Babylonia and left the state intact with a member of the royal family on the throne. According to the same standards there remained no option to him except to put an end to the existence of the Hebrew people. A prompt submission on their part might possibly have been accepted, but an organized resistance could have but one termination.

In due time Nebuchadrezzar assembled an army for the Palestinian campaign. The prophet Ezekiel (21 : 18-22) vividly pictures the king as consulting the omens, on reaching the borders of Gilead, to determine whether he should first attack Rabbah of Ammon or Jerusalem. Deciding to besiege Jerusalem, he crossed the Jordan, invested the city, and ravaged the territory far and near (Jer. 34 : 7). Too late King Zedekiah and his counsellors realized the gravity of the situation. They inquired of Jeremiah what the outcome would be (Jer. 21 : 1-10 ; 34 : 1-7), and attempted spasmodic reforms (Jer. 34 : 8-10). True for once to his pledge, the Pharaoh sent an army against Nebuchadrezzar, who raised the siege of Jerusalem for a while, and marched to meet his foe. Supposing they were saved, the godless nobles of Jerusalem revealed their consummate hypocrisy by promptly annulling the reforms they had just proclaimed. To their dismay the great Egyptian army was soon put to flight, and the victors encamped again around the doomed city. Its miserable inhabitants resisted with all the stoicism of despair. Soon, however, the horrors of famine and pestilence were added to the usual dangers of the siege. The condition of the populace during the six months before the capture was pitiable in the extreme (Lam. 2 : 19-22). At last, in July 586 B. C., the besiegers affected a breach in the northern wall and poured into the city. Zedekiah and a handful of warriors escaped by way of an unwatched private gate and fled toward the Jordan, but were overtaken at Jericho and carried before the great king, where he was forced to witness the slaughter of his sons and of his chief men, and then condemned to blindness and captivity.

After a month's delay, during which the ill-fated city was freely plundered by the brutal soldiery, Nabuzaradan, a royal officer of high rank, was deputed to complete the work of destruction. He took away all the valuable booty that was left, set on fire the temple, the palace, and the mansions of the wealthy nobles, and broke down the city walls. Soon nothing was left of the once splendid city but uninhabitable ruins.

II

OBADIAH'S DIATRIBE AGAINST EDOM

1. *Edom's Hereditary Relations with Judah*

From the dawn of Israel's history as a nation there was traditional enmity between the Hebrews and the Edomites. Of all the foes with whom Israel had to contend, these were the most implacable and untiring. Only a strong hand availed to keep them in retirement and subjection. The traditions of the wilderness wanderings, preserved in Numbers and Deuteronomy, convey the impression that Edom was hostile from the very beginning of their contact, desiring to hold no relations of amity with their kinsfolk. Saul fought against the Edomites, and David made a complete conquest of their land. From Jehoram, one hundred and fifty years later, they successfully revolted. Reconquered again by Amaziah and Uzziah about 760 B. C., they soon regained their freedom and thereafter maintained it.

Between the two nations there was really nothing in common, except that they were both Semitic peoples. Like Jacob and Esau, they were natural antagonists. The relative supremacy of the Israelites for many generations gave a vindictiveness to the enmity of Edom which made it sleepless and bitter. The prophet Amos denounces the sister nation because "he kept his wrath forever." This smouldering hatred, ever ready to break out into a blaze, had a unique opportunity in Judah's day of shame, of which the Edomites seem to have taken full advantage. Lining the hill-tops round about Jerusalem, they jeered at the hapless captives marching by, cut down without mercy the fugitives which they met, and had their share in the plundering of the country. Moreover, they promptly pushed their way up into southern Judah, making it a part of their own land.

The Edomites were the more aggressive because they felt perfectly secure from retribution. Their stronghold and capital, Petra, in the heart of the Mount Seir range, was a remarkable retreat. An irregular, well-watered valley, a mile or two in length, shut in by lofty cliffs, and approached from the desert by a long, narrow winding gorge, afforded a site which was not only capable of easy defence, but adapted, by the soft quality of the rocky cliffs, for the excavation of dwellings in the hill-side. Protected by such a stronghold, the sturdy warriors had long levied tribute on the caravan traffic with South Arabia and with Egypt, and had made themselves rich as well as independent. How soon these conditions were broken up by the irresistible advance of the Nabathaean Arabs cannot certainly be affirmed. The retribution which the prophet looked for was probably not long delayed.

The prophet Obadiah, of whom otherwise we know

nothing, gives expression to the outraged feelings of the exiled Hebrews, as they thought of Edom's base and spiteful mockery of the helpless captives. Yet he uttered no mere invective, but takes the broader ground that Edom is but a type of the hostile influences now blocking Israel's progress, but destined to give way before her.

The book itself, although so brief, raises some interesting problems. Its opening verses are so clearly parallel to passages in Jeremiah 49 : 7-22 as to force the conclusion that they had a common origin. It is quite generally held that Obadiah, and perhaps Jeremiah too, make use of an earlier prophecy against Edom. Obadiah merely introduces his theme by repeating a part of this oracle. The geographical hints of the closing verses are held by many scholars to prove the late post-exilic date of the prophecy, but the spirited references to the scenes that followed Jerusalem's capture seem to point to a period not very remote.

2. *Edom's Apparent Triumph to be Reversed*
(Obadiah 1-21)

Fellow-Israelites, let us not be disheartened and hopeless in this day of humiliation and anguish, but rather think of the coming day of recompense. Recall the prediction, so familiar to us all, regarding boastful Edom. Though still unfulfilled, Jehovah will yet make it a reality. A divine sanction is behind the summons, sent far

The tribes aroused against Edom (1) and wide to the tribes of Arabia, to assemble for war against the haughty Edomites. O arrogant nation, trusting in the security of your rock-hewn city and vaunting yourself among your neighbors, your opponent is no weak commander, but Jehovah himself. Were you as strong as Babylon and as inaccessible, his power could reach you. He will not only frustrate your plans for future conquest but will make you a humble vassal of your tributaries.[1]

Jehovah will humble its pride (2-4)

Edom to be utterly spoiled (5, 6) Sad enough would your plight be, if this were only a raid organized for plunder, for spoilers may be sated with booty. As when grape-gatherers strip a vineyard some clusters are overlooked, so your enemies might spare some treasures to you. What a spoliation, however, there will be! No part of your land will be exempt from search.

And expelled by her allies (7) You shall be expelled, O Edom, by the very ones on whom you rely. Those with whom you have made a covenant shall treat you with mingled treachery and violence. They have been leading[2] you on to your own destruction. How obtuse you are not to perceive this!

Edom's resources of no avail (8, 9) In the day of divine retribution your sages, celebrated far and wide for their wisdom, shall be incapable of suggesting the least expedient for defence; while the hardy warriors, who have been your boast because of their cour-

---

[1] The perfects in this verse and the following may be treated as very vivid forecasts of the future.
[2] The phrase "*they that eat* thy bread" is probably to be omitted.

age and strength, shall become timid and irresolute, an easy prey to the sword of your enemies.

The curse of God will surely be upon you, O Edom, because of your outrageous and merciless violence and unseemly rejoicing over the misfortunes of your sister nation, Judah. You identified yourself with her enemies, seizing the opportunity for plunder and murder. Can Jehovah fail to exact in full the penalty due for such unfaithfulness? *Her treachery the cause (10-14)*

Jehovah's day of recompense draws near for all the world. On that day, O Edom, your deeds will receive the punishment which is their due. As you, my countrymen who inhabit the mountain consecrated by my presence, have not escaped the cup of my chastising wrath, so shall all nations be obliged to drink of this cup, not, indeed, with a passing draught, as you have done, but continuously, until they have drained it to the dregs. Then shall they be utterly forgotten. *She shall receive a full meed of punishment (15, 16)*

The holy land of Judah, on the contrary, shall become the abode of peace, a true sanctuary for Jehovah's people. When we return from this exile we shall repossess our ancient dominion. As a flame devours dry stubble, so speedily and completely shall we drive out of our homes and destroy the children of Edom. *Israel will return and destroy Edom (17, 18)*

Then will cease the ignoble conditions which now prevail. No longer will our foes from every quarter be in possession of the soil of Judah. Those Jews who settle *And obtain control of all Palestine (19, 20)* down in their old homes in the extreme south will add to their territory the land of Edom; those who inhabit the low mountain ranges west of Judah will rule all Philistia; the men of the hill country of Judah[1] will control the mountains and plains of Samaria and Galilee, while to Benjamin will fall the great and fertile grazing land east of Jordan. Thus shall Palestine again revert to its lawful owners. Wherever an Israelite may have been carried he shall find a happy home within the borders of the land. From time to time great national leaders shall be raised up, as in the days of old, to fight Jehovah's battles, subdue all his enemies, and rule them in accordance with his will. At that time, when our foes have become our friends, all will be united in obedience and service to Jehovah.

III

THE STAND-POINT OF EZEKIEL'S FOREIGN PROPHECIES

The predictions of judgments against foreign nations constitute a puzzling feature of Hebrew prophecy until the reader understands the motives which prompted them. If interpreted as expressions of national vanity or jealousy, or as outbursts of vindictiveness, they are grossly misunderstood. Nor are they mere assertions of a just

[1] The Septuagint version thus interprets the indefinite word "they."

Later Prophets
Ezekiel

retribution for injuries inflicted upon the Israelitish nation. As in the hot-blooded message of Obadiah, there is always a broader theme than that of mere revenge; it is the certain movement of events in the future under the guidance of Jehovah's sovereign will that the prophets are forthtelling.

Such prophecies as these are found among the messages of Amos, Isaiah, Nahum, and Jeremiah. They merely voice a standing theme of every prophet, the authority of Jehovah of Israel over all the nations of the world, and the uniformity of his principles of judgment. It is interesting to note that these oracles, although addressed directly to the outside world, are, for the most part, intended for the prophet's own countrymen. They are often to be described as words of consolation rather than of denunciation. They declare that the evils which Jehovah has condemned in his own people, he cannot fail to punish wherever manifested. As an assertion of the supreme sovereignty of Jehovah, Israel's God, over the universe, of his attitude to other nations than Israel, and of his one great purpose to redeem the world, they are highly significant. As affording suggestions respecting the geographical knowledge of a student of affairs in Babylonia in the sixth century B. C., these prophecies of Ezekiel are of unusual value. In characterizing the traits of contemporary peoples, they are often apt and witty.

These particular utterances assume that the fall of Jerusalem is known to the nations addressed, which are situated near the land of Judah. They are grouped in a natural arrangement and have evidently been placed, with literary propriety, between the prophecies relating to the downfall of the city and those which have to do with the upbuilding of the exiled nation.

IV

THE PREDICTIONS OF EZEKIEL AGAINST FOREIGN NATIONS (25 to 32)

1. *Prophecies against Judah's Immediate Neighbors* (25)

Fellow-Israelites, Jehovah has revealed to me his sovereign will regarding the nations on our borders, whose true attitude toward us and toward him these days of our humiliation have made known.

<small>Ammon shall pass into oblivion (25 : 1-7)</small> Against our late allies, the sons of Ammon, whose joy was undisguised when our sanctuary was profaned, our land pillaged, and our people made captives, he pronounces the judgment of national extinction. The ruins of the splendid city of Rabbah shall serve as a stable for the camels of the wandering Arabs, and the whole land shall become a pasturage for their flocks. A nation so devoid of the impulses of true friendship deserves only oblivion.

Against Moab[1] his sentence is less severe. Her scoffing

---
[1] The words "and Seir" should be omitted. Edom is mentioned later.

Later Prophets   Ezekiel 26 : 2

glee over the thought that Judah has been proven by her <small>Moab shall suffer invasion (25 : 8-11)</small> misfortunes to be no better than other nations, deserves a stern rebuke. Her border fortresses, so long an impenetrable barrier against the Arab raiders, shall no longer serve their purpose. From Ammon's fate she shall be spared, but the plundering hordes shall execute a retribution which all will recognize as coming from Jehovah.

Since Edom has ungenerously seized the time of her <small>Edom shall be destroyed by Judah herself (25 : 12-14)</small> rival's weakness as an occasion for avenging her own long-cherished wrongs, Jehovah will empower Judah in the day of her restoration to carry out an exemplary penalty. Edom shall be made a desolation from one end of the kingdom to the other.

Since the Philistines, too, have yielded to their passion <small>The Philistines shall be annihilated (25 : 15-17)</small> for revenge against their rulers, Jehovah declares that he will utterly annihilate them.

2. *Prophecies against Phœnicia* (26 to 28)

(1) *The Coming Destruction of Tyre* (26)

Even Tyre, the queen of the sea, has earned Jehovah's <small>The sin of Tyre— selfishness (26 : 1, 2)</small> displeasure by her exultation over the downfall of Judah. With sordid greed for gold she rejoices that in her inland traffic she will no longer have a rival or a barrier. "O selfish city," declares Jehovah, "nations will come to you in great numbers, but not for trade. They shall be-

Ezekiel 26 : 3

Its punishment
(26 : 3-6)

siege and capture you, destroy your defences, and leave an unsightly and barren rock, fitted only for drying fishermen's nets, where now are splendid palaces."

Nebuchadrezzar to be Jehovah's instrument
(26 : 7-14)

The divine agent shall be Nebuchadrezzar and his mighty army. Having destroyed your dependent cities on the coast, he will persistently lay siege to you. The day will come when the hoofs of his many horses shall raise clouds of dust in the streets of your city, while the rumbling of his chariots will cause the very walls to shake. Then shall he slaughter your citizens, throw down the famous symbols of Melkarth, and give you up to spoil. In that day you will have no heart for exultant song, for your history will be at an end.

The lament of her dependencies
(26 : 15-18)

With what dismay and fear will the groans of your dying citizens be heard throughout your colonies and among your allies. Their rulers, with every outward sign of grief and horror, shall bewail your untoward fate, saying :

> How art thou vanished from the sea,
>   O renowned city!
> Who was strong through the sea
>   She and her inhabitants,
> How didst thou impose thy terror
>   On all her inhabitants.
> Now tremble the coastlands
>   In the day of thy fall.
> And dismayed are the isles of the sea
>   At thy departure.

Amply will their grief be justified, for when the deep waters have swallowed all the traces of your once powerful and populous city, no more shall you have a place and name in the land of the living. *The catastrophe to be irretrievable (26 : 19-21)*

(2) *A Dirge over her Downfall* (27)

Who would not mourn, as he contemplates the ruin of the mistress of the seas, the imperial city, to which the whole world has paid tribute! Fitly may one liken you, O Tyre, to a stately trireme, riding proudly at anchor, attractive to the eye, built of the choicest woods and sumptuously furnished. Skilled mariners of every nation and mercenaries from the remotest quarters of the earth obey your captains, and enable them to bring you wealth. From distant Tarshish to Arabia and the far East traders come to load you with their merchandise. *Tyre a beautiful vessel laden with the wealth of nations (27 : 1-25)*

Thus deeply laden, while on your voyage in the open sea, a wind from the east has caused you to founder. All your cargo and crew have perished in the sea. Alas! what a lamentation arises from the mariners of the deep. With breaking hearts they give way to frenzied exhibitions of grief, uttering a weird wail[1] for the proud vessel, laden with attractive wares, once serving all mankind, but now a miserable wreck. *Her shipwreck (27 : 26, 27) The lament of the mariners (27 : 28-36)*

[1] Verses 32-36 are in elegiac metre.

(3) *Tyre's Opportunity and Well-deserved Fate* (28 : 1-19)

<small>Presumpt-
uous self-
exaltation
deserves a
humiliating
punishment
(28 : 1-10)</small>
Against the prince of Tyre Jehovah announces his judgment. "Because of your wonderful success in gathering wealth and skill in producing objects of use and beauty, and cleverness in making your situation so secure, you have come to think yourself as wise and powerful and great as God. Such impious self-exaltation cannot go unpunished. These very possessions in which you glory shall effect your ruin. By brutal Babylonian soldiers you shall be humiliated and spoiled and given a dishonored grave.

<small>Tyre's
violence and
wickedness
the reason
for her
destruction
(28 : 11-19)</small>
" How appropriate, then, a lament over you ! Once you were worthy in your glorious perfection to live with heavenly beings in the garden of God, adorned with costly jewels and gold ; but you lost God's favor because your pride was so overweening and because you did not hesitate at violence and outrage in your dealings with mankind. He will cast you from your throne of power ; as a fire unexpectedly bursting forth consumes to ashes that which feeds it, so shall your sin become your own destruction."

(4) *The Fate of Sidon* (28 : 20-26)

<small>Sidon shall
yet revere
Jehovah
(28 : 20-23)</small>
For Sidon, also, Jehovah has a message of judgment. Punished by pestilence and bloody invasion, she shall come to acknowledge that he is the great and holy Ruler of the universe. Then shall Israel at last be freed from

the interference and humiliating experience which have thwarted and crippled and harassed her during the centuries past. When her Shepherd brings back his scattered flock and pastures his people once more in the fair fields of Palestine, they shall be free to live a life of true and loyal service. _{Then Israel will attain her true development (28 : 24-26)}

3. *Prophecies against Egypt* (29 to 32)

(1) *Egypt to be Humbled to the Dust* (29 : 1-16; 30 : 1-19)

Not long before Jerusalem's fall, while many were still cherishing a hope that the Pharaoh might possibly extend some aid to the beleaguered city, I received this prophetic word: "Jehovah's curse is against the arrogant dweller by the Nile who, like the huge crocodile of his river, imagines himself to be the creator of that which he enjoys. The Lord will drag him out of his beloved river and leave him on the banks to die, a prey for birds and beasts. Egypt shall be thus treated because she has ever invited the confidence of Israel only to betray it. _{Egypt, the crocodile of the Nile, to meet a crocodile's fate (29 : 1-7)}

"To punish Egypt's overweening pride, the Almighty will transform her boasted fertility into an uninhabited desert and scatter her people, far and wide. For a generation shall her desolation continue, and it shall be universal. Then will Jehovah restore the nation to its home, but not to its former prominence. It shall be of inferior rank, _{Because of her boastfulness and real incapacity (29 : 8-12) Never again to be a leading nation (29 : 13-16)}

no longer able to delude Israel by empty boasts of power and wealth, and to tempt her to distrust her God.

<small>The day of Jehovah will be a day of humiliation for Egypt (30: 1-9)</small>
"O peoples, raise a cry of lamentation, for Jehovah's day draws near, a day of darkness and of grief to all of his foes. Unto Egypt and her allies it will be a day of death and anguish. She shall be humbled to the dust and at last will acknowledge Jehovah as the supreme power in the universe.

<small>Nebuchadrezzar will perform Jehovah's will (30: 10-19)</small>
"Jehovah's agent of judgment will be the mighty Nebuchadrezzar. His ruthless and invincible warriors will spread ruin and desolation throughout the land. Egypt's ruling classes and her strong cities will offer no effective opposition to their advance, and her young men will be carried off as slaves. Then Egypt's pride will completely break down and Jehovah will receive honor and respect."

(2) *The Pharaoh to be Crippled* (30: 20-26)

<small>The misfortune of Egypt (30: 20-22)</small>
When Pharaoh Hophra, having advanced to the support of the people of Judah, had been repulsed by Nebuchadrezzar and driven home, Jehovah announced through me to the wondering people: "The arm of Pharaoh I have caused to be broken; never again shall it wield the sword. <small>Jehovah will only increase it (30: 23-26)</small> His other arm, too, I will disable, rendering him utterly incapable of self-defence. Then shall his pitiless adversary, by me made strong for combat, give him his death-stroke. His people I will disperse far and wide."

(3) *Egypt the Fallen Cedar* (31)

A fitting symbol of the majesty and influence of Egypt's king is a stately cedar [1] of Lebanon of towering height and with spreading branches which shelter all the fowls of air, whose roots strike deep into the earth and drink freely of its waters, surpassing all other trees in the beauty of its foliage and form, and envied even by the trees of Eden. Egypt a stately cedar of surpassing beauty (31 : 1-9)

So overweening is your pride, O Egyptian cedar, that Jehovah will send against you a skilful wielder of the axe. Soon will your huge trunk lie prostrate across the mountain peaks while your branches fill up every valley. Those who have nestled under your protection will make haste to desert you. May your fate be a warning against impious self-exaltation ! Its sure downfall (31 : 10-14)

In the day of your fall, all nature will feel the shock and be moved to grief. Those who have preceded you to the realm of departed shades will rejoice because you have joined them. Superior as you are, you must go down with them and there remain. Her welcome in Sheôl (31 : 15-18)

(4) *Egypt's Coming Desolation* (32 : 1-16)

O king of Egypt, so long regarded by many nations as a devouring masterful lion, Jehovah will prove that you

---

[1] The subject in verse 3 cannot well be " the Assyrian," but was probably originally indefinite.

Ezekiel 32 : 1 *Messages of the*

The capture and death of the river-monster, Egypt (32 : 1-6)

are rather like the powerful crocodile of your rivers, active in display of strength, but successful only in fouling the waters in which you live. He will capture you in his net and expose your carcass to the birds and beasts of prey. Your huge bulk will fill the earth, and the rivers will run red with your blood.

The effect of this calamity upon nature and mankind (32 : 7-10)

All creation will be stirred by the news of your death. The sun in mid-heaven shall be eclipsed, the moon and stars shall withhold their light. Dismay and terror shall fill every human heart, when they see a just retribution overtake you.

The completeness of the ruin (32 : 11-16)

This will Jehovah accomplish by the sword of King Nebuchadrezzar and his invincible warriors. Every living creature shall they sweep away. The streams of Egypt, untroubled by the foot of man or beast, shall run smooth as oil. The once powerful and populous country shall become a desolation, bewailed by all nations.

(5) *The Dirge for the Dead* (32 : 17-32)

Egypt's humiliation in the underworld (32 ; 17-20)

Let this dirge be sung at the burial of Pharaoh and all his host. " Do you go down to the underworld expecting to receive that deference which you have always exacted ? The heroes who are honored among the shades will meet you when you appear and direct you to take your place among the dishonored dead in the lowest portion of the pit.

" There will you find your predecessors, terror-inspiring

82

Later Prophets   Ezekiel 29 : 21

Assyria, fierce and brutal Elam, the violent and blood-thirsty nations of the north. Theirs is not the enviable lot of the heroes of old who went down to Sheôl in their panoply of war, buried with all appropriate rites. Edom also and Syria and Phœnicia, those who perish in battle, will bear their humiliation along with the rest in the lowest abode of the shades. At the sight of these companions in misery you will be reconciled to your lot." She will be comforted by her company (32:21-32)

(6) *Egypt to be Nebuchadrezzar's Reward* (29 : 17-21)

Sixteen years after the fall of Jerusalem, when the thirteen years' siege of Tyre by Nebuchadrezzar had come to a disappointing end, the prophet presented a modified explanation of Jehovah's purpose against Tyre and Egypt. Ezekiel's latest prophecy

"Nebuchadrezzar, my servant, has labored earnestly in my behalf against Tyre. His warriors are worn and weary, yet they have received no pay for their toil. Lo, the land of Egypt shall be their recompense! They shall take its spoil and enslave its people. When Egypt is thus humiliated, Israel will once again become strong and my prophetic teachings will be honored by all." Egypt Nebuchadrezzar's reward for his long service against Tyre (29: 17-21)

JEREMIAH'S MESSAGE TO THE
JEWISH FUGITIVES IN EGYPT

JEREMIAH'S MESSAGE TO THE JEWISH FUGITIVES IN EGYPT

I

THE REMNANTS OF THE JEWISH NATION IN THE LAND OF EGYPT

The deportations of 597 and 586 B. C. carried only a fraction of the total population of Judah to Babylon. Of those who survived the horrors of the sword, of famine, and of pestilence, probably the greater number were found in the land of the Nile. Egypt had encouraged the Judeans repeatedly to revolt against Babylon, and thus had lured the southern Hebrew kingdom on to its final ruin, as it had the northern a century earlier; and yet of all the nations of the earth it alone offered a friendly asylum to the Jews in the hour of their mortal agony. It was also easily accessible from Palestine and therefore doubly attractive to exiles seeking a place of refuge where they might abide until the storm was over and they could return to their beloved land.

As early as 597 B. C. a large proportion of the race had already found homes in Egypt (Jer. 24:8b). When, in 586 B. C., it became evident to every enlightened citizen of Judah that the final disaster was imminent undoubtedly thousands more joined them there. A little later, when the Jewish kingdom, which had been established with its capital at Mizpah, came to an untimely end because of the treacherous murder of its governor Gedaliah, the survivors, notwithstanding the earnest exhortations of Jeremiah, turned to Egypt. The prospect of living in a land where they should " see no war, nor hear the sound of the trumpet, nor have hunger of bread " (Jer. 42:14) was too strong a temptation to be resisted. Jeremiah's warnings that these evils would overtake them there, and his assurances that the Babylonians would treat them justly if they remained in Judah, were of no avail.

The nobles and military commanders of the little Jewish state, with the men, women, and children, with the princesses of the royal Judean house, with Jeremiah and his scribe Baruch, migrated as a body to Egypt. At Tahpanhes, the classical Daphnæ and the modern Defenneh, on its easternmost borders, the colony established itself. In many ways the location of their new place of abode must have been satisfactory to the Jews, for their former homes could be reached by a journey of a day or two, and they were right on the great highway which ran from Egypt to Palestine and the East.

The population of Tahpanhes, as we learn from He-

Later Prophets Jeremiah

rodotus and the results of the excavations which have been made in its ruins, was exceedingly cosmopolitan. While the reigning Pharaohs of Egypt had a royal residence in this eastern outpost of their empire, which they probably visited at rare intervals, Greek and Semitic influences were probably stronger in the life of the city than the native Egyptian. Thus the Jews did not come into very close contact with the religion of the new land of their adoption, and were free to worship unmolested the gods whom they pleased. The dangers which threatened their faith, as Jeremiah's sermons indicate, came not from without, but from within. They had few religious teachers, for most of the priests and prophets of their nation had been carried away by the Babylonians. The refugees in Egypt, therefore, were the rank and file of the nation. Their faith was that of the masses, which, as has been noted in the study of the earlier prophets, differed widely from that of their inspired religious guides. They had never outgrown the old heathen superstitions, and the reactionary reigns of Jehoiakim and Zedekiah had confirmed them in the imperfect faith of their fathers. In their ignorance they also interpreted the disaster which had cast down their nation as evidence of Jehovah's weakness and neglect. Hence it was natural that in their blindness they should endeavor to win the favor of the old Semitic gods. The Queen of Heaven, whose worship had been prevalent in Jerusalem in the days of Jehoiakim, was one of the most popular of these heathen deities. Herodotus states that this cult was common among the Assyrians and Arabs, and identifies the Queen of Heaven with the Assyrian goddess of love Ishtar, the Greek Aphrodite (i. 131). The prominence of the Jewish women in her worship (Jer. 44:17) tends to confirm this identification.

For nearly half a century Jeremiah had preached unceasingly, in the face of apathy and bitter opposition, against the sins of his people. The sweeping misfortunes which had overtaken them were due entirely to their failure to heed his plain warnings. Contrary to his advice his associates had gone to Egypt. Their attitude toward him was one of contempt and defiance. Tradition asserts that they ultimately put him to death. Certainly from a human point of view by his life-long martyrdom he had nobly earned a quiet old age; but, while he was human, he was also a divinely commissioned prophet, so that, as long as his countrymen made mistakes and sinned, he could not keep silence. His latest sermons reflect the same supreme devotion and zeal and courage as do those of his youth.

He probably recognized that, although the mind and soul of his race were in Babylon, its physical strength, which was equally essential for the national reconstruction to which the true prophets looked forward with certainty, was to be sought in Egypt. There were found thousands of Jews able and eager to return and join the struggling few who had remained behind in Judah in reviving the body politic, whenever conditions seemed favorable. Of all the exiles in Egypt, of those located at Migdol, Memphis, and Pathros (southern Egypt), as well as at Tahpanhes, Jeremiah was the pastor, just as Ezekiel was of those in the East. The brief record of his work in Egypt introduces us to a most important, but otherwise unwritten, chapter of Jewish history. Without his faithful ministrations men might not have been found equal to the supreme sacrifice which was demanded of those unknown patriots who first came back without resources and without influence to rebuild the waste places of Judah.

II

PREDICTIONS AND SOLEMN WARNINGS
(43 : 8 to 44 : 30)

1. *The Coming Conquest of Egypt by Nebuchadrezzar*
(43 : 8-13)

Soon after the arrival of the Jewish refugees at Tahpanhes, Jeremiah was divinely led in their presence to take great stones and imbed them in the raised platform, or *mastaba*, in front of the royal residence of the Pharaohs.

The sign prophecy (43 : 8, 9)

While the people stood about in open-mouthed wonder, the prophet interpreted the significance of his strange action : " Jehovah will send to Egypt, even as he has to

Jeremiah 43:10

<small>A symbol that Nebuchadrezzar would invade Egypt (43:10-13)</small> Judah, the agent who executes his righteous judgment, Nebuchadrezzar. On these very stones which I have placed here, at the entrance of the palace of Hophra, will the king of Babylon set up his throne. As a conqueror he will condemn some of the Egyptians to death, and others to deportation to Babylon. Their temples he will plunder and burn. With ease and completely will he become master of the entire land. The obelisks of Memphis and the many temples scattered throughout the land will suffer the fate of the Jerusalem sanctuary. Think not, disobedient Jews, that you have passed beyond the pale of Jehovah's far-reaching influence."

2. *The Certain Fate of Those Unfaithful to God*
(44 : 1-30)

<small>The people have failed to profit by the awful experiences of their past (44:1-10)</small> Again a divine message came to the prophet for all the Jewish exiles living in the different communities in upper and lower Egypt: "You have experienced the misfortunes, and seen with your own eyes the terrible desolation that Jehovah has sent upon your people and land. You also know the reason why: it was because you, as a nation, instead of remaining faithful to him, introduced the worship of foreign gods. In vain he warned you through his zealous, untiring prophets. You would not heed, and so the desolation of Judah and your sad lot are the direct results. Have you failed to learn the simple lesson? Is it possible that by a repetition of the same gross sins you

Later Prophets Jeremiah 44 : 18

will bring still greater evils upon yourselves and your wives and innocent children dependent upon you? I can see from your defiant attitude that you are no more repentant nor inclined to keep Jehovah's laws, which are so plainly presented in the Book of the Covenant, than were your fathers. Therefore, but one course of action is open, even to Jehovah himself. He must continue to execute his righteous vengeance upon you. By the sword and by famine those of you who are faithless to him will die. None shall be spared, until all the world stands aghast at the magnitude of your sin and of its punishment. Think not that you will escape his judgment here in this land of Egypt. It will go on even as in the land of Palestine. You all hope to return in time to Judah. Know that none, except a few faithful ones who escape Jehovah's just wrath, shall realize this fond expectation." *The judgment awaiting the defiant exiles in Egypt (44 : 11-14)*

To the bold, earnest appeals of Jeremiah the exiles, both men and women, who at the time were gathered together from all parts of Egypt in a great assembly, replied, " We will not follow your advice. As we have in this religious convention determined, we will worship the Queen of Heaven as did our ancestors in the land of Judah during the reigns of Manasseh and Jehoiakim, when they enjoyed prosperity, and before any great calamities had overtaken our nation. It was when we, as a people, ceased to worship this powerful celestial deity that these dire disasters came upon us. Charge not the women, O *The defiant reply of the people (44 : 15-19)*

Jeremiah 44 : 19

prophet, with conserving these foreign rites, for in the past, as now, the husbands were in perfect sympathy with the action of their wives."

Jeremiah's counter interpretation of the experiences of his nation (44 : 20-23)

In reply to the deep-seated error of the people, Jeremiah declared: "Your interpretation of the real cause of the calamities which have come to your nation is entirely wrong. They came because Jehovah could no longer tolerate your apostasy to him, your abominable heathen practices, and your contemptuous disregard of his commands.

The fate in store for the guilty exiles (44 : 24-30)

"Hear Jehovah's sentence upon you. You and your wives have deliberately avowed your determination to turn your backs upon him, and henceforth to devote yourselves to worshipping the Assyrian goddess, the Queen of Heaven. Do as you have agreed, only Jehovah commands you never again to pronounce his holy name with your polluted lips. Henceforth his care in regard to you will be to punish and destroy instead of to preserve. War and famine will complete their deadly work. Only a fraction of your number will escape and return to Judah. By bitter experience you will learn the truth of my words and the folly of your own. Let this also be a sign to you: when you behold Hophra, the reigning Pharaoh, a captive in the hands of his conqueror, as was Zedekiah in the hands of Nebuchadrezzar, know the truth of my divine message, and that Jehovah will surely execute upon you the grim sentence which I have just proclaimed."

EZEKIEL'S MESSAGES OF COMFORT
TO THE EXILES IN BABYLONIA

EZEKIEL'S MESSAGES OF COMFORT TO THE EXILES IN BABYLONIA

I

THE SUPREME NEED OF PROPHETIC MINISTRATION

It has already been noted that the prophet Ezekiel, like a pastor of to-day, was deeply interested in the fortunes of the people amid whom he lived. A sufficient evidence of this is his declaration of the responsibility which he felt as a watchman for Israel (3), and the evident bearing of his predictions regarding Jerusalem and of his unsparing criticisms of his nation upon the action and sentiments of his immediate neighbors in Babylonia.

When the downfall of their beloved city and temple became an acknowledged fact, it was natural that he should zealously devote himself to his disheartened countrymen, who had hitherto paid little heed to his words of warning. In spite of what he had repeatedly said, they were unprepared for the crushing news. Some among them attributed their misfortunes to Jehovah's neglect or weakness, and were tempted to renounce their allegiance to him and become like the heathen around them. Others, while seeing in these calamities the judgments of Jehovah for their sins, were overwhelmed by a sense of their guilt (Lam. 1:12) and became almost hopeless respecting the future (Ezek. 24:23). They could only realize that the city was in ruins, the royal house dishonored, the nation uprooted, the people dispersed, and the old home-land either a desolation or in possession of their hated neighbors, who were maliciously exulting over their downfall. Beyond these shocking realities they were not able to see. The prophet, however, found in this condition of affairs the opportunity for which he had been waiting. His work of sustaining, comforting, and upbuilding could now begin—the era of promises rather than threats and of the inculcation of hopefulness instead of fear. He turns the attention of his hearers to the rich possibilities for Israel in the future, at least for an Israel repentant, loyal, and earnest.

One marked result of the confirmation of all that Ezekiel had proclaimed for six long years was his reestablishment as a popular preacher (33:30-32). He was always sure of an audience, and became at once an acknowledged leader in the community. He himself recognized the superficial character of his popularity, and did not expect that his teachings would effect an immediate change of heart. Chapters 33 to 39 doubtless represent the sermons of the next decade, during which the prophet was a faithful friend and helper to his people.

In these chapters the true bent of Ezekiel's mind is revealed. Prominence is given the positive, constructive side of his thinking. The years between 586 and 570 B.C. must have been the happiest of his life, since it was pre-eminently the glory of a prophet to snatch a despondent people from suicidal lethargy and direct them, repentant, into a vitalized, earnest career of service.

II

PROPHECIES OF PROMISE AND CHEER (33 to 39)

1. *The Prophet Appointed to Announce Israel's Possible Future* (33)

Fellow Israelites, Jehovah bids me make clear to you the decisive importance of your attitude toward him and his messenger in these days of reconstruction. I am like a watchman set apart in time of public peril to warn a city of the enemy's approach. If he is faithful to his trust, keeping vigilant watch and sounding the alarm when danger threatens, then those who lose their lives by failing to heed his warning are solely to blame for their death. If, however, he is neglectful, the blood of those who are slain is upon his head. *[The function of a watchman and his responsibility (33 : 1-6)]*

Thus has Jehovah appointed me to proclaim in trumpet tones the doom which I see hanging over my people, if *[The prophet a watchman (33 : 7-9)]* they persist in their evil ways. If I faithfully present my warning message, my responsibility is at an end, but yours, O Israel, will then begin.

<small>The future of Israel to depend upon the character of the people (33 : 10-20)</small>
Do you despairingly conclude that a final destruction has been decreed against you because of your sins and that no effort of yours can avail! Not so, fellow Israelites; you misapprehend the divine purpose. Jehovah wishes that all should live, and ever holds forth the possibility of redemption. A man's past life does not absolutely determine his present or future state in God's sight. A once righteous man who yields to evil impulse must suffer the consequences of his wickedness; a man of evil life who truly reforms, making recompense for the wrong he has done and ordering his life by right principles, can count on divine approval and blessing. Jehovah will hold everyone responsible for his deliberate course of life. Can he do otherwise?

<small>The effect of the news of Jerusalem's fall (33 : 21, 22)</small>
Such is the message which Jehovah now bids me proclaim. There is no need for overwhelming despair because of the startling news of Jerusalem's fall. It enables me to set before you all the real character of your God and his ways of dealing with you. No longer need my lips be sealed, for you will acknowledge that a true prophet is in your midst.

Those who are even now left in the ruined land of Judah are laying claim, as sons of Abraham and heirs of the promise, to the whole territory. Jehovah will point out to them that they are ignoring the true basis of the old covenant and maintaining the very evils for which he has driven the nation from its inheritance. Hence the same judgment must be repeatedly meted out until his righteous will is obeyed. *The remnant in Judah has no right to the land except through obedience (33 : 23-29)*

"As for your fellow exiles," saith Jehovah, "who now crowd to hear my message from your lips, do not set too high a value on their professions of interest. They are curious to hear some sensational preaching, but not eager to repent. They enjoy your artistic sermons as they might a beautiful song. When your words are all fulfilled, these sceptics will discover that you have indeed been a speaker of eternal truth." *The prophet's sermons to be respected (33 : 30-33)*

2. *The True Ruler of Israel* (34)

"Woe," saith Jehovah, "to the rulers of my people, through whose selfish heedlessness they have become weakened and dispersed like sheep which have no watchful shepherd. On every side their enemies have devoured them, while their slothful and self-indulgent guardians were feasting themselves. Such criminal incompetence can no longer be tolerated. *Jehovah will set aside the negligent guardians of Israel (34 : 1-10)*

"Therefore I will interpose and undertake the care of my people. Like a good shepherd, I will seek out those who have wandered far away. I will gently lead them homeward and give them abundant food in their accustomed haunts. There will I lavish upon them the tender *He will himself take their place (34 : 11-16)* care which they have never received from their appointed guardians.

<small>Oppressions will cease (34 : 17-22)</small>
"At that time I will make a sudden end of the oppression of the poor and the weak by those who are wealthy and powerful, who consume the best of everything, and then, in wanton spitefulness, destroy or damage what they cannot use. Such heartless ruffians will receive speedy judgment at my hands.

<small>A true Davidic ruler to be appointed (34 : 23-31)</small>
"When I have thus restored and purged my people, I will appoint over them a faithful shepherd, a second David. Then shall the land be free from foreign foes and beasts of prey. I will give rain in its season, abundant harvests and complete security and happiness. Then at last shall God and his people be reconciled."

3. *The Certain Restoration of Israel's Land* (35 to 36)

(1) *Edom's Usurpation to be Severely Punished by Desolation* (35)

<small>Edom to be a desolation because of her enmity, malice and arrogance (35 : 1-15)</small>
O land of Edom, Jehovah's curse is upon you. A barren waste shall you become because in Judah's day of calamity you exhibited your ceaseless enmity toward her by exulting over her misfortunes, assisting her enemies, and especially by invading with boastful defiance the sacred soil of Israel, Jehovah's abode, as if it had been given up to such as you for spoil. Your acts and your malicious spirit Jehovah cannot pardon.

Later Prophets Ezekiel 36 : 32

(2) *Judah to be again a Fertile and Populous Land* (36 : 1-15)

And you, beloved land of hills and valleys, at once the object of our enemies' jibes and the reward of their evil enterprise, the humiliation that you suffer shall be the lot of those who now possess you. At the time, not far distant, when your own people return, you shall be luxuriantly fruitful and populous. Nevermore will there be a destructive famine, nor shall outside peoples be justified in hurling reproaches against you. Judah to be recovered from its present possessors, purified, and blessed (36: 1-15)

(3) *Jehovah's Motive for Restoration* (36 : 16-38)

Recall, O men of Judah, how necessary it was for Jehovah to act in judgment against you. By your persistent idolatry and acts of murder you forced him, in sheer abhorrence, to mete out the appropriate punishment of world-wide dispersion. The nations among whom you have gone, not understanding the divine method of governing the unwise, dishonor Jehovah by attributing your misfortunes to his inability to protect you. For his name's sake, therefore, he purposes to restore you again to your land, purified from every idolatrous taint, docile, reverent, and disposed to obedience. In response to the shower of blessings from his hand, you will then realize his love and your own iniquities. Both you and the nations will understand his motives and give him honor.

At that time the land will again become as beautiful as

Ezekiel 36 : 33

This redemption will cause all nations to honor Jehovah (36 : 33-38)

Eden and populous as of old. Once more will the people take counsel of Jehovah and ask for his blessing. Every city in the land shall be crowded with thronging multitudes, as was Jerusalem in the past on the great festal days. Looking on such a transformation as this, can the nations fail to glorify Jehovah?

4. *The Revivified and United People* (37)

(1) *The Vision of the Nation's Resurrection* (37 : 1-14)

The despondent exiles (37 : 11)

The vision of the dry bones made into living beings (37 : 1-10)

The greatest obstacle to my ministry of encouragement was the despondency of the exiled people who ever kept speaking of themselves as devoid of hope. One day Jehovah granted me an answering vision. Again I appeared to be in the familiar valley, but it was covered with bleached and scattered bones, which seemed to me truly emblematic of my dispersed and blighted nation. I heard a question, "Weak mortal, can these bones be transformed into living beings?" I dared not deny; I did not venture to affirm; I humbly asked for enlightenment. "Declare boldly," said the voice, "that Jehovah has both the power and the purpose to make a living nation from these bones." On my compliance, the bones began to assort themselves into groups and the groups to become articulated into skeletons and the skeletons to be clothed with flesh, until I saw before me a vast array of inert bodies. Again said the voice: "Call to the four winds of heaven to furnish the breath of life for this great host." I called, the winds obeyed, and there stood up a multitude of living beings.

"Mortal one," the voice added, "these bones which you saw were the remains of the nation Israel. As Jehovah gave life to the dismembered and disintegrated bodies, so he can raise the nation from the very grave, infuse new life, and restore the people to their own land. Then will they be convinced of his power and his love." The explanation of the vision (37 : 12-14)

(2) *The Symbol of its Unification* (37 : 15-28)

Again, under a divine impulse, I took two wooden sticks to represent royal sceptres, which I labelled with names to indicate that they denoted the southern and northern kingdoms of Israel. These I held in my hand as if they had become united into one rod. When questioned about the meaning of this action, I said, "Jehovah is surely purposing to gather all the Israelites from every quarter of the world and to settle them in their own land and to make them a united nation under one king. Purified from idolatry and cleansed from sin,[1] they will serve him alone. Then shall a true representative of the Davidic stock ascend the throne. Like a good shepherd he will faithfully care for them, and they will be obedient and righteous. Jehovah will establish his cove-

The prophetic symbol of the two sticks (37 : 15-17)
The future Israel to be a united kingdom (37 : 18-22)
Its glorious outlook (37 : 23-28)

[1] "Dwelling places" (v. 23) should probably be read, as in the Septuagint, "backslidings."

nant with them forever, and will dwell in their midst to the end of days."

5. *Jehovah's Final Triumph* (38 : 1 to 39 : 24)

<small>The significance of the invasion of Israel by Gog's army (38 : 1-9)</small>

After Jehovah has revealed himself to the civilized world and to Israel by restoring and blessing his own people, there will yet remain one final act in the great drama of universal, divine judgment. The unknown nations of the distant north will need one overwhelming proof of Jehovah's sovereign power, before the whole world will stand in awe of him. Then will he speak to Gog, the leader of those fierce Scythian tribes : " Prepare, O prince of nations, to assemble your forces from every quarter, well equipped and beyond number, ready at my summons to advance, like a cloud of destructive locusts, against my people, Israel.

<small>Gog's motive merely that of plunder (38 : 10-16)</small>

" Your only motive, O robber of nations, will be to plunder unopposed a peaceful, prosperous, populous, but defenceless people. How the merchants of Arabia and Tarshish gloat over the prospects of a rich spoil ! Yet it is not for booty that I bring you to the land of my people, but that my name may be held in reverence by all the world.

<small>His downfall the fulfilment of prophetic expectation (38 : 17-23)</small>

" This will be the invasion to which many of my prophets have looked forward, when I and my nation would be face to face with the embodiment of the heathen world's hostility. In this supreme peril will be my long-awaited opportunity. I will pour out my wrath upon these northern barbarians. By a mighty earthquake the mountains shall be cleft and every lofty object levelled. The panic-stricken soldiers will attack each other, while I complete their destruction by pestilence and hailstorms and fire. Then will my power and the sacredness of my land be known to all.

"Therefore, O representative of uncivilized paganism, I will lead you to this land, but only that you may be annihilated. Making useless your weapons, I will cause you to perish. Even your own home-land shall be ravaged that my glory may be acknowledged by the whole world. Gog to be disarmed and destroyed by God (39 : 1-7)

"Then will the people of Israel go forth from their cities and gather up the spoil. So numerous will be the weapons that for years there will be no need of cutting firewood. In a secluded valley on the other side of the Dead Sea, outside the limits of the holy land, they will bury the corpses. Many months will it take to dispose of the slain which can be readily discovered. Then men will be appointed to search every corner of the land for unnoticed corpses, that it may be wholly freed from defilement. A splendid banquet will I spread on that day for all the birds of the air and for the beasts of prey. They shall eat flesh to the full and drink freely of the blood of princes. The extent of the catastrophe (39 : 8-20)

"After such a manifestation of power as this, the people

Ezekiel 39 : 21

<small>The effect upon Israel and the world (39 : 21-24)</small> of Israel can never again be unfaithful to me. Moreover they and the whole world will recognize that I was obliged to punish them with exile and the sword because of their sins. Thus will my righteous rule be universally acknowledged."

6. *Restored and Purified Israel* (39 : 25-29)

<small>Jehovah's omnipotence and righteousness revealed to the world (39 : 25-29)</small> It will not be long, O Israel, before Jehovah will be ready to restore you to your land. Then will you put away the evil you have practised, and live in obedience and security. Then will you realize why he dealt with you severely. Never again will he need to hide his face from you. Thus will his name be honored throughout the world.

EZEKIEL'S VISION OF THE RE-STORED HEBREW STATE

EZEKIEL'S VISION OF THE RESTORED HEBREW STATE

I

THE CHARACTER AND IMPORTANCE OF THE VISION

The last nine chapters of the book of Ezekiel, far from being, as so many readers treat it, a sort of appendix which may readily be ignored, is really a crowning conclusion to all that precedes. The prophet begins with a vision of God; he concludes with a vision of God in the midst of his purified, reverent people.

There is a real unity traceable throughout the book. In the earlier chapters the prophet unsparingly denounced his unfaithful nation and asserted its destruction because it was in every way misrepresenting its God and ignoring his precepts (1-24). His foreign predictions (25 to 32) were in reality a looking forward to the time when the insolent neighboring states should be cleared away to make room for the new ideal Israel. His hopeful visions of a unified and restored people prepared the way more completely for a sketch of the ideal embodiment of the true relations between God and his people. Perhaps no one but a priest as well as prophet, who knew the old and looked forward to a new and better order, who realized vividly the most dangerous tendencies of the nation before its exile, and who planned in a definite way to counteract them, could have been the medium of so noteworthy a reconstruction.

First of all, however, these chapters are interesting because they contain a remarkably bold prophecy. At a time when the temple and city lay in ruins, when the land was devastated and in the possession of Judah's foes, the people scattered, the empire of their conqueror at the height of its power, and the exiles dispirited and helpless, the prophet draws a picture of a temple to be erected on the old site by a reunited and prosperous people who inhabit a fruitful and populous land without hint of traitor within or foe without. For sublime confidence one can only compare with it Jeremiah's purchase of the field at Anathoth (32 : 1-15) just before Jerusalem's downfall. By such object lessons as these the prophets were wont to challenge despondency and to inculcate their own robust and unswerving faith.

Ezekiel, however, had a broader purpose than merely to awaken a spirit of hopefulness. His aim was constructive. Four ideas seem to have impressed themselves upon his mind as essential to the ideal development of his race : first, the people should make much more of the *forms* of religious life than ever before in order to be responsive to the demands of true holiness; again, the ritual recognized by them should be much more exact and strict than it had been in the past; in the third place, the ecclesiastical power must be independent in matters religious, not subject to royal caprice; and lastly, this power was to be centred in the family of Zadok.

With consummate art Ezekiel presents such a ritualistic constitution, which provides for a temple with priests and servitors, with every appointment and necessary resource, protected and supported but not controlled by the king, its holiness guarded by the provision of an outer court, beyond which only consecrated men could pass, situated in the midst of a reservation allotted to the priests and Levites, which was in turn encircled by a territory where every true Israelite was allotted an equal share. It is a sketch, a ground plan, but its details are also carefully developed. Throughout the author recognizes that his vision has been given by God, an inspiration which is not belittled or gainsaid by the recognition of the prophet's share in its formation.

Two details are new to Hebrew history. The old temple had only one court. Ezekiel provides another, in order to emphasize the distinction between that which is holy and ceremonially clean and, therefore, admissible to God's presence, and that which is common. Not even the king may step within the inner court, where the great altar of burnt offering stands before the temple proper. Again, before the exile, many priestly families had a claim upon the perquisites and the prerogatives of the priesthood at Jerusalem. Ezekiel declares that the Zadokites alone are worthy to serve at the altar, because they had, on the whole, been faithful to the ideals of the priesthood.

There was one element of weakness in this newly formulated policy; it reduced popular religion to a series of forms. A man's access to God was no longer to be direct in any sense; he could only stand afar off and watch, while others performed for him the symbolic rites. No doubt it was felt that the resulting systemization of religion would be a real advantage; but it can hardly be doubted that there was a loss in personal fervor.

Ezekiel's plan was never fully adopted. It was not, in fact, so adjusted to existing conditions that it could be. It is really a sort of Messianic apocalypse, an ideal picture of what ought to come to pass, intended rather to suggest broad lines of progress than to indicate exact details.

Ezekiel has been properly termed the father of Judaism, for by his keen insight into the needs of the times and by his clever formulation of his proposed policy in this striking vision, he helped materially to shape the growth of the Jewish polity which resulted in the adoption of a strict ritual. His suggestions seem to stand half-way between the free and popular ritual of Deuteronomy and the elaborate technicalities of the Levitical code. In this

Later Prophets Ezekiel 40 : 4

work he probably also represents other thoughtful minds which were intent upon the religious problems of their race, and yet among them all he was as conspicuous as one of the stately cedars of which the prophets love to think. His was the master mind through which was given the impulse toward the most important transformation that ever a nation was called upon to undergo.

II

THE DETAILS OF THE VISION

1. *The New Sanctuary on Mount Zion* (40 to 43)

(1) *Its Gateways and Outer Court* (40 : 1-27)

In the fourteenth year after the fall of Jerusalem Jehovah graciously revealed to me a vision of such an abode as he would delight to inhabit. When the prophetic ecstasy came over me, I seemed to be carried back to my native land and set down in the sacred city, Jerusalem. Upon the old temple hill, conspicuous above all other elevations, was an imposing group of buildings, like those of a city. Directly before me in the eastern gateway stood a man of glorious appearance like a heavenly messenger, holding in his hand a cord and rod for taking measurements, who said to me: "Mortal man, pay strict heed to all that I show you, that you may be able to reveal Jehovah's purpose to your nation."

Introduction : the vision of the new temple at Jerusalem (40 : 1-4)

Ezekiel 40 : 5

The surrounding wall (40 : 5)
My attention was first drawn to a wall, nine[1] feet high and broad, which encircled all the buildings.

The eastern gateway of the outer wall (40 : 6-16)
Then we came to the great gateway facing the east. It was seventy-five feet long and half as wide. Ascending the outer steps, we entered, through a portal as wide as the outer wall, a passage-way fifteen feet wide and forty-two feet long. On each side of this were three guard-rooms for officers, each nine feet square and provided with windows. At the other end of the passage-way was a second portal, similar in size to the first, from which we passed into a large vestibule, and then into the courtyard.

The outer court and the outer gateways (40 : 17-27)
Around the outer margin of this court were thirty chambers fronting upon a pavement which extended to the vestibule of the gateway. The court was one hundred and fifty feet wide. It had two other gateways fronting to the north and south, exactly similar in construction and size to the one through which we had passed.

(2) *The Inner Court* (40 : 28-47)

Its three gateways (40 : 28-37)
Crossing the outer court, we came to the gateways leading into the inner court. They were three in number, facing south, east, and north. Their dimensions and construction were exactly like those of the outer gateways, except that their vestibules faced the outer court. The

[1] For purposes of convenience the cubit will be reckoned at eighteen inches in the following estimates. Quite probably one-sixth should be added to every such estimate.

level of the inner court was reached by a flight of eight steps.

Connected with a vestibule of the inner gateway¹ by a door was a chamber in which the burnt offering was washed. *The sacrificial tables (40: 38-43)* In the vestibule itself stood four tables, two on either side, and outside the vestibule two other pairs of tables, all for use in the slaughter of sacrificial victims. With each pair of tables was a smaller one of hewn stone, on which the sacrificial implements were laid.

In the inner court were two apartments, one by the north gate facing southward, the other by the south gate facing northward. *The two apartments for priests (40: 44-46)* The former was the residence of the priests who took care of the temple; the latter was for those of the family of Zadok, who ministered at the altar.

The inner court itself was one hundred and fifty feet square. In the middle, so that it could be seen through the gateways, and immediately before the temple, was the great altar of burnt offering. *The great altar (40: 47)*

(3) *The Temple and its Adjuncts* (40: 48 to 41: 26)

On the western side of the inner court was the temple on an elevated platform approached by ten² steps. Ascending these, we entered a vestibule thirty feet wide and eighteen feet long by an entrance twenty-one feet wide. On either side of the entrance was a huge pillar. Beyond *The porch (40: 48, 49)*

¹ The text does not indicate which gateway it was.
² So the Septuagint.

Ezekiel 41 : 1 *Messages of the*

The main hall (41 : 1, 2)
the vestibule was the main hall of the temple, sixty feet in length by thirty in breadth, entered through a doorway fifteen feet wide.

The most holy place (41 : 3, 4)
Beyond this hall was the innermost shrine of the temple, the holy of holies. It was exactly square, with a doorway nine feet in width. Within this hallowed spot, the abode of Jehovah's glory, I could not enter.

The chambers at the side (41 : 5-7)
The wall of the temple was nine feet thick. Round about this wall on each side except the east was an outer wall seven and a half feet thick, the interval between them at the base being six feet. Between these walls were built small cells in three tiers, thirty chambers in each tier. The cells of the second and third tier were somewhat broader than those at the base, their supporting beams resting on the ledges made by the recession of the wall.

The raised platform (41 : 8-15a)
The tiers were connected by winding stairways, and opened into the terrace on which the temple stood. Thirty feet west of the temple was a large building, the purpose of which I did not ask. Its area as well as that of the temple court and that of the inner court were each one hundred and fifty feet square.

The interior of the temple (41 : 15b -26)
The whole interior of the temple was panelled and ceiled with wood. From floor to roof this woodwork, in the holiest place and in the main hall, was ornamented with carved work representing cherubs and palms. Before the holy of holies stood an altar-like wooden table

for the shewbread. Swinging doors led into the hall and into the most holy place, each door being made in two sections and elaborately carved.

(4) *Other Buildings of the Inner Court* (42 : 1-14; 46: 19-24)

On the northern and southern sides of the inner court were two three-story buildings, each one hundred and fifty by seventy-five feet, with a passage-way fifteen feet wide in front. The uppermost stories included a gallery. The walls which faced the outer court extended only half of the length of the walls that faced the temple. These buildings could be entered from the passage-ways and from the outer court. In these chambers the priests who minister at the altar were to store and eat their portions of the sacrificial offerings, and to lay aside their sacred garments before going into the outer court of the people.

The chambers for the priests (42 : 1-12)

Their use (42 : 13, 14)

Entering these chambers from the outer court, we noted in the western corners of the inner court kitchens for the exclusive use of the priests in preparing their share of the sacrifices for food. Passing thence, we saw in each corner of the outer court four kitchens sixty by forty-five feet in size, surrounded by pillars, where the Levites boiled the sacrificial meals for the people.

The kitchens for the priests and people (46 : 19-24)

(5) *The Whole Temple Area* (42 : 15-20)

Having completed the inspection and measurement of the interior arrangement of the temple area, we passed

Ezekiel 42 : 16   *Messages of the*

The outside measurements of the whole enclosure (42: 15-20)
out of the eastern gateway and measured the exterior wall. The whole enclosure was seven hundred and fifty feet square. A wall encircled it, shutting in the sanctuary from the outside world.

(6) *The Return of Jehovah to His Abode* (43 : 1-12)

The third vision of Jehovah's glory (43: 1-5)
We then returned to the eastern gate, and there I beheld the glory of Jehovah approaching from the east with a noise that resembled the roar of a rushing stream and a radiance that illumined the earth and sky. It was like the splendid visions I had seen before on the river Chebar and at Jerusalem. I fell on my face in awe, while the glory passed through the gateway. Transported to the inner court, I saw that it filled the temple. At the same

The conditions of its permanence (43: 6-9)
time a voice announced : " Mortal man, in this truly sacred temple I will be pleased to dwell. No longer shall my abode be defiled by the immediate presence of a royal palace and a royal burial-place, and by the abominations which kings are wont to practise. It must be wholly free from contact with that which is profane.

The new temple to be built according to the vision (43: 10-12)
" Proclaim, therefore, to the men of Israel exactly how the new temple is to be erected, describing its true dimensions and noting all its ordinances and ritual, that everything may be done in perfect keeping with the divine ideal. No part of the mountain top is to be given up for a royal residence, or for any other secular use. All is to be consecrated to the worship of Jehovah."

(7) The Great Altar and its Consecration (43 : 13-27)

In the very centre of the inner court was the great altar of burnt-offering, a huge structure of stone, rising in three regularly diminishing terraces to a height of seventeen feet from a base twenty-seven feet square and one and a half feet in height. The steps by which the priests ascended to the altar-hearth faced the east. *(Description of the altar (43 : 13-17))*

"Mortal one," said the voice, "in the day when the altar is completed it shall be consecrated for its sacred service in the following manner: Let the priests of the family of Zadok, whose service is acceptable to me, apply the blood of a freshly slain bullock to the prominent parts of the altar, in token of its dedication to the service of Jehovah. The bullock shall then be burned in the proper place outside the temple area. For six days thereafter the altar shall be ceremonially cleansed with the blood of a he-goat, and a burnt offering made of a bullock and a ram. When the altar has thus been set apart and sanctified, the sanctuary will be holy, and there will I accept the offerings of my people." *(The method of its dedication (43 : 18-27))*

2. Ordinances Regarding the Temple (44 to 46)

(1) The Use of the Outer Eastern Gateway (44 : 1-3)

We now returned to the great eastern gateway of the outer court but found it closed. The voice then said: "Since Jehovah has entered by this gateway, no mortal *(The prince alone to enter it (44 : 1-3))*

Ezekiel 44 : 3   *Messages of the*

shall pass through it. Let it remain forever closed. The prince¹ may enter the vestibule from the outer court and there partake of the sacrificial meal."

(2) *The Functions of the Levites and the Priests* (44 : 4-31)

The regulations in the interests of sanctity (44 : 4, 5)

Returning to the inner court, I again saw the splendor of Jehovah's glory filling the temple. The voice bade me pay good heed to the ordinances and regulations about to be promulgated for the preservation of the sanctity of the house of God.

Servants of foreign birth to be replaced by Levites (44 : 6-14)

No longer, forgetful Israel, shall you profane the sanctuary by permitting foreigners, whose service is purely mercenary, to be present while sacrifices are being offered and to have charge of the temple. Hereafter the members of the priestly families, which ministered at the high places and promoted Israel's unfaithfulness, shall be responsible for the service of the sanctuary. They shall guard the gateways, serve the priests, slay the animals for sacrifice, and wait upon the worshippers. They shall not, however, be permitted to act as priests.

Priests to be Zadokites (44 : 15, 16)
Their clothing (44 : 17-19)

The members of the priestly family of Zadok alone shall act as priests in the temple, for they have always been faithful to me. In the service of the sanctuary they shall wear, for the sake of coolness and purity, only linen clothing. Before mingling with the people they shall change these garments, leaving them in the appointed

¹ For some reason Ezekiel uses this word in preference to "king."

122

chambers. They shall neither shave their heads nor let their hair grow long like the Nazirite. They shall refrain from wine while on duty. They shall marry no one but a virgin or the widow of a priest. They shall not approach a dead body except that of a blood-relative. They shall then remain unclean, not serving at the altar for seven days, and shall thereafter present a sin-offering. {Further regulations promotive of sanctity (44 : 20-22, 25-27)}

They shall instruct the people in ceremonial obligations, deciding difficult cases. They shall also arbitrate in disputes between man and man, control public worship, and enforce the due observance of sacred days and seasons. {Their duties (44 : 23, 24)}

They shall not be expected to support themselves, but shall subsist entirely upon the offerings brought to the sanctuary. It is lawful for them to eat whatever is not to be consumed by fire. Theirs also is all property consecrated to Jehovah, the best of the first fruits and the thank offerings. They must carefully avoid eating meat which has not been slaughtered. {Their support (44 : 28-31)}

(3) *The Apportionment of their Land* (45 : 1-7)

On the return from exile, when the land is reapportioned, you shall mark out a tract about seven miles square. Of this land, set apart two-fifths for the Levites and their cities.[1] Another two-fifths allot to the priesthood, the domain required for the temple and an open space of seventy-five feet on all sides of it being taken from its {The sacred reservation (45 : 1-7)}

---

[1] So the Septuagint in place of "chambers."

Ezekiel 45 : 6 *Messages of the*

centre. The remaining strip, about seven miles by one and one-half, shall belong to the people who live in Jerusalem. All the territory east and west of the reservation shall belong to the prince.

(4) *The Rights and Duties of the Prince*
(45 : 8-17; 46 : 16-18)

The prince subject to property laws (45 : 8; 46: 16-18)
Having received a portion of his own, the prince must not take or give away the property of a subject. He may only allot the land to the tribes in accordance with Jehovah's will. His own property he may give to one of his sons in perpetuity. If granted to a subject, the land reverts to the prince in the jubilee year. He shall establish a correct scale of weights and measures, so that all robbery of the people in his name shall cease. They shall pay over to him for the support of the ritual one-sixtieth of their produce of wheat or barley, one-one-hundredth of their oil, and one out of every two hundred lambs. The prince shall in turn provide that which is needful for all the stated public sacrifices.

To regulate weights and measures (45 : 9-12)

The support of the ritual (45 : 13-17)

(5) *The Stated Offerings* (45 : 18 to 46 : 15)

The atonement for the sanctuary (45 : 18-20)
On the first day of the new year[1] and on the first day of the seventh month the priests shall formally cleanse the temple by applying the blood of an unblemished bullock to the doorposts of the sanctuary, to the corners of

---

[1] According to our calendar about the fifteenth of March.

the altar and to the posts of the gateway of the inner court. Thus shall it be kept absolutely sacred.

In the middle of the first month [1] shall be held the feast of the Passover. On the first day the prince shall offer in atonement for himself and the people a bullock, and in addition, daily burnt offerings for a week, with the appropriate cereal offerings and oil, and a sin-offering for each day. The offerings at Passover and Tabernacles (45 : 21-25)

Similarly, at the feast of Tabernacles, six months later, shall be provided all that is needed for the public offerings throughout the sacred week.

In ordinary weeks the eastern gate of the inner court shall be open only on Sabbath days and the days of the new moon. At such times the people shall assemble for worship in front of the gate, while the prince may ascend the steps, pass through the gateway, and stand at the threshold which opens upon the inner court. Every Sabbath the prince shall offer a burnt offering of six rams and one lamb, with the suitable proportion of cereal offerings and of oil. On the day of the new moon he shall make the same offering with the addition of a bullock Regulations for Sabbaths and new moons (46 : 1-7)

After performing his duties in the temple, the prince shall return as he entered. The multitude, however, to prevent confusion on a festal day, shall enter the outer court by one gate and depart by the opposite one. Both prince and people shall worship at the same time. If the Various regulations (46 : 8-12)

[1] About the first of April.

prince desires to make a special offering, the eastern gate of the main court may be opened for the purpose.

<small>The daily burnt offering (46 : 13-15)</small>
For every day in the year the prince shall provide a yearling lamb as a morning burnt offering with the suitable offerings of flour and oil.

3. *The Renewing and Allotment of the Land* (47 ; 48)

(1) *The Fertilizing Stream from the Temple* (47 : 1-12)

<small>Its source (47 : 1, 2)</small>
Again my celestial guide brought me to the inner court and showed me a stream of pure water issuing from beneath the porch of the temple, passing the altar on the south side and emerging from the temple near the <small>Its size (47 : 3-7)</small> outer eastern gate. Fifteen hundred feet away from the gate the water was ankle-deep; farther on it covered the knee; soon the stream became an unfordable river that could be crossed only by swimming. Along its banks <small>Its effect (47 : 8-12)</small> grew an abundance of trees. "Mortal one," said my companion, "behold this river of life-giving water springing from the very presence of God. Down the barren slopes of the Judean wilderness it will pour, restoring them to productiveness. It shall freshen even the Dead Sea, so that fishermen shall ply their trade there as on the Great Sea. Its desolation shall disappear. Only so much shall remain unchanged as will supply the salt which human life demands. All along the banks of the river shall grow every kind of useful tree, perennially fruitful. Thus shall the land be made a paradise."

Later Prophets   Ezekiel 48 : 14

(2) *The Boundaries of the Land* (47 : 13-20)

This is the will of Jehovah, O Israel, respecting the ex- <small>Only terri-
tory west of</small>
tent of the fertilized land, which you shall equally share <small>Jordan to be
included in</small>
among the twelve tribes. Its northern boundary shall ex- <small>the new land</small>
tend from the sea, not far from Tyre, and run eastward <small>of Israel
(47 : 13-20)</small>
to the vicinity of Dan. Its eastern boundary shall be the
river Jordan and its connected seas. The southern boundary shall extend from Tamar below the Dead Sea, through Kadesh, along the Brook of Egypt to the Mediterranean Sea, which shall constitute its western boundary.

(3) *The Allotment of the Land* (47 : 21 to 48 : 29)

Although this land shall be divided among the tribes, <small>The rights
of proselytes</small>
strangers not of Israelitish blood, who have adopted the <small>(47 : 21-23)</small>
worship of Jehovah and abide by all the ordinances, shall
have equal rights with those who are of Israel. They
shall have an inheritance among the members of the tribe
in which they sojourn.

Seven tribes shall be given allotments north of the por- <small>The tribes
north of the</small>
tion set apart for sacred purposes : Dan, Asher, Naphtali, <small>reservation</small>
Manasseh, Ephraim, Reuben, and Judah. Each tribe shall <small>(48 : 1-7)</small>
occupy a zone extending from the Jordan to the sea.

South of Judah's allotment shall be the sacred reserva- <small>The reser-
vation itself</small>
tion, inhabited by the Levites and by the priests. None <small>(48 : 8-22)</small>
of it shall ever be sold or exchanged or alienated by them,
for it is Jehovah's land.

Ezekiel 48 : 15-35

South of the portion allotted to the priests shall be a zone, one-half as large, in which the city Jerusalem shall be built. It shall be about a mile and a quarter square. Its public lands shall extend three hundred and seventy-five feet on every side. The rest of the territory, about nine square miles, shall be devoted to agricultural purposes. The inhabitants shall come from all Israel. On both sides of the sacred reservation, that he may protect it, shall be the domain of the prince.

The tribes south of the reservation (48 : 23-29) South of the reservation five tribes shall be given allotments: Benjamin, Simeon, Issachar, Zebulon, and Gad. This territory, two hundred miles by an average of fifty, shall be the possession of the tribes of Israel forever.

(4) *The Holy City* (48 : 30-35)

The circuit, gates, and name of the new city (48 : 30-35) The city shall have three gates on each side named after the ancient tribes. Its whole circuit shall be about five miles.[1] The city shall no longer be designated by its old familiar name, but shall be worthy of a new one, indicating that God dwells with his people. All shall call it, "Jehovah is there."

[1] The present city, excluding the suburbs, has a circuit of 2½ miles.

SONGS OF EXULTATION OVER BABYLON'S APPROACHING FALL.

SONGS OF EXULTATION OVER BABYLON'S APPROACHING FALL

I

THE RISE OF CYRUS

Ezekiel's latest prophecy is dated 570 B. C. Probably before that time Jeremiah's long life-work came to an end. From the middle of the period of the Babylonian exile no prophecies which can be dated with certainty have been preserved. While the strong hand of Nebuchadrezzar ruled the Babylonian empire the Jews were apparently subjected to no serious persecutions, nor was there anything in the political outlook to arouse hopes of deliverance; the prophets therefore were silent.

Although under the immediate successors of Nebuchadrezzar there was no radical change of policy to the close observer, the internal weakness of the empire began to be apparent. The accession of the usurper Nabonidus in 555 B. C. marked the beginning of the end. He had none of the prestige nor executive ability of the conqueror of Jerusalem. His interests were with the gods and traditions of the past rather than with his subjects and the problems which pressed upon them. While dangers threatened, he devoted himself to excavating the sites of ancient temples, neglecting his duties as king. The inevitable result was that the civil and military organization of the state fell into decay, while the confidence and loyalty of the people toward their antiquarian king waned, so that when the crisis came the empire collapsed suddenly and completely.

Its strength and vast resources might have preserved it intact had not a powerful and energetic foe arisen in the north. The rise of Cyrus from comparative obscurity to the rule over all of southwestern Asia was so sudden and unexpected that it took the ancient world completely by surprise. In 549 B. C. this king of the little kingdom of of Anzan, located among the mountains to the northeast of Babylonia, espousing the cause of the older Aryan population, defeated his overlord, the Scythian king Astyages, and by this act became master of the large but loosely organized empire which the northern invaders had built upon the ruins of Assyria.

The new conqueror was quickly able to amalgamate the varied elements under him and by his personal ability and energy to develop an efficient army. Fortunately for him the strongest rivals, the Babylonians under Nabonidus, were inactive. He was, therefore, able to meet his foes in succession and to strengthen his position on every side before attacking the proud mistress of the lower Euphrates. He appears also to have instituted intrigues in Babylon calculated still further to alienate the subjects of Nabonidus and to prepare the way for their ready submission when the attack came.

After having conquered in 547 B. C. the territory of Mesopotamia lying to the north of Babylonia, he turned westward in the following year to meet the attack of the rich, powerful Lydian king Crœsus. After fighting an indecisive battle, he followed up his rival, defeated him, and within an incredibly short time was in possession of his wealthy capital and kingdom.

He next attacked the opulent Greek colonies on the coast of the Ægean Sea. Many of these were not lacking in courage, and so offered a desperate resistance, but the rapid advance of Cyrus gave them no opportunity to effect a general organization against their dread foe. The result was that most of them quickly submitted, while those who refused were not able to hold out long against such overwhelming numbers as the Persian king was able to launch against them. In the end, after a series of signal victories, Cyrus returned to his capital, supreme lord of all of the states of Asia Minor.

The restless, half-civilized peoples to the east of his empire next commanded his attention. Here again he and his army secured not only vast territory and spoil, but also great prestige, so that by the autumn of 538 B. C., when he turned his armies against Babylon, victory was practically assured.

II

THE DATE AND AUTHORSHIP OF ISAIAH 13 : 2 to 14 : 23 ; 21 : 1^{b}-10 ; JEREMIAH 50 : 1 to 51 : 58

The period following the overthrow of the rule of Astyages by Cyrus in 549 B. C. furnishes the most probable background of a series of brief prophecies, appended to the original writings of Jeremiah and Isaiah, which treat of the approaching downfall of Babylon. In Jeremiah 50 : 1 to 51 : 58 the prophet and his readers behold in the north the people who are to deliver them. They are clearly the Medo-Persians under Cyrus, although in accordance with the terminology which continued in use even after the death of the great conqueror, they are styled simply the Medes. Babylon's destruction is looked for in the future, so that the prophecy must have been written before 539 B. C. In the middle or earlier part of the decade is found the most probable date of the original sections.

The prophecy was, without much doubt, in time attributed to the great Jeremiah, or at least joined to the collection of his sermons, because of the tradition preserved in the closing verses of chapter 51, to the effect that " he wrote

Later Prophets   Isaiah

in a book all the evil that should come upon Babylon"; that he made a prediction concerning that great worldpower is undoubtedly historical. Several of his prophecies respecting the Babylonians have been preserved, but a study of them makes it probable that Jeremiah was not the author of the present one. Not only is the style different, but the point of view also is quite other than that of Jeremiah. A familiarity with Babylon and with the politics of the East, which would be impossible to a Jew who had never crossed the Euphrates, is also apparent. The prophet who wrote these chapters had obviously not, like Jeremiah, received special favors from the Babylonians, but instead recalled only wrongs and insults received from their hands. He was also familiar with certain of Ezekiel's prophecies, written probably after the death of Jeremiah. He was, perhaps, a disciple of one of the great prophets. Although his prophecy lacks the originality, literary finish, and permanent value of his master's, it affords a glimpse into the hearts of the faithful exiles and records the triumph of inspired faith at a critical moment in the history of the Jewish race.

    The same date, although probably not the same author, has given us the prophecy found in Isaiah 13 : 2 to 14 : 23. The political problems which were insistent in the days of Isaiah the son of Amoz have long been forgotten. The Babylonians instead of being fellow-rebels with the Hebrews, as they were in the time of Hezekiah, are the masters and hated oppressors of the Jews. The exile, which Isaiah at the most only hinted at as a distant danger, has long been a reality; and the promise of restoration to Judah is presented by the prophet. The Medes are already crossing the northern frontier of Babylon. Many ideas peculiar to the exilic and post-exilic writers also find expression in this section. The style likewise is not that of Isaiah but of the later prophets.

Striking points of contrast between Jeremiah 50: 1 to 51: 58 and this prophecy suggest that the author of the one influenced the other. If so, the passage in Isaiah is the more original and, therefore, probably slightly earlier.

To the same group belongs the short section, Isaiah 21: 1-10. Its theme is the fall of Babylon. Media and Elam (from whence Cyrus came) are urged to advance against the oppressor. The end, however, is seen only by aid of the prophetic vision. The language of the passage has many points of affinity with that of Isaiah, but the extreme obscurity of its thought is in striking contrast with the clear, direct messages of the pre-exilic prophet. While the exile and the years immediately following the appearance of Cyrus furnish the only satisfactory historical setting, its indefiniteness suggests that it is the earliest of the three prophecies.

Later Prophets   Isaiah 21 : 10

III

PREDICTIONS OF THE FALL OF BABYLON (ISA. 21 : 1ᵇ-10 ; 13 : 2 to 14 : 23 ; JER. 50 : 2 to 51: 58)

1. *The Vision of Coming Overthrow* (Isa. 21 : 1ᵇ-10)

Like the dreaded wind-storm from the desert came Content of the vision (21: 1ᵇ-2)
to me a revelation of desolation and judgment about to fall upon the destructive robber-nation, Babylonia. Advance, O Cyrus, from your mountain home in Elam at the head of the Medo-Persian army which you are forming. Babylon shall soon cease to afflict the nations.

As I contemplated the overwhelming catastrophe which Effect upon the prophet (21 : 3-5)
was about to overtake the proud city, I was overcome with mingled regret, dismay, and terror. While I observed the display and luxury of its inhabitants, I thought of the deadly attack which its rulers would soon be obliged to meet, when least they expected it.

At the divine command I stationed a watchman to report Report of the prophetic watchman (21 :6-10)
the first appearance of the hostile Persian army As he carefully scanned the political horizon he saw the cavalry in double rank advancing. Then by anticipation he raised the cry : " Fallen is Babylon, and all the images of her gods are broken in fragments." O exiles, objects of Jehovah's crushing judgment, victims of Babylonian greed and cruelty, learn from this vision the message of

hope and promise which your God thus announces to you.

2. *Jehovah's Judgment upon Babylon* (Isa. 13 : 2 to 14 : 23)

<small>The agents of Jehovah's judgment (13 : 2-6)</small> The divine decree has gone forth to raise in a conspicuous place the standard of war, and to send forth the proclamation. Already Jehovah has consecrated and commissioned the victorious Persians to carry out his righteous purpose. They advance, a great host enlisted from many and distant nations. They are his agents, appointed to execute his judgment upon mankind.

<small>The horrors of the day of Jehovah (13 : 7-16)</small> When the day of Jehovah comes, the strong shall be powerless, the stanchest hearts shall quail, and men shall be seized with mortal agony. Then toward those who have defied his laws, Jehovah will show not mercy but fierce indignation. All nature will join with him in carrying out his just sentence against the guilty, arrogant, and tyrannical. So universal shall be the destruction that only a few men will be left to people the earth. The thunder, the lightning, and the earthquake shall be messengers of his wrath. Men shall flee like sheep without a shepherd, each seeking a refuge in his own land, but in vain. Those who are captured will be slain by the conquerors, their children ruthlessly slaughtered in their presence, their wives ravished, and their houses pillaged.

The agents of Jehovah's judgment are already at hand;

they are the victorious Medes, now organized and led by the strong hand of Cyrus. Bribes will not turn them back. To none do they show mercy. Before them, proud, imperial Babylon shall go down in ruin, as complete as that which Jehovah visited upon the corrupt cities on the plain beside the salt sea. Uninhabited, its desolate ruins shall be avoided even by the wandering shepherd. Foul beasts and birds of prey and vile spirits shall infest its luxurious palaces. {The Medes to execute vengeance upon Babylon (13: 17-22a)}

That day is near; you will not have long to wait, O exiles. [Soon Jehovah will take pity upon his afflicted people, and will restore them to their land. Foreigners, as proselytes, will join themselves to the Jews and thus swell their depleted ranks. The heathen nations, their present foes, will then aid in restoring them. Then Jehovah's people will be, not the slaves, but the masters of their present captors. Then shall they enjoy peace and immunity from the tasks and pains of the present. Upon their lips will be this song of derision over fallen Babylon:] {The restoration of Jehovah's people (13: 22b to 14: 3)}

"Behold how the proud city, rich from the spoil of countless nations, has at last come to an end! Because these Babylonians sought only to destroy and to crush other peoples who fell under their sway, Jehovah has broken their power. As a result peace and joy have come to all mankind. The whole universe joins in exulting over the fact that just retribution has at last overtaken {Ode of triumph over fallen Babylon (14: 4-21)} you, O cruel Babylon. Sheol has eagerly received you, and all your pomp and vain glory have gone down to the land of shades. You have been brought low, you who were the most distinguished among the great nations of the earth; you who purposed not only to conquer all the habitable earth, but also to mount the heavens, and, ejecting God from his throne, to rule omnipotently. To the lowest depths of degradation shall you fall. Succeeding generations, observing your humiliation, shall inquire wonderingly, 'Can this be the people who caused the whole world to tremble with fear, and who carried away so many captives into unending confinement?' Other conquerors have been honorably interred by their subjects, but you shall be cast forth, dishonored and unburied, because you have brought only ruin to your own and other lands. Your descendants will also be the objects of divine judgment, lest the corrupt and destructive race overrun the entire earth."

Jehovah's doom (14:22, 23) Jehovah solemnly declares that he will completely extinguish the Babylonian nation, so that no offspring shall survive in future ages. After his sentence of destruction has been executed, its land shall be a desolate, deserted ruin.

3. *Retribution for Babylon and Restoration for Israel* (Jer. 50:2 to 51:58)

Let all the nations know that Babylon's doom is sealed. Her gods, in which she now places implicit trust, are soon to be subjected to ignominy and disgrace. Already from the north the foes are approaching which are destined to break her power and devastate her land. *Babylon's impending doom (50: 2, 3)*

In the new era just dawning, the chosen people of Jehovah in true penitence will seek their God. The descendants of the northern and southern Israelites shall earnestly crave the restoration of the old life about the sacred temple mount, and the establishment of a close and binding relationship between them and Jehovah, which they will not disregard as did their fathers. *The true repentance of Israel (50: 4, 5)*

Tragic has been their history, and pitiable is their present condition, for they are as lost sheep, misled by their natural leaders. Scattered far and wide, they have forgotten their home-land. They are the helpless victims of their enemies, who declare that it is no crime to destroy them because their gross sins have made them the objects of Jehovah's wrath. *The present sad condition of Jehovah's people (50: 6, 7)*

At last escape, O Jewish exiles, from the land of your captivity. Vie with each other in the alacrity with which you flee from the midst of this condemned people. For Jehovah is about to array hostile hordes from the north against them, whose might and military equipment shall be irresistible. Babylon shall prove a rich spoil to the conqueror. This judgment shall fall upon the Babylonians because they took a heartless pleasure in plundering and destroying Judah. They in turn shall experience the same horrors. As they did to others shall it be done to *Relief shall come through the overthrow of Babylon (50: 8-16)*

Jeremiah 50:16 — *Messages of the*

them. In the days of their humiliation, the nations which they wronged shall turn against them. Desolation, destruction, and terror shall overwhelm them.

<small>Israel's tragic past contrasted with its glorious future (50:17-20)</small>

In the past the chosen people of Jehovah have been the prey, first of the fierce Assyrians and then of the Babylonians, but now the course of their history is about to change. Jehovah has determined to take vengeance upon the Babylonians, even as he did upon the Assyrians. Then will he bring back his scattered people to the fertile land of Canaan, there to satisfy alike their physical and their spiritual wants, for he will completely pardon the sins of those who then survive.

<small>The divine vengeance awaiting Babylon (50:21-32)</small>

Advance, O agents of Jehovah's judgment, against Babylon, the most defiant and guilty of people; slay and spare nothing, for it is the divine command. Already the great conflict is on and the destruction of this destroyer of nations has begun. Already Jehovah has begun to bring low this mighty kingdom which has so long bade defiance to him. Against it he is sending the strong people who are to execute his vengeance. Spoil, plunder, spare neither man nor beast, for its guilt leaves no place for mercy. Soon fire and the sword will complete the work of destruction. Long, and with no visible prospect of escape, have the descendants of the northern and southern Israelites been held as captives by their oppressors, but Jehovah their deliverer is omnipotent. He will vindicate them and grant them peace and prosperity, through the overthrow of the Babylonians. The might and wisdom of these arrogant rulers of the world will not deliver them from Jehovah's wrath. The avenging sword is about to cut off all their power, pomp, and wrath. The destructive forces of nature shall assist in their undoing. The land shall become a barren waste, like the site of the cities of the plain. *The completeness of the destruction of Israel's oppressors (50 : 33-40)*

Babylon's destroyers are already approaching from the north. They are a mighty nation, formed by the union of many peoples from far and near; they are well equipped and show no mercy to their foes. The sound of their advance is like that of the surging sea. The king of Babylon loses all courage as he hears of their approach. Terror and distress destroy his power of action and chill his heart. Like a strong lion they are about to leap upon their helpless prey. All this is but the carrying out of Jehovah's omnipotent purpose. They are the agents of Babylon's overthrow. Soon the whole earth shall be shaken by the great catastrophe. *Picture of the approach of the destroyers summoned by Jehovah (50 : 41-46)*

Since Jehovah so plainly reveals to his guilty but now forgiven people the overwhelming fate awaiting Babylon, let them hold themselves in readiness to flee, lest they suffer in the time of universal destruction. Babylon has been an agent of judgment in Jehovah's hand, but now she has completed her work. Her fate is sealed, since she refused to learn from the ambassadors of Jehovah. It only remains for us, the foreign exiles in her midst, to *Let Israel therefore leave doomed Babylon (51 : 1-14)*

Jeremiah 51 : 9

return to our own lands, and so avoid the consequences of the far-extended judgment which will come upon her. Our God by her overthrow is vindicating our righteousness. Therefore let us devote ourselves to re-establishing our nation in Judah, thereby making known the glorious deliverance which he has effected. The Median princes are already completing their plans for the destruction of Babylon. O nation, rich in resources, surrounded by huge walls and deep moats, confident of your strength, Jehovah has determined to lay you waste ; it is vain for you to hope to escape !

Jehovah alone is God supreme (51 : 15-19)

Jehovah it is who by his omniscience and omnipotence created and now rules the universe. Its forces are completely under his control. Man is weak and ignorant in comparison with him. The images which the heathen worship as their gods are vain delusions, the inanimate products of the hands of mortal men, while Jehovah is the supreme creator and ruler of everything in heaven and on the earth.

Israel to be Jehovah's instrument of judgment (51 : 20-24)

[You, O chosen people,[1] are the instrument with which Jehovah will realize his purpose in human history and wherewith he will break the power of the mighty nation which now with iron hand rules the world. Upon the

[1] Verses 20 to 24 interrupt the context and probably were interpolated. It is doubtful whether they were addressed to Israel, Cyrus, or Babylon. In view of the thought in verse 24, the first interpretation has been adopted.

Later Prophets Jeremiah 51 : 58

Babylonians, who so long have wronged you, he will visit the punishment for their crimes.]

    To complete the destruction the warlike nations of the north draw near. In their terror the Babylonians make no attempt at defence. All is confusion. The rapacious people who swallowed up, like a great fish, little Judah at last are atoning with their own life-blood for the violence done. Let the Jewish exiles flee from the doomed city, already given over by Jehovah to the spoilers. *Detailed description of the destruction of Babylon (51 : 25-58)*

THE MESSAGES OF THE GREAT
PROPHET OF THE EXILE
(ISAIAH 40 TO 55)

THE MESSAGES OF THE GREAT PROPHET OF THE EXILE
(ISAIAH 40 TO 55)

I

THE AUTHORSHIP, UNITY, AND DATE OF ISAIAH 40 TO 55

In the entire field of Old Testament prophecy there are found no more striking contrasts in style, vocabulary, and thought than exist between the extracts from the sermons of the great statesman-prophet, preserved in the first part of the Book of Isaiah, and the glowing messages of comfort and encouragement contained in chapters 40 to 55 of the same collection. The condensed, forcible, and often abrupt diction of Isaiah the son of Amoz is exchanged for a flowing, poetical, and, at times, redundant style. In general, the one is the product of the public orator, adapting his form of expression, as well as his thought, to the listening audience before him, while the other is that of the student, who writes in private, developing his elaborate figures and parallels at his leisure. The vocabulary and idioms peculiar to each also differ widely.

No great prophet who followed the imperial Isaiah failed to be influenced more or less by his inspired teachings. The majesty and omnipotence of Jehovah, the supreme Ruler of the universe, are emphasized in every part of the Book of Isaiah, but many new conceptions of God appear for the first time in chapters 40 to 55. Many of them are peculiar to this section, but others reflect the experiences of the Hebrew nation, or of individual members of that commonwealth, during the century and a half following the death of Isaiah the son of Amoz.

Especially do the life experiences and teachings of Jeremiah reappear in the noble setting of these chapters. Principles first proclaimed by Ezekiel are re-emphasized. The characteristic style and thought of this section are unmistakably not those of the earlier period, but of the exile.

The point of view also is clearly not that of Isaiah, who dealt with the national problems forced upon Judah, and who spoke of captivity as only a distant possibility, conditioned upon the action of his people and their leaders, but of the latter part of the Babylonian exile. The prophet is speaking not to an organized nation, but to a handful of disheartened, afflicted exiles. The denunciations and warnings of the past are no longer repeated. Instead, his watchword is comfort. His aim is to encourage and to inspire within doubting hearts faith in Jehovah and in the future of their race. Captivity is no longer held up as a threat; for years it has been an awful reality; but now,

Later Prophets — Isaiah

at last, the prophet proclaims, in a hundred varied forms, that deliverance from Babylon, where his hearers are living, is at hand. It is certain, and the deliverer has appeared; he is Cyrus, whose career the Jewish exiles, like all the peoples of that ancient world, were watching with terror and expectancy.

These, and a vast array of kindred facts, have led modern students generally to recognize in chapters 40 to 55 one of the many appendices, added during the exilic and post-exilic periods by chance, or, more probably, intentionally, because of their intrinsic beauty of thought and expression, or because of their logical connection to the earlier sermons of the prince of prophets. The associating of later anonymous pieces of literature with the name of some prominent personality, like Moses or David or Solomon, was a liberty freely taken by the editors of the Old Testament writings.

The name of the author of these chapters, like that of many of the later prophecies, will probably never be known. Because they are found in the Book of Isaiah, the author has been designated by many writers as "the Second Isaiah," or "the Deutero-Isaiah." This term, however, does not affirm that he actually bore the name Isaiah, although, if his writings were not one of many appendices in the present book, identity of name might furnish the simplest explanation of the association. By some, in recognition of the fact that his work was anonymous, he has been styled "the Great Unknown." The originality and grandeur of his message, his surpassing beauty of expression, and the profound impression which he made upon the minds of succeeding generations certainly entitle him to the designation "great." To distinguish him from other contributors to the Book of Isaiah, we have spoken of him as "the great prophet of the exile."

As will be shown later, chapters 56 to 66 of the book, in all probability, come from the post-exilic period. The unity of the section 40 to 55 has also been seriously questioned. Professor Cheyne, for example, assigns chapters 49 to 55 and the passages describing the servant of Jehovah to the Persian period. The recurring cycles of thought and the frequent repetition of the same ideas in nearly the same words suggest that the section was not all written at once. It seems rather to represent extracts from tracts sent out to the exiles on different occasions. The editing may have been done by the author himself, but it is more probably the work of some of his disciples. Later editors also made certain additions, but in the spirit of the original author, so that, with the exception of a few passages, the different divisions constitute literary units, and will be treated as such in the paraphrase.

Notwithstanding these evidences of editorial revision, the testimony of the data, on the whole, strongly confirms the conclusion that these chapters are all the product of the same inspired mind, and come from the closing years

Later Prophets Isaiah

of the exile. The brilliant literary style, which makes each of them a classic, was imitated by later writers, but never equalled. Although presented in many varied forms, the same distinctive messages of immediate deliverance from exile, and of victory through self-sacrificing service, reappear in every chapter. There are also no suggestions that the revival of the Judean community had been partially realized. The way is being prepared for the return, and the Restoration is proclaimed with a confidence which is in striking contrast with the discouragements of the Persian period. The exuberance of hope which characterizes the entire section is peculiar to the great prophet and to the last decade of the Babylonian rule.

Two main divisions can be distinguished. In chapters 40 to 48 the doubts and temptations of the exiles are met. By authoritative statement and by arguments the prophet strives to dispel their fears that Jehovah has forever forsaken them. He calls their attention to the omnipotence and universality of the rule of their God. He then points out the many reasons why Jehovah will surely deliver them. To confirm their wavering faith by visible evidence he pictures the weakness of Babylon, and boldly declares that Cyrus is Jehovah's appointed agent of deliverance.

The victorious advance of this great conqueror can be traced with comparative definiteness. The distant peoples who are in their terror resorting with blind zeal to their gods of wood and metal, in the hope that they will reveal the future and deliver their devotees, are without much doubt the Greek colonies of western and southern Asia Minor. The chapters can, therefore, be dated with reasonable certainty in the years immediately following the conquest of the kingdom of Crœsus, in 546 B. C.

In the second section, chapters 49 to 55, there are no direct references to Cyrus. He has apparently about completed his work of preparing for the deliverance. The ironical invectives against the powerless gods of the Babylonians are also silenced. The inference is that their incapacity has been demonstrated to the minds of all by the impending or already accomplished conquest of their worshippers by Cyrus.

Henceforth the energies of the prophet are devoted to arousing the enthusiasm and patriotic zeal of his fellow-exiles sufficiently to lead them to face the hardships of the return to the land of their fathers, and the great privations and discouragements which certainly awaited them at the end of their journey. The date of the second section is, therefore, to be found not far from 538 B. C., when Cyrus by the conquest of Babylon removed all political barriers which hitherto had deterred the exiled peoples, whom he found in the captured city, from returning to their homes.

Later Prophets Isaiah

II

THE IDEAL OF SERVICE PRESENTED IN THE POR-
TRAITS OF THE TRUE SERVANT OF JEHOVAH

The Babylonian exile shattered many dogmas long cherished by the Hebrew race, and in so doing prepared the way for the acceptance of nobler doctrines. The old popular belief that the children of Israel were chosen by Jehovah simply to be the objects of his especial solicitude and the recipients of his favor no longer satisfied the thoughtful among the exiles in view of the calamities which had overtaken their nation. The salutary conviction was also forced upon them by the evidence of their eyes that they were only insignificant members of the great human family. The burning question: "In what sense are we the chosen people of Jehovah?" found its true answer in the inspired teachings of the great prophet of the exile. "Your greatness and superiority consist not in what you possess, nor in your character, but in the fact that you have been selected to be Jehovah's representatives before the world, and to be his witnesses. To that end you have been carefully educated by him. You are chosen, therefore, to give, not to receive."

After the destruction of the Hebrew kingdom in 586 B. C., largely as the result of the incapacity and crimes of the kings and princes of the house of David, the future hopes of the race, for a period at least, ceased to centre, as much as they had in the earlier days, about the royal Messiah. Cyrus is the only Messiah to whom the great prophet of the exile refers, and he is anointed by Jehovah to bring deliverance to the Jewish exiles in Babylon.

As the breadth and greatness of the mission of his race were revealed to the inspired author of Isaiah 40 to 55, he employed the already familiar but marvellously felicitous term, "servant of Jehovah," to describe the agent by whom God's beneficent purpose for mankind was to be realized. It had before been applied to individual prophets, priests, and kings, as well as to the nation collectively, so that it called up a host of inspiring memories in the mind of every Jew who heard it. It was a word which had the ordinary meaning of slave. It suggested complete possession by the master. The title "servant of Jehovah," therefore, implied, on the one hand, that the life, the energies, the all of the one so designated, were devoted to the service of his God, and on the other, that the Lord stood in a peculiarly intimate relationship to his slave. Its essential thought was the same as that of a Messiah who was anointed, and thus commissioned to perform a specific service.

Like his predecessors, the prophet frequently designates his nation, as a whole, as the servant of Jehovah. "Thou Israel, my servant, Jacob, whom I have chosen, seed of Abraham my lover, whom I brought from the ends of the

Later Prophets Isaiah

earth and called from its remotest parts. To whom I said: My servant art thou; I have chosen and have not rejected thee" (41:8, 9). To interpret the broader meaning of this term, and to lead his race to recognize all the obligations which it entailed, was the chief aim of the prophet.

As he considered the real character and thoughts of the representatives of his nation in Babylon, he realized with deep regret that they were by no means the perfect servants of Jehovah who were called for at that great crisis of human history to carry out the divine purpose. In dismay he exclaims in the name of Jehovah: "Ye deaf, hear; and ye blind, look up, that ye may see. Who is blind but my servant and deaf as my messenger?" (42:18, 19) and yet, he adds a little later: "Ye people with eyes, but blind, and ye with ears, but deaf. . . Ye are my witnesses, says Jehovah, and my servant whom I have chosen" (43:8, 10ª).

Like the great prophets who had preceded him, the author of Isaiah, 40 to 55, did not stop after having denounced the sins and incapacity of his people, but also set before them in glowing colors the ideal which he wished them to attain. Side by side with the portraits of the exiles, who were as a whole very imperfect servants of Jehovah, he places, in a series of remarkable passages, pictures of the ideal servant. The value and effectiveness of this type of teaching are obvious. That the prophet aimed thereby primarily to influence his contemporaries so that they would, if not completely, at least in part realize that ideal of devoted, self-sacrificing service, is also evident. Naturally he had in mind especially the more faithful ones among the exiles, who though persecuted and oppressed, were still asking what is the will of Jehovah. This fact of the intended immediate application of the teachings respecting the perfect servant of Jehovah, is well illustrated in the fiftieth chapter, where, after declaring in the name of the true servant that he must be the victim of cruel wrongs and insults, but that he will be upheld and vindicated by Jehovah, the prophet turns to his hearers and says: "Whoso among you fears the Lord, let him obey the voice of his servant; whoso walks in darkness with no light, let him trust in the name of Jehovah and lean upon his God" (50 : 10).

In portraying the ideal servant, the prophet clearly derived certain elements from the experiences of the spiritual heroes of his nation's past. The prophets as a class are prominently before his mind, and especially Jeremiah, whose life and words are vividly recalled by many of the passages; but it is the lot of the faithful in the exile, the persecutions, the reviling, and the doubts which he himself shared, that furnish the background and the darker outlines of the portraits. With these elements he set forth in immortal form the essential character and experiences of the man or men who alone would perfectly carry out the divine will. The originality and completeness of the picture are conclusive evidences of its divine origin. With his inspired sight the prophet saw, not the man or men of flesh and blood, but the type of servant required for the realization of the divine purpose in human history.

His own and succeeding generations in part—but only in part—realized the ideal of service. Those in Babylon who never ceased to trust and serve Jehovah, although in so doing they were the objects of the taunts and persecutions of their conquerors and their apostate brethren, belong to that number. It also includes such men as Joshua the priest and Zerubbabel the Davidic prince, who in 520 B. C. undertook the difficult task of rebuilding the ruined temple. Apparently recalling these chapters, Haggai addresses Zerubbabel as the servant of Jehovah (2 : 23). The ideal was ever before the minds of the faithful in the post-exilic period. Nehemiah and the others who later followed him from the East, leaving behind their own interests in order to revive their prostrate nation, proved themselves, just in so far as they were faithful, servants of Jehovah. No one man, however, nor group of men, completely realized this ideal of service, until Jesus of Nazareth, acting in perfect accord with the divine will, not only fulfilled it, but also revealed still more clearly by his life and words God's purpose to redeem mankind from its unnatural sins. Hence those who disregard their historical setting and see in these servant passages pure predictions of the Christ have grasped the essential fact. They fail, however, to profit by that fuller light which is shed upon these marvellous chapters by a sympathetic appreciation of the immediate aims of their author and by a knowledge of the existing conditions with which he was dealing. They also fail to recognize with Paul (Acts 13 : 47) that the exalted ideal of service is a constant divine appeal and command to every human being, irrespective of age or nationality, to become a perfect servant of Jehovah.

III

THE CERTAINTY AND THE REASON OF THE RELEASE OF JEHOVAH'S PEOPLE (ISA. 40 TO 48)

1. *The Proclamation that Deliverance is at Hand* (40 : 1-11)

The prologue: comfort, the keynote of the following prophecies (40 : 1, 2) Jehovah's message to his people through his prophets is now not one of denunciation, but of comfort. With infinite tenderness he speaks to the sad hearts of the exiles, assuring them that their period of affliction and discipline is at last nearing its close and that they have paid the full penalty for the sins of their nation.

Jehovah's triumphal restoration of his people (40 : 3-5) The proclamation has already gone forth to prepare a royal highway, straight and smooth, through deserts and mountains for Jehovah, our God, who like a conquering king will come bringing back his people. Thus before the eyes of all mankind his divine might and majesty will be manifested. It shall be, because he, the supreme Ruler of the universe, has decreed it.

Scattered, afflicted and weak though they are, let not Jehovah's people doubt the fulfilment of this proclamation. As a prophet, I am commanded to remind them that before Jehovah these great and powerful nations, beneath whose iron hand they are crushed, are but as the grass or delicate flowers which fade before the first hot blast which he sends. All their material power and pomp are ephemeral; the only permanent thing in this world is his divine purpose, revealed to his people through the promises and teachings of his prophets. Man shall not frustrate the purpose of the Infinite (40: 6-8)

Let those whose duty it is to announce to desolate Jerusalem the triumphant return of Jehovah begin to watch, for the great event is at hand. Let them declare to the cities of Judah that their divine Deliverer, like an invincible conqueror, is already advancing to vindicate those who have been faithful to him and to punish the wicked. With the tenderness of a shepherd he will lead and uphold in the long and wearisome journey the weak and helpless of his people. Jehovah will soon return to Jerusalem with his people (40: 9-11)

2. *Deliverance Certain because the Deliverer is Omnipotent* (40: 12-31)

Do you sometimes, O exiles, question Jehovah's ability to deliver you from your powerful heathen foes? Con-

Isaiah 40 : 12   *Messages of the*

No other being in the universe to be compared with Jehovah (40 : 12-17)
sider his infinite might and wisdom ; he it was who alone created and regulates this universe. No other mind can comprehend its intricate and stupendous mysteries. Much less can any other being advise and instruct the omniscient Creator of all. Compared with his omnipotence, the might of these great nations which you fear is as a drop in the limitless sea, and the lands which they inhabit are but atoms in his great universe. All of the wood and beasts of Mount Lebanon would not suffice to make for him an appropriate burnt-offering. In his eyes the nations, instead of being objects of fear, are only so many particles in the world of matter.

The folly of representing him by means of images (40 : 18-20)
Consider the superlative folly of trying to represent such a deity as Jehovah by means of idols, carved by human hands out of wood and covered with gold or by rude wooden images which the impoverished owner sets up with great care lest they tumble over.

Human insignificance and divine omnipotence (40 : 21-26)
Remember that it was Jehovah who created the earth. Its wonders all reveal his transcendent power. He it is who spanned the earth with its blue canopy. From his heavenly throne on high he rules the world. The powerful earthly potentates, before whom you tremble, and these great empires, which seem eternal, are in his sight as chaff borne hither and thither on the breast of the tempest. Cease to gaze upon these works of frail man and look up with the eye of faith to the Incomparable One who created and rules the universe with omnipotent might.

Later Prophets Isaiah 41 : 7

Say not, O disconsolate group of exiles, that Jehovah pays Jehovah's unceasing care for those who need and trust him (40 : 27-31) no heed to your misfortunes. In your time of distress do not forget that he is all-knowing, all-powerful, and that he is subject to no human limitations. Instead of forsaking, he gives strength and help to those who, like yourselves, are weak and defenceless. Young men and brave warriors lose their vigor, but those who trust in Jehovah shall grow stronger and stronger.

3. *Jehovah's Irresistible Purpose to be Realized through Cyrus* (41 : 1-7, 21-29)

Let the distant nations, which are now trembling before Jehovah alone has sent Cyrus upon his career of conquest (41 : 1-4) the advance of the invincible conqueror Cyrus, stand in awe before Jehovah's tribunal. He it was who sent this obscure prince upon his triumphal course and has given him his victories. The same omnipotent God has made the peoples helpless before him, so that his advance is unobstructed. Jehovah, the ever-existent, the source of all, has brought these things to pass in order that his divine purpose may be realized in human history.

In their terror the distant nations encourage each other The foolish confidence of the heathen in their idols (41 : 5-7) to be brave in face of the great danger. Blindly they turn to their false gods. They think to save themselves by putting their idols in good repair. They hope to be delivered by inanimate images, which will fall over unless securely fastened.

Let the representatives of heathenism vindicate their

Isaiah 41 : 21

<small>Jehovah alone knows the future (41 : 21-29)</small>
claims. With the aid of their idols, let their prophets and soothsayers foretell the future. Or let them do at once some marvellous deed to illustrate their supernatural power. They will do no such thing, for they and their claims are vanity. Jehovah alone has proved that he is God. He it is who has summoned Cyrus, his worshipper, from the east to destroy and overthrow these heathen peoples. While the oracles of the pagan world were silent, he announced from the first the coming of this conquering prince. To his people he gave the promise of deliverance. In the presence of the sweeping victories of Cyrus, the Gentile world is dumb with amazement. The utter uselessness of their idols is obvious. By the clear testimony of history Jehovah is shown to be the supreme Lord of the universe.

4. A Personal Message of Encouragement to Jehovah's Servant Israel (41 : 8-20)

<small>Jehovah will surely deliver his helpless, oppressed servants (41 : 8-14)</small>
Do you, O exiles, the true representatives of my people Israel, share the alarm of your present masters? Jehovah declares: "I have chosen your race from the earliest days of your national history, and ever stood in the closest and most intimate relations to you, leading you forth from the distant parts of the earth, that you might perform for me a unique and important service. Notwithstanding your sins as a nation, I have not annulled that peculiar relationship. You are still my servants; therefore be not

Later Prophets   Isaiah 41 : 20

terrified in the presence of the great world-powers; for I will ever protect you with my omnipotence. The nations which attack you will do so at the cost of their life. So completely will they be destroyed that you will look for them in vain. Weak though you are and ground down under the heels of your conquerors, fear not, O people, for like a loving earthly father I will uphold and deliver you.

"In my hands you shall become an effective instrument of vengeance. You will smite your powerful oppressors and crush them; and I, Jehovah, by my natural forces, will complete the work of destruction. By my righteous, irresistible might you will accomplish this, and in me will you glory. *(They shall in turn execute judgment upon their foes (41 : 15, 16))*

"Although you now lack all of those material comforts which give pleasure to life, I, who am the source of all, will respond to your cry for deliverance, and will not leave you to perish. In rich measure everything will be supplied which can contribute to your happiness. The barren places through which you must pass and where you must live, shall be transformed into veritable Edens. When men behold the great transformation they will know at once that your God, the one supreme and altogether righteous Being, has effected it." *(The glorious future in store for the suffering exiles (41 : 17-20))*

5. *The Contrast between the Ideal Servant whom Jehovah Seeks and the Actual Israel* (42)

The character and methods of the servant whom Jehovah desires to perform his service (42 : 1-4)

"The only question, O exiles, is whether you will prove the kind of instrument which I can use in carrying out my purpose in the world. Consider carefully the type of servant whom I would uphold and who would realize the desire of my heart and to whom I would so impart my own divine purpose and spirit that he would effectively declare by word and life my will to all mankind. Not by violence nor by loud public proclamation will he accomplish his mission. To the weak—physically, mentally, and morally—he will prove, not a destroyer, but a saviour. In all faithfulness he will make known my gracious commands. He will not lose heart nor relax his efforts until all mankind know and do my will. For his message of truth and light the heathen world now in error and darkness is waiting."

Jehovah's commission to the Jewish race (42 : 5-9)

Listen, O chosen race, to the declaration of your God who created the earth and its inhabitants and who imparted the breath of life alike to all mankind, and who therefore is the divine Father of all : " In accordance with my righteous purpose expressed in my covenant, I called you to my service; I cared for you in your earliest days ; I formed you into a nation. All this preparation was that you might be the mediator of a solemn covenant between me and the entire human family, to impart the knowledge

Later Prophets Isaiah 42 : 17

of me to the heathen peoples who now are in the darkness of ignorance, and thus to give full life and liberty to those now living in physical and spiritual bondage. I am the supreme God of the universe, and I will not tolerate the paying of divine honors to idols of wood and metal. Already those things which I proclaimed through my prophets have become realities. Now I announce a new and fuller revelation of my purpose. Before the events transpire, I tell them to you, my chosen servants."

In view of his new revelation, let all the world join in praising Jehovah. Let the inanimate voices of nature unite with the inhabitants of the distant Gentile lands in a song of thanksgiving. Let the dwellers in desert and on mountain raise their joyful acclamations; for Jehovah, like an invincible warrior, is at last going forth to reveal his true character as the avenger of wrong, and as the champion of the right. *A lyrical ode of praise to Jehovah (42 : 10-13)*

" Long have I kept silent in the presence of evil," proclaims Jehovah, " but I will withhold my judgment no longer. I will reveal my real purpose. The proud, dominant world-powers will I overthrow, and those who are groping in darkness, with no one to lead them, I will conduct back to their land by means which they know not. I will change their present distress and doubt to joy and prosperity, and all obstacles shall be removed from their way. These promises will I surely fulfil; but terrible shall be the fate of those who worship images, *The coming deliverance of Israel and judgment upon idolaters (42 : 14-17)*

Isaiah 42 : 18 — *Messages of the*

trusting that these will deliver them in the hour of affliction and judgment."

The actual servant Israel (42 : 18-25) Give heed, O careless exiles, to the ideal of service which Jehovah holds up before you, and to his purpose which he desires to realize through you. Alas! instead of being responsive, you are slow to comprehend, and fail to grasp the message which he wishes to give to the world through you. Through the events of history and the mouths of his prophets he has revealed many precious truths to you, and yet you have not appreciated nor appropriated them. If you had only proved receptive, he would have imparted to you still greater and more glorious teachings. As it is, this people, alas! oppressed by their conquerors, the prey of their foes, with no champion to deliver, have lost all spirit and energy. The ultimate cause of their moral obtuseness is to be found in the earlier waywardness of their race. Will some of you more thoughtful ones give heed to this great truth and hand it on to coming generations? Because of the crimes of your nation, Jehovah delivered it over to its hostile foes to be punished and disciplined. Hardened by sin, this people have not recognized the true cause and source of all their afflictions, and consequently have failed to learn the great lessons which they were intended to teach, and which must be learned before they can fully realize the ideal of the faithful servant of Jehovah.

Later Prophets   Isaiah 43 : 11

6. *The Preparation and Mission of the True Israel*
(43 : 1 to 44 : 5)

Jehovah, who created and led you, O chosen race, says to you: " Have no fear, for I will vindicate you. You are my peculiar people. When calamities come to you, I will be at hand to deliver you, for I am your God. If necessary to ransom you from the hands of your masters, I will give the richest lands, like Egypt and Sheba, in exchange for you, for I love and prize you dearly. From every quarter of the earth I will command the nations among which you have been scattered to bring back my sons and daughters. Thus shall all the members of that race which I have called to serve and honor me be restored to the land of their fathers." *(Israel will be protected, ransomed, and restored by Jehovah (43 : 1-7))*

Can you not, O blind people, understand that Jehovah unceasingly cares for you in order that you may perform for him a great service? Can you not appreciate his character and purpose, as revealed in history and through his prophets? All of the heathen oracles in the world cannot prove the divinity of their gods nor produce evidence to substantiate the claims of their devotees. Jehovah is the only true God, and you are his witnesses before mankind. He has chosen you to serve him by believing and by recognizing in him the one supreme and universal Lord. He establishes his claim to absolute supremacy by incontestable evidence. He alone possesses the divine *(Israel is Jehovah's witness to the heathen world (43 : 8-13))*

Isaiah 43 : 12   *Messages of the*

power to deliver his worshippers. He alone reveals the events of the future before they transpire. Your high duty and privilege it is to make known to the world his character and demands. You are safe, for no one can take you away from him. His divine purpose and acts no power on earth or in heaven can annul.

<small>The overthrow of Babylon and the second exodus (43 : 14-21)</small> For your sakes Jehovah announces that he will soon bring low proud Babylon. He who cared for and led his people in the past, who destroyed completely the military strength of your oppressors the Egyptians, will perform for you an even more remarkable act of deliverance. Can you not already behold the signs of its early accomplishment? He will speedily turn the desert into a fruitful, well-watered land, that his chosen people may return through it with songs of thanksgiving on their lips.

<small>Israel's poor return in the past for all of Jehovah's mercies (43 : 22-28)</small> Notwithstanding all of the blessings and promises which Jehovah has given so freely to you his people, you have not turned to him in gratitude, showing by your generous offerings that you recognized in him the great source of all. He did not demand of you so many offerings that to have given them would have been a burdensome task; and yet you set aside nothing for him out of the abundance which he gave you. The only things which you brought to him were your sins of ingratitude and apostasy. But he is a forgiving God and will not remember those crimes of the past. Review that past, if perchance you may find some justification of your conduct. From the first your

Later Prophets   Isaiah 44 : 8

ancestors sinned against him, your priests and prophets were disloyal to him, and your rulers introduced heathen cults into his sacred temple, so that he was compelled to give his people up to judgment and to make them an object of scorn in the eyes of the world.

Black as is your past record, O race with an exalted ideal and destiny, Jehovah, who chose you to be his people and trained you, will not abandon you. He still calls you to service. Therefore fear not your foes, nor doubt your own ability to witness for him, for he will revive you physically and spiritually. Your descendants at least will enjoy his blessings in such rich measure that the heathen world will be eager to associate themselves with you and to be known as the people of Jehovah. *[Jehovah will yet make his name and that of his people honorable in the eyes of mankind (44 : 1-5)]*

7. *Jehovah's Incomparable Superiority to the Gods of the Heathen* (44 : 6-23)

Jehovah, Israel's King and Deliverer, proclaims : " Before creation's dawn I existed, and shall continue to exist through all eternity, and there is no other God beside me. If there is any other being in the universe comparable to me, let him prove his superiority, as I have done, by announcing the events of the future through the mouths of his prophets. Be not alarmed by the claims advanced for these heathen deities. I long ago revealed to you, my people, your destiny. Since you are my representatives *[The declaration of monotheism (44 : 6-8)]* before the world, be assured that the one supreme Lord of all will watch over and protect you."

<small>The inanity of idol-worship (44 : 9-20)</small>
The heathen idols have no worthy representatives, for their devotees are deluded by foolish superstitions. When it comes to a real test they are filled with confusion. Consider how these gods, which men regard as so sacred, are made. A smith heats the metal over the coals and then with a strong arm hammers it into the form of an image. This maker of gods suffers from hunger and thirst like all finite beings. Or, if the idol be made of wood, the carpenter by the use of line and rule carves out an object of human form, first selecting suitable material from the trees of the forest, which are dependent, like the image-maker, upon Jehovah's bounty for their life. Out of the same log from which he hews a god he secures fuel with which to cook his bread. Before an inanimate idol thus manufactured he prostrates himself in worship and prays for help in the time of need! Such folly reveals a mind hopelessly deluded, totally incapable of distinguishing between truth and falsehood.

<small>Jehovah's intimate relation to his people (44 : 20-23)</small>
Remember, O Jewish race, that you are the witnesses of the living God, and that for that service you have been prepared. For that reason Jehovah has forgiven your gross sins against him, and now is about to deliver you from the hands of your foes. Let heaven and earth rejoice over the salvation of his people Israel which is at hand.

Later Prophets Isaiah 45 : 5

8. The Real Purpose and Significance of the Conquests of Cyrus (44 : 24 to 45 : 25)

To you, the chosen people, your divine Creator and Redeemer proclaims : " The entire universe is my work. I am he who makes evident the falsity of the pretensions of those who worship heathen gods. I am he who confirms the predictions of my true prophets by the events of history. In conformity with my promises through them, I will again cause Jerusalem and the desolate cities of Judah to be rebuilt and repopulated and my temple to be restored. All obstacles will I remove. Cyrus, whose career you are watching with deepest interest, is my agent, who will prepare the way for the accomplishment of my gracious purposes." <small>Jehovah the creator and supreme ruler of all (44 : 24-28)</small>

To Cyrus, his anointed, whom he has called and commissioned to serve him, Jehovah declares : " I will subdue kings and kingdoms before you. The strong defences of the nations will I break down. Vast and hidden treasures will I cause to fall into your hands, all in order that you may know and acknowledge me as the one true God. <small>Cyrus called that he may recognize Jehovah as supreme (45 : 1-3)</small>

" Also that you may deliver my chosen people Israel, that they may be at liberty to serve me as I desire, I have without your knowledge prepared you to be my Messiah. <small>That he may deliver Israel (45 : 4)</small>

" I, who am the one true Lord of all, will commission you to make known to mankind my real character and demands. In nature and in human affairs I am the sole

173

Isaiah 45 : 6

That the whole world may acknowledge Jehovah (45 : 5-8)

Creator and absolute Sovereign from whom all authority emanates. There is not (as the teachers of your race contend) an antagonistic spirit of evil who is gifted with divine power; but I alone am the source both of light and darkness, of good and evil. Let heaven and earth join with their Creator in the redemption of Israel and the salvation of humanity.

In his own good way Jehovah will deliver his people (45 : 9-13)

"Do some of you find fault with the means whereby I am going to deliver you? Does the clay criticise the work of the potter who moulds it? Equally presumptuous is it for you, whom I created, to dictate to me how I shall act. I who made the heavens, the earth, and all mankind upon it, have raised up that foreign conqueror, Cyrus, in accordance with my righteous purpose, to rebuild Jerusalem and to liberate you, my exiled people. Voluntarily, without ransom shall he do this."

The southern nations shall acknowledge Jehovah's sovereignty (45 : 14-17)

In the future days the tall men of the south, from Egypt and Sheba, shall come to you as suppliants to confess that your God, Jehovah, is the only true God who is able to deliver his people. Then all who put their trust in idols will be filled with shame and dismay. You alone will be saved from calamity and enjoy unending peace and prosperity.

Jehovah's salvation for all mankind (45 : 18-25)

Jehovah, who created the earth for the habitation of man, claims undivided homage. Openly has he declared his promises to his people. He has inspired no vain hopes. Whatever he has said shall surely come to pass.

174

Later Prophets Isaiah 46 : 2

Only through ignorance and folly can men put their trust in deities of wood and stone which they can carry around on their shoulders (as do the Babylonians)—in idols which have no power to realize what their representatives promise in their name. Jehovah, he alone is God, he alone can deliver. Therefore let all the nations, even the most distant, in this time of their distress, accept his gracious invitation and turn to him and be delivered by his omnipotent might. He solemnly proclaims that the time shall yet come when every human being will acknowledge him as Lord supreme. Then shall not only the Jewish race but all mankind recognize that he is the one source of strength. Those who are hostile to him shall be filled with shame, while his people, who faithfully serve him, shall be vindicated and glorified.

9. *The Contrast between the Deities of Babylon and Jehovah of Israel* (46)

Already the chief gods of Babylon are bowing down before the conqueror. Their images, which their devotees have been wont to carry about in solemn procession, will soon be carried off as spoil on the backs of weary beasts. They will be only a burden to be borne away into the captivity from which they are powerless to deliver their worshippers. *The impotence of the Babylonian gods (46 : 1, 2)*

You, O Israelites, have been borne by Jehovah, your

<small>Isaiah 46 : 5</small> *Messages of the*

<small>Jehovah's omnipotent care for his people (46 : 3-5)</small> God, from your earliest days as a nation, although you have proved a heavy burden. He who changes not declares that he will never cease to uphold and protect you. What other deity in all the universe is like him?

<small>The impotence of all heathen deities (46 : 6, 7)</small> Consider the origin and nature of all other gods. They are manufactured through the expenditures of the money and energy of their worshippers. They are dead things, dependent upon their devotees for care and transportation, and entirely incapable of answering the petitions which are directed to them.

<small>Jehovah a living God, active in human events (46 : 8-12)</small> Forget not the real nature of your God and that of the no-gods of your conquerors, O apostate Jews. Remember what he has done for your nation in the past. He alone of all the gods has shown through the predictions of his prophets that he knew and ordered the events of the future. He has selected Cyrus to carry out his divine purpose. The deliverance which he promises will surely come. Consider and be encouraged, you who have lost faith in Jehovah's justice and ability to deliver. The hour when he will lead you forth and vindicate his true character by restoring you to your native land is near at hand.

10. *A Taunt Song Commemorating the Impending Fall of Babylon* (47)

<small>The captivity of Babylon (47 : 1-4)</small> At last your turn has come, proud Babylon, to taste the horrors of captivity which you have in the past ruthlessly inflicted upon so many helpless thousands. Leave your

luxuries behind, cast aside your royal garments, like a common slave, half-clad, sit in the dust and perform menial labor; for Jehovah, Israel's deliverer, is about to execute vengeance upon you.

Nevermore will you recover your lost authority. Forevermore your lot shall be that of a captive, for when Jehovah delivered his people to you for a time, since he wished to discipline them, you betrayed the trust and cruelly enslaved them, showing no mercy to the aged and helpless. In your overweening pride you shut your eyes to the possibility of judgment, and regarded neither the principles of justice nor your own future. *Punished because of its cruelty to Jewish captives (47:5-7)*

Your pride and false confidence in your own resources shall bring ruin upon you. Your citizens and defenders shall be torn from you. All your magical incantations will not deliver. Trust in these has misled you, so that you think that your acts will escape the eye of the supreme Lord of all. You even claim divinity for yourself. Useless will be your formulas and spells to avert the sudden and overwhelming ruin which shall come. The conflicting prognostications of your astrologers only confuse you, and reveal nothing respecting your future. Your worthless religious guides, to whom you have always devoted so much attention, will think only of themselves in the hour of calamity, and you will be left without helper or deliverer. *Because of pride and trust in magic (47:8-15)*

11. *A Recapitulation of Preceding Arguments, Culminating in an Exhortation to Flee from Babylon* (48)

<small>The new revelation about to be given (48: 1-8)</small>

O remnants of the Hebrew race, exiles from Judah, followers of Jehovah in name but not in faithfulness, heed the message of your God: "The events of the past I announced to you by the mouth of my prophets before I brought them to pass, that you might have no excuse for unbelief; for I knew your obtuseness and pride and wilfulness. Long ago I predicted that which is now transpiring before your eyes, lest you should say it is the work, not of Jehovah, but of the gods of the heathen. Now I am about to give to you a new and broader glimpse of my divine purpose which is being unfolded in human history.

<small>Not deserved but because Jehovah wills it (48: 9-11)</small>

"Because of my infinite mercy, and because I desire to realize that purpose, not because of your merit, have I spared and preserved you. For my own sake will I bring about this great deliverance so that through you, and not through another race, will my true character be revealed to the world.

<small>Cyrus the agent of the new revelation (48: 12-16)</small>

"Listen with the ear of faith to me, the Creator and Ruler of all. None of the heathen deities announced to their devotees that the whole world was to be turned upside down by the advent of this unknown prince, Cyrus. I am the one who raised him up to lay low this proud city of Babylon. I have called him, given him his victories.

Later Prophets Isaiah 48 : 19

From the first I have made known that the ultimate end of his work was the liberation of you, my people. Do you still doubt that I will carry it to completion?
"Remember that I stand in the closest and most inti- mate relations to you and am ever looking out for your best interests. By each new experience which comes to you, I am leading you on. Can you not learn the plain lesson and obediently do my will? By so doing the peace and prosperity for which you are longing would be secured in richest measure. Then would the disasters of the present be no more." Believe Jehovah's clear statement and read the signs of the times; prepare to leave this doomed city. Instead of grovelling in the dust, arise and triumphantly spread abroad the good news of the deliverance at hand. Recognize the glorious fact that Jehovah at last has redeemed his people. Supplying their every need, he will lead them back through the hot deserts which lie between them and their native land. Peace awaits the faithful, but the rebellious shall seek it in vain.

If the nation would only learn to obey Jehovah (48 : 17-19)

IV

THE REDEMPTION OF ISRAEL AND OF MANKIND TO BE SECURED THROUGH SELF-SACRIFICING SERVICE (49 to 55)

1. *The Preparation and Mission of the True Servant of Jehovah* (49 : 1-13)

Call and preparation (49: 1-4)
Let all the world, even the most distant peoples, hear the declaration of Jehovah's true servant respecting his call and mission: "From the earliest days of my existence the Lord appointed and equipped me for the performance of his service. He has given me an authoritative message and ability to deliver it forcibly. Although confronted by bitter opposition, I have ever been securely protected by Jehovah. He has found me useful in his service. He has commissioned me the true Israel to be his official representative before the world. Although I feel at times that all my efforts have been in vain, I am assured that Jehovah will surely vindicate and reward them.

The broader mission of the servant (49: 5, 6)
"He who created and trained me that I might by my loyalty and devotion restore and reclaim my people as a whole, and who has honored and upheld me, further declares that my mission will not be limited to the Jewish race, but that it will also be my high duty and privilege

Later Prophets Isaiah 49 : 15

to proclaim his life-giving truth and salvation to the entire heathen world."

Jehovah, Israel's God and Deliverer, also assures his faithful servant, now ground down by forced servitude to foreign kings and despised and loathed by all peoples, that the time is surely coming when he will be so exalted that the rulers of the earth will come to pay to him reverential homage; for the omnipotent God who has called him to his service will not fail to reward. *The future glory of the true servant (49 : 7)*

In his own good time Jehovah promises to deliver his servant and institute through his agency a new era in the history of his chosen people. He shall revive the prosperity of the land of Palestine and restore the captive exiles to their homes. They shall be relieved of all of the hardships incidental to the return by their loving God. From all quarters shall the scattered remnants of their race come streaming back. In view of the great deliverance which Jehovah is about to bring to his afflicted people, let all the universe join in a hymn of praise. *The servant's part in the restoration (49: 8-13)*

2. *Jehovah's Assurances that he will Surely Restore his People* (49 : 14 to 50 : 3)

Do some of you sad exiles fear that Jehovah has abandoned you to your hard fate? A human mother's affection for her child, strong as it naturally is, may grow cold; but the divine love of Jehovah for you will never wane. You are indelibly impressed upon his memory, so *Jehovah's love soon to find glorious expression (49 : 14-21)*

181

Isaiah 49 : 16　　　　　　　　　*Messages of the*

that he cannot forget you for a moment. He is ever planning to restore your ruined city and nation. The hostile foes who have laid them waste shall depart, and in their stead shall come hastening back the exiles and fugitives of your race. They will revive the ancient glories of your nation. Soon the cities and lands now desolate and uninhabited shall be so densely crowded that there will not be room for all. Joyful wonderment shall fill your hearts at the sight of the sudden and marvellous revival.

The way in which the restoration shall be accomplished (49: 22-26)　Do you question how this glorious restoration is to be accomplished? Jehovah declares that he will signal to the heathen nations who now hold in captivity the scattered members of your race and they shall carefully bring them back to Judah, eagerly supplying with reverence their every need. Then shall those who now faithfully serve me, striving to realize the ideal of the true servant, cease to be objects of scorn. Instead they shall be treated as the princes of the earth. Do you question the fulfilment of this prediction because the peoples who now hold you are seemingly invincible? One mightier than they, even Jehovah, will wrest from them their unlawful prey and thus rescue his people. By the overthrow of your tyrannical masters he will demonstrate to all the world that he is your deliverer and redeemer, able to save from all foes.

Jehovah has for a time turned you over to your enemies to be disciplined, but he has by no means rejected you forever. Your calamities, individual and national, are self-imposed. Now that he offers to you the opportunity to be restored, do not lose it for lack of faith and responsiveness. Surely you cannot for a moment doubt Jehovah's ability to deliver you, or question the power of the God at whose command the character of the entire universe is transformed. {Jehovah still willing and able to deliver his people (50: 1-3)}

3. *The Experiences of the True Servant of Jehovah and their Lesson* (50 : 4-11)

Listen, O people called to service, to the united testimony presented by the lives and experiences of Jehovah's true prophets, and catch the spirit of the perfect servant whom he would approve: "Jehovah, my Lord and Master, has given me the eloquence and facility as a teacher which are alone possessed by well-trained pupils, in order that I may relieve by messages of comfort the distress of those who are needy, and therefore eager to listen. He daily and constantly imparts to me, as a teacher to a disciple, a fuller and clearer knowledge of his character and purpose. Eagerly have I striven to learn the lessons which he has taught. If the way of instruction and duty leads through persecution and contumely, I do not flinch nor turn back. I will never fail, because Jehovah will uphold and give me strength. Confident of his help, I calmly face opposition and assault. He who will vindicate me is ever at hand. Foes, who assail me, when I have such a champion as he, will only do so to their ruin." {The methods and confidence of the servant (50: 4-9)}

The lesson of encouragement and warning to be learned from the servant (50: 10, 11)

Learn from the past and present experiences of the true servant of Jehovah, O faithful ones among the exiles, the lesson of trust, so that, while you grope in darkness, without a prospect of deliverance, you may receive help from the same God. You also, who taunt the righteous, assailing the loyal servants of the Lord, take warning. Judgment will surely overtake you, for Jehovah always executes vengeance upon those who attack his faithful followers.

4. *Words of Exhortation and Encouragement in View of the Coming Restoration* (51 : 1 to 52 : 12)

The lesson of Israel's past (51: 1-3)

Consider and learn the lesson from your nation's past, you who are seeking to know and do Jehovah's will. Recall how he from a single family of nomads reared up a powerful people. He who accomplished these wonders with such an insignificant beginning, assures you that again from you, the humble remnants of your race, he will raise up a mighty nation, and again make the desolate land of Judah richly fruitful, so that joy and praise will fill your hearts.

The fulfilment of Jehovah's gracious purpose certain (51: 4-8)

Know also, O chosen people, that Jehovah purposes to reveal his character and will to all mankind, and that a knowledge of his eternal principles will be given the heathen for their enlightenment. Quickly and unexpectedly will the Lord appear to vindicate and deliver his people, and to bring justice to all nations far and near. The

Later Prophets   Isaiah 51 : 18

visible heavens and earth shall dissolve and their inhabitants, like insects, shall pass away; but Jehovah's tender care for his people and his just rule of the universe shall never cease. Therefore, O exiles, be not terrified by the threats and insults of mortal men, for your afflictions and the foes who cause them will soon cease to be; but your vindication and deliverance by Jehovah shall be for all time.

    Again as at the creation, when thou didst separate the light from the darkness, and the land from the waste of waters, or as when thou didst lead thy people forth from Egypt reveal, O Jehovah, thine omnipotence. [Then will thy people, freed from captivity, return with rejoicing to their native land, and their present sorrow will be no more.] An appeal to Jehovah to deliver at once (51 : 9-11)

    Jehovah assures the doubting exiles that they have no cause to fear mortal men, since he, the Creator and Ruler of all things, animate and inanimate, is their protector. He will speedily release them from their painful slavery, for he has given them, as his servants, a message for humanity. He has protected and cared for them, since through them he purposes to inaugurate a new epoch in human history and to effect the complete restoration of his people to Palestine. His assurance of speedy deliverance (51 : 12-16)

    Arise, O prostrate nation, for your period of punishment and discipline is over. Pitiable indeed is your fate, since no one of your citizens has proved himself able and willing to lead and comfort you in this time of humiliation Promised relief from present woes (51 : 17-23)

Isaiah 51 : 19   *Messages of the*

and distress. With your land desolate and you yourself the victim of famine and the sword, who can comfort you? Your bravest and noblest citizens are unable to relieve you, for they are helpless and the objects of Jehovah's vengeance. But now, O afflicted and prostrate nation, he assures you that your days of judgment are past. From his hand your oppressors shall in turn receive their punishment, because in the time of your weakness and humiliation they crushed you to earth and showed no mercy.

<small>The righting of the great wrongs (52 : 1-6)</small>
Arise to new life and power, O Jewish race! No longer shall you be the prey of your heathen oppressors. Cease to bewail as captives your bondage, which is now at an end. Unjust have been the different captivities to which you have been subjected. Egypt abused the laws of hospitality in its treatment of your fathers; Assyria oppressed them without cause; and now you are held here as slaves for whom your masters, the Babylonians, have paid nothing to Jehovah. Thus his name is constantly being dishonored; but in the coming day, when he fulfils his promises of deliverance, his people and the whole world will appreciate his true character.

<small>Deliverance at hand (52 : 7-12)</small>
If you had the enlightened prophetic sight you might even now see hastening over the mountains to Jerusalem the herald of peace and deliverance, proclaiming that Jehovah, Israel's God, has again assumed the direct rule over his people. Already the watchmen of the holy city

Later Prophets Isaiah 52 : 15

are beginning to rejoice, for they can behold him returning to his former abode. The desolate ruins of Jerusalem will now be rebuilt, for Jehovah is about to reveal his omnipotence to the nations by restoring his people. Already he commands you, O Jewish exiles in Babylon, to leave the polluted land. Guard yourselves carefully from anything which may render you ceremonially unclean, for it is your sacred duty to bear back with you the holy vessels which were carried away by Nebuchadrezzar after the destruction of the temple. Go not forth as fugitives, but as victors, as becomes a people escorted and guarded by Jehovah, your divine Guide and Protector.

5. *The Mission and Future Vindication of Jehovah's Martyr Servant* (52 : 13 to 53 : 12) [1]

" By virtue of his wise action," Jehovah declares, " the one who shall fully realize my ideal of service, shall in the end attain highest honor. As many were appalled because of the overwhelming misfortunes which befell him and which they regarded as evidence of my displeasure aroused by his sins, so shall they stand—kings and humblest subjects alike—before him in awe-struck silence, astounded by the greatness of his exaltation. Then shall they realize what they had never before suspected, namely,

Jehovah's testimony respecting the work of his servant (52 : 13-15)

[1] In the original this section is a poem consisting of stanzas of four lines each.

Isaiah 53 : 1   *Messages of the*

that affliction, voluntarily, nobly borne in my service, leads to glory."

The testimony of later generations (53 : 1-6)
Later generations, appreciating the full significance of the work of Jehovah's servant, shall exclaim : " Who believed the revelation respecting the servant which was announced to us by the prophets, and who realized that God's purpose was being accomplished by his sacrifice and sufferings? The victim of adverse circumstances, he possessed no external attractions. Abandoned by his fellows, afflicted with wasting disease, avoided as an outcast, we depised him, never suspecting his true character and the nature of the service which he was performing for us all. And yet it is now clear that he whom we regarded as the especial object of Jehovah's righteous wrath, was afflicted that we might thereby be delivered from pain and disease. The repeated disasters that fell upon him were the consequences, not of his, but of our, crimes. Peace came to us instead of judgment, because our punishment fell upon him. We all as a nation had ceased to follow Jehovah and to obey the divine commands, but in accordance with God's mysterious purpose, the punishment of our apostasy and disobedience fell, not upon our guilty heads, but upon this ideal servant."

The testimony of the inspired prophet (53 : 7-12)
" Although the object of cruelly unjust persecution, he submissively, voluntarily, and in silence endured. By an unjust sentence was he put to death ; while no one of his contemporaries recognized that he was thus struck

Later Prophets   Isaiah 54 : 3

down in his innocence because of the sins of Jehovah's people. Even after his death, he was buried as a common criminal, although he was perfectly guiltless in thought and deed. All this seeming injustice, however, was no accident. In accordance with Jehovah's gracious purpose, he was allowed to offer himself as a sacrifice for others' guilt, that thus he might beget spiritual offspring, and through them live immortally. After his pain and trial is over, he shall enjoy the perfect consciousness of having been instrumental in delivering many from the consequences of their sins. His shall be the glory and the rewards of a mighty victor, because he voluntarily sacrificed his all, even his life and his reputation in the eyes of his contemporaries, in order that he might thereby deliver many from their load of guilt and bring them into harmony with the eternal God of love.

6. *Renewed Promises of Restoration* (54)

O nation desolate and without children, sing the pæan of victory, for without undergoing the pains of childbirth, you will suddenly find that the numbers of your citizens are far greater than during the days of your national independence and prosperity in Canaan. Prepare for this great increase; extend your borders, for in the coming restoration your descendants will possess the territory of the heathen nations and rebuild the now desolate ruins of Palestine. Do not fear that you will again be humiliated

[The period of affliction is over (54 : 1-10)]

Isaiah 54 : 4

in the eyes of mankind. Soon will you forget the shame of the past and present, for Jehovah, who is Lord of all, has covenanted to love and care for you. He will surely deliver you. Because of the intimate relationship which has existed between you and him from your earliest history, he will never entirely reject you. For a brief period he has severely disciplined you because of your infidelity to him, but the infinite love and compassion which he feels toward you will find eternal expression. This period of exile is to you as a nation what the deluge was in the days of Noah to the human race. As Jehovah promised to Noah and his descendants that never again would he destroy mankind by a flood, so he now solemnly assures you who are faithful that he will never again visit his vengeance upon you. The eternal mountains may be shaken from their foundations, but his mercy and the abundance of life which he will give you shall never cease.

The re-establishment of the nation (54 : 11-14a) To the faithful members of the race now scattered hither and thither, the victims of calamity and persecution and without a comforter, Jehovah declares: " I will re-establish you and your capital city, Jerusalem, firmly and gloriously. Strength and beauty shall characterize you as a nation, instead of the present weakness and shame. Your descendants shall enjoy in rich measure peace and prosperity, for I will instruct them in the principles of righteousness and truth.

" Then shall the possibility of oppression and the terrors which constantly haunt you, be no more. Calami- ties, such as have swept over you, shall never come again. Instead of falling a prey to those who attack you, you will be able to overthrow them. I, the Creator of everything, raised up the foes who destroyed you. Surely now that you have been disciplined and I am reconciled, you have no cause to fear any nation or power in all the universe. The arms of your enemies shall be raised in vain against you. From every contest you will emerge victors. These shall be the rewards and permanent possessions of those who have proved themselves my true servants, for thus will I vindicate them." The future invulnerabil- ity of the nation (54 : 14b-17)

7. *A General Invitation to Participate in the Blessings of the Coming Restoration* (55)

Let all who long for restoration and a fulfilment of their spiritual aspirations accept freely Jehovah's gift of prosperity, of reconciliation, of deliverance and the satis- faction of their soul's desires. Do not expend all your energies in attaining the mere material comforts and pos- sessions offered by this land of your exile. They will never satisfy your higher cravings. Listen to Jehovah's call to service; leave Babylon behind; go back, even though it calls for great sacrifices, to the land of your fathers; and you have the divine assurance that your highest hopes and aspirations shall be completely ful- filled. Heed this call to duty, for only in responding to it The call to spiritual life and service (55 : 1-5)

Isaiah 55 : 3   *Messages of the*

will you find your true spiritual development. If you do heed, Jehovah will enter again into an intimate and solemn relationship with you and realize through you the gracious promises which he gave to David and to his house. By uniting the Hebrew race and by extending the rule of Israel throughout Palestine, your first great king brought his race and religion prominently before the ancient world. Even so you, by your faithful service, will proclaim Jehovah's character and demands to distant peoples, now unknown to you. Foreign nations shall come hastening to you because of Jehovah, your God, and because of the glory which he will confer upon you.

Neglect not Jehovah's gracious invitation (55 : 6-9)

Do not lose this supreme opportunity when Jehovah calls you and is so eager to be reconciled with you. Let those who have been following their own selfish, wicked ways, neglectful of his commands, turn to him in true penitence, and be assured of his free and full forgiveness and a share in his promises. Your aims and purposes are far different from those of Jehovah; for while you are thinking of the material things of the moment, he is preparing for you and for mankind everlasting spiritual and national blessings, far surpassing your power to comprehend.

Jehovah's promise of restoration will surely be fulfilled (55 : 10-13)

As he provides with infinite care and wisdom by means of the processes of nature for the material needs of man, so will he also realize in human life and history his eternal promises and commands. None shall fail to be fulfilled. Therefore be assured, doubting exiles, that without opposition and with songs of praise in your hearts you will go forth from the land of your captivity. The whole universe will rejoice with you in your deliverance. Your present misery shall be exchanged for joy and prosperity. Judah, to which you will be restored, will cease to be an unattractive desolation and become a paradise. Thus in the deliverance and restoration of you, his chosen people, Jehovah's true character shall be revealed once and for all time to mankind.

THE MESSAGES OF HAGGAI AND ZECHARIAH TO THE TEMPLE BUILDERS

THE MESSAGES OF HAGGAI AND ZECHARIAH TO THE TEMPLE BUILDERS

I

THE FIRST TWO DECADES OF THE PERSIAN PERIOD

After becoming master of the old Median and Lydian empires, Cyrus, the Persian, in October of the year 538 B.C., completed his remarkable career of conquest by the capture of the city of Babylon. This victory, which extended his rule at one stroke to the borders of Egypt, was won almost without bloodshed. The decisive battle was fought in northern Babylon, between the Babylonian forces, led by their king, Nabonidus, and the Persian, led by one of the generals of Cyrus, and resulted in a sweeping victory for the latter. After this first defeat the overwhelming prestige of Cyrus, the attractive promises which he held out to the conquered, and the dissatisfaction which they felt toward their king because of his religious innovations influenced the Babylonians to open their gates to the conqueror. Within a week after the first engagement he was, according to the inscriptions, in possession of the proud mistress of the lower Euphrates.

While Cyrus lived the Babylonians had no cause to regret their ready surrender. A universal amnesty was granted to all; the rights of his new subjects were carefully guarded; building enterprises were instituted; the temples of the Babylonians, which had been neglected by Nabonidus, who was interested only in the ancient gods of the race, were repaired and adorned. In public inscriptions Cyrus declared himself and his son, Cambyses, to be devoted worshippers of the gods of Babylon. Toward the peoples formerly subject to the Babylonians he showed like favor. As soon as they had acknowledged his rule, he restored to their homes all captives whom he found in Babylon. He also assisted in rebuilding their ruined temples and sent back their gods which had been carried off by earlier conquerors (Cyrus Cylinder, 31, 32).

Although the Jews are nowhere mentioned in the inscriptions of Cyrus thus far discovered, there can be no doubt that the same free permission was granted to them to return that was given to all exiles deported to Babylon by the Chaldeans.

It was also in perfect accord with his well-known policy of conciliation to encourage the Jews to rebuild their ruined temple. The quotation from the old Aramaic document (Ezra 6 : 3-5) contains the Jewish version of a decree attributed to Cyrus in which he gives command that "the house of God at Jerusalem be builded, the place where they offer sacrifices," that the expense be defrayed from the royal exchequer, and that the vessels which Nebuchadrezzar carried to Babylon be returned. The same source also states that the restoration of these vessels was assigned to a certain Sheshbazzar, probably one of the Jewish royal line (1 Chr. 3 : 18), who was appointed governor of the province of Judah. These concessions were no greater than those which Cyrus himself states he made to conquered people who came under his rule. In the case of the peoples of Palestine there was a still further reason why he was especially eager to insure their loyalty to him, as well as to develop the resources of this frontier province, for already he was contemplating the conquest of Egypt.

The decree contained in the old Aramaic document (Ezra 6 : 3-5) makes no reference to a general return of the Jews in Babylon to Palestine. Cyrus aimed rather to win the loyalty of the remnants of the Jewish nation, who had been left behind in Judah or who had soon returned from the adjacent lands where they had taken refuge. That their numbers were much larger than is generally supposed is indicated by a variety of references (compare Jer. 24 : 8; 40; 44 : 15; Ezek. 33 : 24). Never had they ceased to regard the temple site as the one sacred spot where Jehovah could rightly be worshipped. Before the close of the Babylonian exile they had reared an altar and instituted sacrifices there, as the decree of Cyrus plainly states (Ezra 6 : 3). Permission to rebuild the ruined temple was, therefore, well calculated to secure their grateful attachment to the Persian rule.

There is no evidence in the oldest records that many Jews in Babylon heeded the impassioned exhortations of the great prophet of the exile. He indeed seems to have feared that the superior attractions offered by the land of the great rivers, to which they had already become attached, would deter them from returning. The prospect of leaving behind their comfortable homes and opportunities for a life of comparative luxury to enter upon the long, painful journey which would bring them back to desolate Judah with its barren hills, with its poverty-stricken, ignorant population and with its treacherous, malignant foes, who had already seized nearly half of the territory held by the Judeans before the exile, was far from inviting.

Few appear to have been equal to the great sacrifice. Their numbers were too small to secure for them any mention in the sermons of Haggai and Zechariah. The latter speaks in 519 B. C. of a small deputation "of them of the captivity who had come from Babylon" bringing gifts to the Jewish community in the west (6 : 9, 10); but in addressing their audiences these prophets always call them either the "people of the land" or the "people who have been left." These were the exact terms used by Jeremiah to distinguish the Jews who were left behind after the Babylonian deportations from those who had been carried away (Jer. 42 : 2, 15, 19; 43 : 5; 44 : 7, 12, 14). In 519 B. C. Zechariah evidently regarded the exile as not yet ended (1 : 12), and earnestly exhorted the Jews in Babylon to return (2 : 7). Also, in 445 B. C., Nehemiah knew of no general return, but only inquires from a deputation of his race from Palestine which waits upon him, "How are the Jews who escaped, who were left of the captivity?" (1 : 3).

The opening chapters of the Book of Ezra furnish the only basis for the generally accepted conclusion that thirty or forty thousand Jews returned from Babylon soon after 539 B. C. These chapters are from the pen of an author who lived in the Greek period, centuries after the men to whom Haggai and Zechariah spoke had passed away, and they, therefore, present the later conception of this earlier age. A careful study of the lists preserved in Ezra 2 (and also introduced again in Nehemiah 7) demonstrates that they represent a census of "the children of the province," in all probability, taken not at the beginning, but during the last century of the Persian period (see pp. 276-278; compare Kent, *History of the Jewish People*, pp. 128, 130, 225, 228).

These facts suggest the true historical background of the prophecies of Haggai and Zechariah. The decree of Cyrus had given the Jewish community in Palestine full permission, and even encouraged them to rebuild the ruined temple. Governors from the royal Judean line—

first Sheshbazzar and then Zerubbabel—had been placed over them. Joshua, a lineal descendant of the priestly family who had been in charge of the pre-exilic temple, also performed their sacrifices. With these leaders had probably returned certain Jews of Babylon, zealous to see the temple rebuilt and imbued with the superior religious spirit which characterized those of the dispersion. But, notwithstanding all these encouragements, really nothing had been done toward rearing Jehovah's sanctuary. Unproductive seasons had reduced the scant resources of the Jewish community. Those who were able had devoted themselves to building better houses for themselves and their families. Although they recognized the obligation to begin the restoration of the ruined temple, they excused their inactivity by the plea that the favorable moment had not yet arrived. If they were familiar, as they probably were, with the glowing predictions of Ezekiel and the great prophet of the exile, the reality must have seemed all the more hopelessly discouraging because of the contrast. Thus the struggling, poverty-stricken community was losing its confidence, its faith, and its ideals; while the golden opportunity for rebuilding the temple and so establishing a common bond with which to unite the scattered Jewish race was slipping away. Neither Zerubbabel nor Joshua possessed the energy and influence required to arouse the people to action.

In the years 522 to 520 B. C. the entire ancient civilized

world was shaken from the lethargy which had seized it after the conquests of Cyrus were completed, by the death of his son Cambyses. Already the Persian throne had been seized by a pretender, Gomates, who succeeded only for a short time in holding together the great empire. When he was slain by the hands of conspirators, Darius, a descendant through a collateral branch of the same family to which the great Cyrus belonged, was placed by his fellow-conspirators on the throne.

Many of the subject peoples improved the opportunity to renounce the Persian rule and to rally about princes of their own blood. From one end to the other the empire was torn asunder by rebellions. That Darius would ever succeed in quieting them seemed an utter impossibility.

The reports of revolt inspired the hearts of the dependent people everywhere with hopes of freedom and national glory. The Jews in Palestine were not unaffected. During the summer of 520 B. C. the rebellions in the east were at their height. The moment was a critical one in Jewish history, for then, if ever, the hopes of the people were calculated to inspire action.

II

THE PERSONALITY OF HAGGAI AND ZECHARIAH

Respecting the personal life and character of the two prophets, Haggai and Zechariah, the biblical record furnishes no information beyond what is contained in their prophecies. Although one in purpose and closely associated, each possessed an individuality which was in marked contrast to that of the other.

Haggai's language and message indicate that he was a layman. His appeal to the priest for an official decision (2 : 11-13) confirms the conclusion, for if he had belonged to the priestly class, like Zechariah (Zech. 7), he would himself have given the formal deliverance. There is no evidence to support the late Jewish tradition to the effect that he was an old man when he delivered his prophecy. His appeal to the old men who had viewed the former temple (2 : 3) suggests that he was young rather than advanced in years. His energy, courage, and enthusiasm all, as in the case of Isaiah and Jeremiah, are characteristic of the opening rather than the closing years of life. He was also a man of action, not of quiet meditation. He seems to speak as a native of Judah, and his sermons furnish no evidence that he had ever been in Babylon, so that he may well be regarded as the enlightened conscience of the resident Palestinian community.

Zechariah's great interest and familiarity with priestly matters confirm beyond doubt the statement of the superscription to his prophecy that he belonged to the priestly family of Iddo (Neh. 12 : 4). There is a depth and spirituality in his thought and teaching which suggest maturity and a wide experience of life. The religious conditions and problems of the community command his attention. He is also a careful student of Israel's past and of the messages of the earlier prophets. His sermons betray an intimate familiarity with the writings of Ezekiel and with the great prophet of the exile. His political outlook extends far beyond the borders of Palestine. His use of elaborate vision suggests that he received his youthful training in the calm and leisure of the exile rather than in unsettled Judah. He also manifests close acquaintance with the commercial life of Babylon. Being a priest, his ancestors were, without much doubt, among the captives carried to Babylon by Nebuchadrezzar, so that he, like Joshua and Zerubbabel, was one of the few faithful exiles who came back to Judah to lead and to instruct the poor ignorant community in Palestine.

Together these two prophets, widely different in character and training, but like Elijah and Elisha, each incomplete without the other, labored, not only for the rebuilding of the temple, but also for the reorganization of the community and the revival of its spiritual life and hope.

III

THE OPENING ADDRESSES OF THE PROPHETS
(HAG. I : I to 2 : 9 ; ZECH. I : 1-6)

1. *Haggai's Call to Begin Building the Temple*
(I : 1-11)

The occasion (1 : 1)

In September of the year 520 B. C., on the first day of the month, when the members of the discouraged Judean community were gathered at Jerusalem to celebrate on the ruined temple site the feast of the new moon, the prophet Haggai improved the opportunity to appeal to the civil and religious leaders of the people. "Hear Jehovah's message to you, selfish, faint-hearted people! Cease urging for your continued failure to rebuild this desolate temple the excuse that the opportune time has not yet arrived. You have found time to build comfortable homes for yourselves. Are you not ashamed to live in well-built houses, while you allow my house to lie here in ruins? You cannot plead ignorance of my wishes; for consider the recent fortunes—or rather the misfortunes—that have come to you. The enterprises into which you have put your best efforts have ended in disaster; your labors have been in vain; your hard-earned savings have been dissipated. Are not these calamities plain evidence that I am displeased with your conduct?

Jehovah's condemnation of the delay in rebuilding the temple (1 : 2-6)

Later Prophets   Haggai 2 : 1

"Since you are too obtuse to interpret the significance of his dealing with you, Jehovah, the Omnipotent, gives you this plain command: 'Forthwith go out upon the hills and secure the necessary timber and begin the repair of my temple, that I may no longer be dishonored by the disloyalty of my chosen people, and that they may become as pleasing to me as now they are displeasing. The hard times which you have experienced were no mere chance. I it was who caused a curse to rest upon the scanty fruits of your toil; and why? Because every one of you was so eagerly intent upon building his own house that you have allowed my house to remain a desolate ruin. For this reason I have sent no rain to fructify the earth, but instead drought, which has destroyed your means of support and brought you face to face with starvation.'" Build the temple and avert Jehovah's displeasure (1 : 7-11)

The strong appeal of Haggai touched the consciences and aroused the religious zeal of Zerubbabel, the governor, of Joshua, the high priest, and of the people, so that before the twenty-fourth day of the same month, the work upon the temple was begun. Effect of Haggai's appeal (1 : 12-15)

2. *Haggai's Encouragement to the People to Persevere* (2 : 1-9)

In November, about a month and a half after he delivered his first sermon, when the people were beginning to grow discouraged, Haggai again addressed the leaders The occasion (2 : 1)

207

and people, probably as they were assembled to observe the Feast of Tabernacles:

<small>Jehovah's promise that he will richly bless the efforts of the temple builders (2 : 2-9)</small>
"Naturally, as you behold the extent of the ruins of the ancient temple, and as some of you with gray beards recall its splendor as you saw it before its destruction, sixty-six years ago, you feel that in comparison the structure we are rearing is mean and insignificant. 'But be not discouraged, O Zerubbabel and Joshua, be not discouraged O people of the land,' is Jehovah's sure message to you. 'Persevere in the noble task that you have undertaken and be assured of my blessing and help; for my spirit is ever present with you. Though you are weak and struggling in the midst of many dangers, do not lose heart. Soon I will transform existing conditions, so that instead of being obliged to send your paltry earnings as tribute to the distant people which rules over you, you shall behold all the nations bringing to Jerusalem their richest possessions to adorn my temple. Do you doubt the realization of this promise? Remember that all the wealth of the world is mine. Even though the present outlook is dark, the future glory of the sanctuary shall be greater than that of the past. Above all, to it and to every one who has been active in rebuilding it, I will grant my peace, which is far more valuable than any earthly possession.'"[1]

---

[1] The last sentence is based upon a reading which has been preserved in the Septuagint.

Later Prophets Zechariah 1 : 6

3. *Zechariah's Lessons from the Past* (1 : 1-6)

About two months after Haggai made his opening address to the people, Zechariah delivered his first recorded sermon. In the name of Jehovah he declared: "Do not make the fatal mistake of your fathers, who incurred my fierce displeasure because they utterly disregarded the plain warnings and exhortations of my prophets and paid no heed to my demands. Your fathers have passed away, and likewise the prophets who proclaimed my will; but the fate which overtook your fathers, as well as their testimony, have demonstrated that although the form of my message may vary, its content is unchanging, and they who defy my commands and break my eternal laws will surely pay the penalty of their misdeeds. Therefore, avoid the fatal sins of past generations, seek faithfully to know and do my will, that thus it may be consistent for me to bless and prosper you as my unbounded love for you prompts."

Disobedience to Jehovah's commands means death (1 : 1-6)

IV

HAGGAI'S SERMONS IN CONNECTION WITH THE LAYING OF THE FOUNDATION OF THE TEMPLE (2 : 10-23)

1. *The Former Uncleanness of the Community and the New Promise of Blessings* (2 : 10-19)

<small>The setting of the sermon (2 : 10)</small> During the latter part of December, in the memorable year 520 B. C., the foundation of the temple was formally laid. Of the two messages of encouragement which Haggai delivered upon that day, the first was intended for the community as a whole. Since the written law had not yet been expanded as it was in later times, the people consulted the priests for a formal decision in regard to all questions not answered in the book of Deuteronomy, which was evidently still the code of the Jews in Palestine (Deut. 17 : 8-13).

<small>Contaminating influence of the unclean (2 : 11-13)</small> Turning in public to the priests, the prophet demanded an official decision : " Does anything holy, as, for example, the flesh of the sacrifice, communicate its holiness beyond these objects which it immediately touches ? " When the priests answered " No," the prophet further inquired : " Does anything which has touched a thing ceremonially unclean, as, for example, a corpse, communicate

Later Prophets   Haggai 2 : 20

the defilement to everything with which it comes in contact?" To this the priests answered "Yes."

"According to the same principle," the prophet declared in the name of Jehovah, "this people, all of their work, and the sacrifices which they offer on the altar, which they have reared there on the old site, are unclean before Jehovah. Their sacrifices certainly will not effect their cleansing, while that ruined, polluted temple communicates its defilement to offerers and offerings alike. Think, people, of your past experience up to the present day, until, by laying the foundation of the temple, you manifested a genuine desire to remove this source of pollution from your midst. Surely the return from your fields and vineyards has not half fulfilled your reasonable expectations. The reason why is obvious: Jehovah it was who sent the blight and hail to destroy the unclean work of your hands. While you were all defiled, in consequence of your selfish neglect of his temple, it was foolish for you to expect immediate prosperity; but now that the fundamental work of cleansing has begun, Jehovah declares that he will show you his favor." _{Their failure to rebuild the temple has polluted the people (2 : 14-19)}

2. *The Revival of the National Hopes of Israel* (2 : 20-23)

To Zerubbabel, the governor of Judah and legal heir to the throne of David, the prophet on the same day declared in the name of Jehovah: "I am about to overturn the existing world-powers and to break their military strength _{Promise to Zerubbabel of a prominent rôle in the new kingdom to be established on earth (2 : 20-23)}

by means of the widespread insurrections which even now are convulsing the Persian empire; and when that general overturning comes, and I establish my kingdom on earth, you, O Zerubbabel, my servant, will stand in a peculiarly intimate relation to me, and will be the earthly representative of my authority."

V

ZECHARIAH'S VISIONS OF COMFORT AND PROMISE (1 : 7 to 6 : 8)

1. *The Prophet's Use of the Vision as a Form of Teaching*

In verses 1-6 of the first and in the seventh and eighth chapters of his prophecy Zechariah deals directly with vital questions which concerned the Judean community. His language is remarkable for its simplicity, and contains no obscure or complicated figures. It is noticeable that in these chapters he quotes most frequently from the preexilic prophets. In fact, he does little more than reapply their teachings to the peculiar problems of his day. It would seem that he had in these passages caught their habit of simple, forcible address.

In the remaining sections, however, in which he presents his distinctive messages to his readers, his style is entirely different. The language and figures which he employs suggest that he was striving to make the truth more impressive by employing an elaborate symbolism. The constant, almost excessive use of the phrase "thus saith Jehovah of hosts" or "the word of Jehovah of hosts came unto me," which characterizes the sermons of Haggai and Zechariah, perhaps indicates that they were conscious that their hearers and readers no longer received the prophetic message with the childlike faith of earlier days. Four times also in his brief prophecy Zechariah pauses to assert that, when his predictions come true, his audience "will know that Jehovah of hosts had sent him to them" (2 : 9^b, 11^b; 4 : 9^b; 6 : 15^b). Educated in the distant exile, where Israel's teachers were far removed from national problems, where they were obliged to reconstruct with their imagination the life of the past and of the future, and where they had unlimited leisure for dreaming, it was natural that Zechariah should use the apocalyptic form of teaching. Like Ezekiel he was by birth a priest, and so from his infancy was taught to represent the real and spiritual by symbols. This fact alone undoubtedly goes far to explain why it was that these two prophets were so fond of the vision as a form of teaching, while their contemporaries, the author of Isaiah 40-55 and Haggai, never employed it. It is safe to say that the growth of apocalyptic literature was closely related to the corresponding development of legalism which characterized the exilic and post-exilic periods. The former represented the spirit of legalism carried over into prophecy. Both movements were the results of the dominant influences of the age, and both were popular with the people. Amos recognized the value of the picture method of teaching, for in the closing chapters of his prophecy he reiterates, by means of a series of graphic visions or word-paintings, the same truths that he had presented in his oral addresses. With the masses pictures are always the most profitable and accepted form of presenting truth. To many modern readers the apocalyptic literature seems cumbersome, mechanical, and often grotesque, but by the Jews, in the post-exilic period, it was highly esteemed. It aroused their curiosity, and so commanded their attention; it appealed powerfully to their imagination, and at the same time compelled them to think in order to interpret its inner meaning. Its indefiniteness commended it to the prophets as a medium for prediction, for it enabled them to create a desired impression without committing themselves to details respecting which they themselves were ignorant. During the centuries when the Jews were ruled by the Persians and Greeks, it enabled the prophets at many critical moments in their history to impart to their audiences messages which, if expressed in plain language, might have compromised them in the eyes of their foreign rulers.

Although, as a result of this peculiar training and type of mind, the divine messages which came to Zechariah may from the first have been clad in apocalyptic form, yet his visions or word-pictures bear the evidence on their face of conscious elaboration. Like Ezekiel, he draws his motives and coloring from the life of his age. The figure of the smiths was a familiar one, which had already been employed by Ezekiel (21 : 31). The angelic horsemen and chariots were suggested by the military organizations of the Persian empire; the symbolism of the golden candlestick was taken directly from the temple.

The belief in angelic beings was not new to the Hebrew and Semitic thought, but in the apocalyptic literature it suddenly became very prominent. Contact with the Persians, who had a highly developed system of angelology, may partially explain the fact. The thought that Jehovah had temporarily withdrawn from his sanctuary and people also took firm possession of the minds of the Jews during the exile, and finds frequent reflection in the sermons of Ezekiel and Zechariah. The result was that even the prophets lost the old sense of his immediate presence, and consequently felt the need of angelic messengers or interpreters to communicate between them and the Deity.

In the visions of Zechariah, Satan, or the Adversary, the heavenly being whose duty it was to test men and to report their shortcomings to Jehovah, is mentioned for the first time in Hebrew literature. Already his functions and general attitude are well known, which suggests that the belief, which is dimly reflected in the vision of Micaiah ben Imlah, who prophesied in the presence of King Ahab

(1 Kgs. 22 : 19-23), had taken definite form in the popular mind during the intervening centuries. The malicious zeal in leading men into sin, which was attributed to the Adversary by later ages, is also foreshadowed in this book.

When the fundamental teaching of Zechariah's complex visions is reached it is found, like that of his other writings, to be remarkably broad, simple, and spiritual. Although frequently passed by because of their obscure symbolism, the first eight chapters (which alone come from the present prophet) are exceedingly valuable both from an historical and religious point of view. The eight visions contained in these chapters are dated in February of the year 519 B. C., which appears to have been the exact time when Darius succeeded in turning back the first great wave of rebellion that had swept over the Persian empire as soon as he attempted to mount the throne of Cyrus. To the Jews the news of the victories of Darius seemed the blighting of all the fond hopes of national independence, which they had cherished and which the prophet Haggai had encouraged. By his symbolic pictures Zechariah sought to inspire them with higher and more spiritual hopes.

2. *The First Vision—The Report of the Angelic Horsemen* (1 : 8-17)

As I meditated in the calm and quiet of the night upon the future of Jerusalem and Judah, I seemed to see the

Later Prophets   Zechariah 1 : 18

angelic messengers, whom Jehovah had sent out, coming in from every quarter of the earth; and they brought the report that the revolutions, which had inspired in the minds of us all eager hopes of national exaltation, had been quelled and that the entire civilized world was again inactive. The report that peace had been re-established throughout the whole Persian empire (1 : 8-11)

To the natural question, How much longer will the inhabitants of Jerusalem and Judah, whom Jehovah has already for sixty-seven years given over to be the victims of heathen conquerors, be thus punished for their sins? came the encouraging reply from Jehovah: "I have never ceased to love and cherish my people, and now the tyranny of their arrogant oppressors has aroused my righteous indignation, for the punishment which they have inflicted has been far greater than I desired—therefore I will return to deliver and pardon Jerusalem. The temple, the symbol of my abiding presence in your midst, shall again be built and the sacred city restored. Proclaim abroad that this land shall again be prosperous, the present sadness of its inhabitants turned to joy, and Jerusalem, once rejected, shall be the especial object of my favor." Jehovah's promise yet to exalt and bless his holy city and people (1 : 12-17)

3. *The Second Vision—The Destroyers of the Four Horns* (1 : 18-21)

Again I saw in imagination four horns, which were the symbols of the mighty nations which from different

Zechariah 1 : 20   *Messages of the*

<small>The destruction of all of the foes of Jehovah's people (1 : 18-21)</small> sides have attacked and scattered the people of Judah. In the same connection I saw four smiths, who symbolized the mighty powers which Jehovah was soon to raise up to break the strength of Judah's destroyers.

4. *The Third Vision—A Picture of Restored Jerusalem* (2)

<small>Jerusalem yet to be populous, prosperous, and protected by Jehovah (2 : 1-5)</small> As I meditated upon the complaints of the people because Jerusalem was poverty-stricken, possessed of but few inhabitants and not provided with walls to protect it from its assailants, there arose before my mind a vision of a young man going forth to measure the city with a view to rebuilding it on its old lines, thus symbolizing the narrow, material ambitions which now fill and embitter the hearts of its citizens. As I watched, Jehovah's message came to me through his interpreting angel: "The Jerusalem of the future shall not be confined within narrow walls as of old, but like a huge village shall extend far out into the surrounding country. No walls of stone will be required, for Jehovah himself will guard it with his invincible might from all hostile attacks, and his abiding presence within will be the true source of its exaltation and renown."

<small>Exhortation to the Jews in Babylon to return to Jerusalem (2 : 6-9)</small> Listen, exiles of the Jewish race in the distant lands of the captivity. Although Jehovah has scattered you to the four corners of the earth, he now summons you to escape from Babylon and return to participate in the restoration

of Jerusalem. He announces—and the fulfilment of the prediction will bring honor to me his prophet—that he is about to overthrow the nations which prey upon you, forgetting that in wronging you they are injuring Jehovah's most cherished treasure. When you see your oppressors the prey of those who now serve them, you will know that Jehovah has revealed to me that which I now proclaim. Instead of complaints because of your woes, let a glad song of rejoicing be upon your lips, O citizens of Jerusalem; for Jehovah is returning to dwell in your midst. Instead of being alone among the nations, in the days that are coming many shall unite with you in worshipping him. When you have the evidence of your eyes that he has redeemed his promise to abide in your midst, then you will believe my prophetic word. Then will Jehovah restore to his people the holy soil of Judah and make Jerusalem the centre of his worship and the chosen place of his abode. Let all mankind be hushed in silence, for the Lord of the universe is about to enter again into his restored and reconsecrated temple.

The future glory which Jehovah will bring to Jerusalem (2 : 10-13)

5. *The Fourth Vision—The Vindication of the Community and Re-establishment of the Priesthood and Nation* (3)

As I listened to the complaints and doubts of the people because misfortunes, which they regarded as conclusive evidence that they were guilty in the eye of Jeho-

Zechariah 3 : 1 — *Messages of the*

<small>The misfortunes of the community not an evidence of its guilt (3 : 1-2)</small>
vah, still rested heavily upon them, I saw in imagination Joshua, the religious representative of the community, standing for trial before Jehovah's tribunal with the Accuser at his side accusing[1] him. Then Jehovah, as the champion of his people, condemned the Accuser because he had interpreted their misfortunes as evidence of their sin, ignoring the fact that the Judean community was made up of the few survivors of the great disaster which had overtaken the nation, and that their misfortunes were only the inevitable consequences of that overwhelming calamity which had left an indelible impression upon them.

<small>Reconsecration of the priesthood (3 : 3-5)</small>
Joshua was clad in foul garments, which symbolized the sins of the past and the incomplete and unclean service, which alone had been possible while the temple lay in ruins. At the command of Jehovah's messenger he was clothed with clean instead of foul garments, and was assured that the guilt of the past had been removed. A clean turban was also placed upon his head, as an emblem

<small>Promise of the Messianic King and Kingdom (3 : 6-10)</small>
of his high-priestly office, and he was told that, if he faithfully discharged his duties, he should direct the service of Jehovah's temple and be received whenever he brought, as the religious head of the community, petitions to Jehovah in its behalf. Furthermore, the assurance was given him that he and those who participated with him in the service of the restored temple should be

---

[1] The same root "*Satan*" appears in both the Hebrew words for the Adversary or Accuser and in the verb.

an earnest of the greater national restoration in which Jehovah would at last fulfil his promises, given through earlier prophets,[1] by raising up an offspring of the royal house of David " to reign as king over his people, to deal wisely and to execute judgment and justice in the land." Behold also the stone, with its seven facets, which shall be in the royal crown! Upon its face I will engrave the name of my chosen servant, the son of David (Zerubbabel[2]). When he is established on the throne, all evidence of the nation's guilt will be removed, for prosperity shall take the place of present misfortunes. Then will be inaugurated that blessed era of peace and plenty of which the earlier prophets sang.[3]

6. *The Fifth Vision—The Temple Candlestick and its Sources of Supply* (4)

As I meditated upon the relations between the high priest and the king, whom Jehovah was about to raise up, and upon their rôle in the life of the restored community, I was led to see with my inspired vision a seven-lamped golden candlestick. This was fed by seven pipes leading from a reservoir which was supplied in turn directly from two olive trees standing on either side. Not understanding the full meaning of these symbols, the ex- {The two inspired leaders of the community (4 : 1-6a, 10b-14)}

---
[1] Jer. 23 : 5; 33 : 15-17; Ezek. 34 : 23-31; 37 : 24.
[2] Compare Hag. 2 : 23; Zech. 6 : 10-14 (restored text).
[3] Compare for example Micah 4 : 4.

Zechariah 4 : 10ᵇ *Messages of the*

planation was given me :[1] The seven lamps represent the omniscient, omnipotent God of the universe, and the symbolism as a whole, like the temple, represents his presence among his people. The olive trees, the sources of the supply of oil, represent Zerubbabel and Joshua, the respective heads of the monarchy and priesthood, the two national institutions which support the temple and its service, and who, in turn, stand before Jehovah, and, like the olive trees, derive from him their life and power.

A special message of encouragement to Zerubbabel (4 : 6ᵇ-10ᵃ)

Jehovah also gives this promise to Zerubbabel: " Not by your own strength nor energy, but by means of my omnipotent power, you shall succeed in the great work which you have undertaken. Do the obstacles seem unsurmountable? Before Zerubbabel they shall entirely melt away. He shall put on the top-stone of the temple, while the assembled multitude joyfully praise the beauty of the completed structure." Zerubbabel's hands laid the foundation of this temple, and I have Jehovah's assurance that his hands shall complete it. When that is done, O doubting people, you will believe in my God-given message. Then those of you who sneered at our limited resources, when we began the seemingly impossible task of building, will rejoice with us all to see the finished structure.

[1] Since the special message to Zerubbabel in verses 6ᵇ-10ᵃ interrupts the logical sequence in the thought of the passage, it is introduced in the paraphrase at the end of the section.

Later Prophets Zechariah 5 : 11

7. *The Sixth Vision—The Winged Volume* (5 : 1-4)

Again I beheld, flying through the air, a huge volume which represented the curse which was about to fall upon the land of Judah because of the sin of the thieves and perjurers in its midst. But henceforth, Jehovah declares, "the consequences of their guilt shall rest, not upon the community as a whole, but upon the sinners themselves, destroying their homes and driving them from the land." *The curse of sin to rest only upon the sinner (5 : 1-4)*

8. *The Seventh Vision — The Woman within the Ephah* (5 : 5-11)

Still again in my mental vision I saw a great bushel-measure. When the cover was removed I beheld a woman sitting within, who symbolically represented the power of sin and temptation. Soon she was shut up in the bushel-measure and borne away through the air by superhuman beings to the land of Babylon, there to find her true home among that corrupt and avaricious nation of traders. Thus Jehovah in his mercy will remove, not only the consequences, but also the causes of sin from the midst of his people, who are now showing their loyalty to him by rebuilding his temple. *The removal of sin and temptation from the land (5 : 5-11)*

9. *The Eighth Vision — The War-Chariots of Jehovah* (6 : 1-8)

In my last, as in my first, vision, my thought went beyond the boundaries of Judah, and I considered the future

Zechariah 6 : 1 *Messages of the*

Jehovah's omnipotent rule over the nations (6 : 1-8)
relations between the Jews and the great Gentile nations. Again I saw different colored horses going forth in all directions; but this time they drew war chariots, and those who went out toward the north, toward Persia, executed Jehovah's vengeance upon that great conquering power, indicating that he is soon going to overthrow the mighty nation which now holds the people in subjection.

VI

THE SYMBOLIC RE-ESTABLISHMENT OF THE HEBREW MONARCHY (6: 9-15)

1. The Messianic Hopes Centring Upon the Prince of the House of David.

It was but natural that the Jews should hope that they might be able to make Zerubbabel, who was their governor and the legitimate heir to the royal house of Judah, their king as well. Until Darius reorganized the empire, after putting down his rivals, the policy of the Persians had been to place native princes over the peoples subject to them. The revolutions in the empire, the successful beginning of the temple-building, and the presence of a deputation from Babylon, bringing gifts from the Jews in the east, all encouraged the Jewish community in Palestine to believe that the opportune time had arrived, and that the promises of the earlier prophets that an offspring of the house of David would again reign gloriously on the throne of Judah were on the point of being fulfilled. The prophecies of the great prophet of the exile had raised their hopes to a white heat. Haggai and Zechariah also shared the general expectation. Both addressed Zerubbabel in language which, it is true, was somewhat indefinite, but its purport was unmistakable. Haggai's prophecy that Jehovah had chosen and would make Zerubbabel his signet (2 : 23) was rendered still more definite by Zechariah. That he hoped and wished to inspire in his hearers the belief that during the high-priesthood of Joshua the prophecies of Jeremiah and Ezekiel respecting the " branch " or offspring of the Davidic house, would be realized in Zerubbabel, is clear from 3 : 8-10. What was there presented in connection with a vision is in 6 : 9-15 symbolically represented by the prophet.

Later editors of the book, who realized that Zerubbabel was not actually crowned king, but that instead the high-priestly family absorbed the power once vested in the monarchy, regarding the name of Zerubbabel as a mistake, substituted that of Joshua. The text, even as it stands, suggests the original reading. The designation "branch" or "shoot" (6 : 12), in the light of its original use in Jeremiah and Ezekiel, applies only to an offspring of the house of David. To Zerubbabel, and to him alone, was given the promise that he should complete the temple (4 : 9). According to the reading of the Septuagint

Zechariah 6:9

the priest was to sit, not on the throne, but on the right hand of the king (6:13^b). The statement that "the counsel of peace shall be between them both" (6:13^c) indicates conclusively that, not only the name of the priest, but also that of Zerubbabel, stood in the original text. Restoring this, the otherwise unintelligible passage becomes very clear.

2. *The Crown Prepared for the Head of Zerubbabel* (6:9-15)

The preparation and conferring of the crown (6:9-11) The divine command came to me to take some of the silver and gold, which had been brought by the deputation of Jews who had returned from Babylon, and make therewith a crown [1] and place it on the head of Zerubbabel, the rightful heir to the throne of David. I was also **Its significance (6:12-15)** impelled to declare: " Behold the man in whom shall be realized the promise of earlier prophets respecting the 'shoot' from the house of David! He shall be the founder of a prosperous dynasty. He shall build Jehovah's sanctuary. He shall exercise royal authority and reign on the throne of Jehovah. At his right hand, supporting and co-operating with him, shall ever be the priestly house of Joshua. In perfect harmony shall they together further the best interests of the nation. Let the

[1] The Hebrew plural evidently is not to be translated "crowns," for in verse 14 it is followed by a singular verb, but refers to the many bands out of which it was made.

Jews who have returned from the dispersion lay up within the temple, until the opportune time comes to place it on the head of Zerubbabel, the crown which has been made from the silver and gold, sent as a gift from the Jews in distant Babylon. Soon these also will return and join in rebuilding the temple and thereby confirm my prophetic words. If you will give heed to the commands of Jehovah, he will redeem his promise to you.[1]

VII

ZECHARIAH'S PRACTICAL EXHORTATION AND ENCOURAGING PROMISES (7, 8)

1. *The Judean Community at the Close of 518 B. C.*

The two years that intervened between the publishing of the visions recorded in 1-6 and the brief addresses in 7 and 8 of Zechariah's prophecy brought only a partial fulfillment of the earlier hopes. The quotation in Ezra 5 and 6 from an old Aramaic document states that after the work on the temple had progressed so far that the timbers were being placed on the foundation, the Persian satrap of the trans-Euphrates province, to which the sub-province of Judah belonged, visited Jerusalem and demanded the reason for the unwonted activity of the Jews. They

---
[1] The last part of the sentence has been lost. It is here supplied by conjecture.

appealed to the permission granted them by an earlier decree of Cyrus to rebuild their sanctuary. Without stopping the work, the satrap, at their suggestion, referred the matter to the central government, and the claim of the Jews was supported by the discovery of the decree of Cyrus, so that the building went steadily on, until in 516 B. C., as Zechariah had predicted, the temple was completed.

There is no evidence that the crown which was to be prepared for Zerubbabel ever rested upon his head. The insinuation of Nehemiah's foes: " It is reported among the nations that you and the Jews plan to rebel; and you would be their king. And you have also appointed prophets to preach of you at Jerusalem, saying, There is a king in Judah " (Neh. 6 : 7ª), may have been suggested by events in the days of Zechariah, seventy-five years before. There is, however, no direct evidence to support the theories of a recent writer, who claims that Zerubbabel was actually made king and paid for this passing honor by dying the death of a martyr (Sellin-*Serubbabel*, 1898). Neither Haggai nor Zechariah urged the people to raise their governor to the kingship, but only proclaimed that the matter was in the hands of Jehovah. It was for this reason that they scanned the distant political horizon with such keen interest. The calm tone of the later sermons of Zechariah, chapters 6 and 7, and the fact that the Jews were allowed to complete their temple are rather conclusive proofs that no great upheaval came to the community before 516 B. C. By that time Darius had succeeded in putting down all of the mighty revolutions which had first aroused the hopes of the Jews, so that there was no longer the slightest encouragement to rebel.

If the earlier political ambitions of the Jews became public, Zerubbabel was probably removed from the governorship soon after the visit of the Persian satrap, whose suspicion had evidently been aroused. If not, then the Jewish prince may well have been set aside in connection with the general reorganization of the empire by Darius in which Persian officials were substituted for native rulers. Thus, without receiving any notice in Jewish literature, the house of David disappeared forever from public life.

In 518 B. C., when Zechariah delivered his closing addresses, the temple building had so far progressed that a form of service had been instituted. Large numbers had not yet been returned from the lands of the dispersion, and the privations and constant petty warfare, to which those who had remained behind had been subjected, had made it impossible for men to live to a ripe old age, or for them to develop large families (8 : 4, 5); but notwithstanding all these discouragements, there were indications of progress. Jerusalem was no longer abandoned, as in the years immediately following 586 B. C. This raised the practical question whether the fasts observed by the remnants of the Israelites and Judeans in Palestine—that of the fourth month, commemorating the capture of Jerusalem by Nebuchadrezzar (Jer. 39 : 2 ; 52 : 6, 7); that of the seventh, in remembrance of the murder of Gedaliah (Jer. 41 ; 2 Kings 25 : 25); that of the tenth, in which Nebuchadrezzar began the siege of Jerusalem (Jer. 39 : 1; 2 Kings 25 : 1); and especially that of the fifth month, which commemorated the burning of the temple and city (Jer. 52 : 12-14)—should still be observed. The question was naturally referred to Zechariah, since he was both priest and prophet. In answering it, he improved the opportunity to enforce upon the minds of Judean and Samaritan communities, which during this early period worshipped together at Jerusalem (Jer. 41 : 5; Zech. 8 : 13), certain most salutary and fundamental prophetic truths.

2. *The Mistakes of the Past and the Glorious Possibilities Awaiting Jehovah's People* (7, 8)

Jehovah demands deeds of kindness and mercy, not ceremonialism (7 : 1-14)

When a deputation came from the town of Bethel to consult the priests and prophets of the temple as to whether or not they should continue to fast and lament in the fifth month over the destruction of the city and sanctuary, I was inspired thus to deliver this address to the people and priests of the land : " What has been the real motive which has led you to fast during the past seventy years ? Has it been to worship Jehovah or to give expression to your own selfish feelings ? What is it also that makes you so punctilious in observing all religious fasts and ceremonies? Is it not because you enjoy the eating and drinking and the formal ritual? Recall the teachings of the earlier prophets like Amos and Isaiah, who prophesied in the days when this land was at peace and inhabited, and before southern Judah and the plain lying on the coast had been seized by our hated foes, the Edomites. Through[1] them Jehovah commanded our fathers to give just decisions in the courts, to do deeds of kindness and mercy to one another and not to wrong the helpless, but instead to cherish true love and charity in their hearts. You know how they defiantly, persistently refused to heed the plain teachings of his prophets, until he was compelled to punish their rebellion against him by an overwhelming judgment. Desolation of their land, slaughter, and exile came simply because they would not listen to his commands. Will you follow in their footsteps, or, profiting by their awful example, will you worship him by your righteous deeds, as well as by your fasts and sacrifices?

Although in the past Jehovah made Jerusalem a ruin, he now proclaims: "The city where my temple stands is the object of my love and my watchful, zealous care. Woe to those who attack it. Again have I taken up my abode in its midst. Sanctified by my presence, Isaiah's prediction shall now be realized (Isa. 1 : 26), and it shall be a city where truth and fidelity are the ruling principles.

What Jehovah purposes to do for Jerusalem (8 : 1-6)

[1] Verse 8 is omitted, since it obviously is a later interpolation, and adds nothing to the thought of the passage.

Zechariah 8 : 4 — *Messages of the*

Again its unoccupied spaces shall be filled up. Its former peace and prosperity shall return, so that men and women shall live to a ripe, contented old age, and its half-deserted streets shall again swarm with happy children. Do these predictions seem impossible of fulfilment to you who have been left behind, you who have endured hardships far worse than exile? Remember that nothing is impossible to the omnipotent God who guarantees their realization.

The coming return of the exiles (8 : 7, 8)

"The first step toward their fulfilment will be a general restoration of the scattered exiles. From the distant lands of the dispersion I will bring them back, to people Jerusalem, their true home. Then at last I shall again have a people toward whom I shall stand in a personal and peculiarly intimate relation.

Blessings to take the place of past misfortunes, if the people prove faithful (8 : 9-17)

"Be courageous and hopeful. Note the progress which has already been made in the two years since the foundation of the temple was laid. Then all your enterprises were fruitless. You were constantly attacked by your ever-present foes, and, worst of all, contention and mutual suspicion within your ranks made life almost unendurable. Now your condition is radically changed. Now these remnants of a nation are united in the accomplishment of a noble purpose, and as a result the fruits of peace instead of discord are beginning to appear. Your vines and fields are also beginning to bear abundantly. Soon, instead of making you objects of scorn and contempt among the nations, O survivors of the Northern Israelites and Judeans, I will prosper and exalt you, so that all shall highly esteem you. Be not daunted by present obstacles. Be brave, be hopeful, be faithful, for instead of devising judgment against you, as I did against your disobedient, unrepentant fathers, I have in store for Jerusalem and Judah rich blessings, if you will only prove worthy. Do not lose confidence. Be open and honest toward one another. Pronounce just decisions in your courts. Do not try to wrong and cheat each other; do not pervert the truth; for such sins as these arouse my righteous indignation.

"The time is coming when these fast-days, by which you commemorate the overthrow of your nation, shall be celebrated as joyful feasts, provided only you learn genuinely to love honesty, uprightness, and that kindly attitude toward each other which will make your civic life harmonious, strong, and healthful. Then shall the peoples of the earth, citizens of great and opulent cities, be attracted by the peace and beauty of Jerusalem. Sickened by the corruption and contention with which they daily come in contact, they shall say. 'Let us go and worship Jehovah and join ourselves to his people.' Then shall strong, powerful nations come trooping to Jerusalem to array themselves under my banners. Instead of despising and persecuting the Jew, the heathen will court him and press about him in their eagerness to be led to a knowledge of the true God of the universe." _{The future glory and universality of the religion of Jehovah (8 : 18-23)}

ANONYMOUS REFORM SERMONS

ANONYMOUS REFORM SERMONS

I

CONDITIONS WITHIN THE JUDEAN COMMUNITY BEFORE THE INSTITUTION OF THE PRIESTLY LAW OF EZRA

The completion of the second temple in 516 B. C. gave a centre and a habitat to the religion of the Jews, but it did not mark, as they had hoped, the beginning of the realization of their political expectations. The next seventy years are passed over by the Jewish historians with a silence that is ominous. Had the prophets failed to give us vivid pictures of conditions within the Judean community, even then it would be possible, with our knowledge of the character of the Judean colony in 520 B. C., to reconstruct the probable course of events. The firm re-establishment of the Persian empire by Darius quietly but effectively blighted the aspirations of the Jews for political independence. It preserved them from complete destruction at the hands of their hostile neighbors, but at the same time condemned them to a narrow, petty existence. Henceforth they were only one of the many units which together made up the great empire. Their political responsibilities were reduced to supporting the Persian governor who was set over them, and to paying their allotted tribute. No great crisis, no great opportunity, no great need, called forth deeds of self-sacrifice or patriotism. Their contact with their neighbors was close and always galling. Upon them the Ammonites, and Edomites, and Arabians vented the bitter hatred which was the product of centuries of hostility and wrong. Whereas in earlier times the Judeans usually had been the masters, now they were the victims. Deprived by the Edomites of the southern half of the territory once held by their ancestors, the Jews were confined to a few square miles of barren hills and narrow valleys, from which they were able to extract only a meagre subsistence. Grinding poverty pressed to earth men whose minds were filled with dreams of prosperity and wealth and world-wide dominion.

It was inevitable that a dangerous reaction should come. Years grew into decades, and the outlook only grew darker. Expectations disappointed became doubts, and hopes long deferred made the heart sick. A state of apathy, new to the Jewish character, took possession of all classes. The leaders of the community ignored their duty and devoted themselves simply to gratifying their own selfish ends. Their ambitions became mercenary, and they did not hesitate to employ base means to realize them. Even the priests set the example before the people of despising the temple and its service, and of neglecting the sacrifices.

Scepticism for the first time in the history of the race found open expression. People asked, "What gain is there in serving God faithfully?" Those who sacrificed most and who were the most loyal worshippers of Jehovah were the poorer and more unfortunate members of the community. Their very misfortunes seemed, according to the mistaken thought of the age, evidence either that Jehovah did not care for his servants or else that they were secretly at fault. Comparative prosperity came to those who spent none of their substance on sacrifices, who defrauded their neighbors whenever they had a chance, and used their authority to increase their wealth. The faith of the Judean community—never very strong—was being sorely shaken. They began to ask whether or not the prophets' teaching about Jehovah's especial favor toward his people was not all a fiction. The very foundations of morality and religion were beginning to give way. It was a critical moment in the faith of Judaism and of mankind.

Influenced by the desire to ally themselves with their powerful neighbors, who otherwise would be very unpleasant foes, the leading priestly and noble families were beginning to marry heathen wives. If necessary they did not hesitate to put away their native Jewish wives. Thus the purity and integrity of the Jewish race in Palestine, its natural stronghold, were seriously threatened. The Jews were in danger of being absorbed by the larger and far more powerful heathen or half-heathen communities about them. The peril was all the greater because the leaders did not recognize its true character. The moral and religious deterioration had been so gradual, and was such a natural result of the environment and narrowing influences to which the survivors of the Jewish race in Palestine had been subjected, that few appreciated it. At the same time it was so great and dangerous that it is not strange that the enlightened prophets who noted it with horror felt that a special divine intervention and judgment would be necessary to purify and transform the community.

The faithful preaching of the prophets under divine guidance prepared the way for reform; while from the Jews in the East were destined soon to come men and influences which would complete the noble work, first of material development, and then of moral and spiritual evolution.

II

THE MESSAGE OF THE BOOK OF MALACHI

1. *The Date and Authorship of the Prophecy*

That the undated Book of Malachi comes from the discouraging, degenerate period following the rebuilding of the temple is obvious from its contents. The sacred structure has been standing for some years, for the priesthood has had time to grow corrupt and careless. The popular scepticism, of which there was little trace in the sermons of Haggai and Zechariah, has attained an alarming development. Foreign marriages have become common, and ample opportunities have been given to observe their dire consequences. Traces of class distinctions begin to appear within the Judean community. The poor and faithful are forced to bow before the rich and arrogant. The evils which the prophet attacks are those which Nehemiah and Ezra devoted themselves to correcting (Ezra 9, 12; Neh. 5, 13). There are no suggestions, however, that the work of these great reformers had as yet begun. Scepticism and vice are triumphant. The prophet looks to the future for the messenger of reform, the second Elijah.

The Book of Deuteronomy, which was adopted as the law book of the nation in the days of Josiah, and not the expanded Priestly Code introduced by Ezra, is still, as in the days of Haggai and Zechariah, the standard legal authority. The prophet, for example, knows nothing of the later distinction between the sons of Aaron and the Levites; but, like the Book of Deuteronomy, classifies all of the priests as the sons of Levi. He also uses the expressions, not of the Priestly Code, but of the earlier law book.[1] As the Book of Deuteronomy provided, questions

[1] Compare Mal. 3:5 with Deut. 5:11-33; 18:10; 24:17; Mal. 4:4 with Deut. 5:31; 12:1; 26:16.

not decided by it were referred to the priests for an official decision, which was regarded as authoritative (Mal. 2 : 7). The law therefore which Ezra later instituted was still in the process of development.

There is also no suggestion that the party of the righteous had yet found a strong champion in Nehemiah. The joy and hope which filled the hearts of the Jews after they had rebuilt the walls of Jerusalem in 445 B. C. find no reflection in the book. The reference in 1 : 8 to the custom of bringing gifts to their Persian governor also points to a period before Nehemiah was appointed over them, for he distinctly states that he accepted no such presents (Neh. 5 : 14-18). Thus all the internal evidence indicates that the little book was written during the dark years immediately preceding the new era in Jewish history inaugurated by Nehemiah in 445 B. C.

Like the other prophecies written at this time, when "the wicked" within the community were in the ascendency, it appears to have been issued anonymously. The directness with which the sins of the leaders, priests, and people are attacked suggests the reason. The title "Malachi," *my messenger*, which appears in the present superscriptions was probably taken from 3 : 1, where it appears in the prophecy, "Behold, I send my messenger." It is never used elsewhere as a proper name. The oldest versions do not treat it as such. The Septuagint reads: "By the hand of his messenger." The absence of any statement in the superscription respecting the father or place of residence of the prophet confirms the conclusion that it was originally anonymous.

The peculiar title, " Burden of the Word of Jehovah," is found elsewhere only in the superscriptions of the anonymous appendices to the Book of Zechariah (9 : 1 ; 12 : 1). Since the present prophecy, as it stands, is really a third appendix to the same book, it is exceedingly probable that the three titles all came from the hand of some later editor.

The character of the author is revealed in his message. His carefully wrought out, argumentative style indicates that the prophecy was first written, not spoken. In his spirit and aim he was a worthy successor of the earlier prophets. Like them he addresses himself directly to the problems which concern the community. It is because they are so sordid and petty that the prophet does not attain to the grandeur and sublimity of certain of the pre-exilic prophets who were dealing with far greater questions.

In his simplicity and directness he resembles Haggai. The apocalyptic form of expression appears, however, in 4 : 1-3. His surprisingly generous estimate of the religion of the heathen (1 : 11, 14) suggests an intimate familiarity with Persian thought ; for the degenerate cults in vogue among the heathen in Palestine were not of such a character as to impress favorably a faithful prophet of Jeho-

Malachi 1 : 2

vah. The thought of Jehovah's sending a messenger to his people in Palestine, which finds frequent expression in the book; the ancient title of the prophecy, "By the hand of his messenger," preserved in the Septuagint; and the tradition found in the Targum of Jonathan to the effect that Ezra, the scribe, was that messenger—all suggest, not that the prophet was Ezra himself, but a faithful Jew who was educated amidst the more favorable religious influences of the East and who subsequently returned to Judah. The horror which conditions there aroused in him is the same as that which they evoked later from Nehemiah and Ezra. Whether born in Judah or in the East, the author of this brief prophecy was certainly one of the most important of pioneers, who, by their faithful, patient efforts, prepared the way for the restoration and the birth of the true Israel.

2. *The Evidence of Jehovah's Love and his People's Shameful Ingratitude* (1 : 2 to 2 : 16)

The fate of their hated foes evidence of his especial love for his people (1 : 2-5)

Do you complain, O Jews, that Jehovah gives you no evidence of his love and care for you? He declares that his love toward you has never ceased. Of that fact you have proof at hand, if you will only open your eyes. Compare your history with that of your brother nation, Edom. Jehovah, after disciplining you, has given you back a portion of your land; but the defiant, lawless attitude of the Edomites has evoked only his just vengeance. Their

Later Prophets Malachi 1 : 8

native mountains are desolate, and the land which their race has occupied for centuries has been seized by the Arabians. Vain are their hopes of re-establishing themselves in their lost territory. Try as they may, Jehovah declares that he will thwart their purpose. Their true character shall also be generally recognized, and they shall be famous among the nations for their deeds of lawlessness. The calamities which shall overtake them shall be conclusive evidence to every observer that they are the objects of his righteous judgments. You yourselves shall behold and be convinced that Jehovah's authority and rule extend far beyond the limits of Palestine.

What return have you made for the favors which the Almighty bestowed upon you? Have you shown toward him that deep, filial reverence which alone is befitting your peculiar relation? Instead, you, who minister at his sanctuary and stand as examples before the people, have openly shown your contempt for his holy character and claims. Do you ask "How?" By sacrificing unclean offerings upon his altar and by saying to yourselves, "It makes no real difference whether or not in the temple service we faithfully observe the ceremonial laws." You practically declare that anything is good enough for Jehovah, for you say that it matters not if the animals which you sacrifice are blind or lame or sick. Would you take such gifts as these to your Persian governor, and would you with them hope to win his favor? Do you

Their base requital of his love (1 : 6-14)

think for one moment that with these you are honoring Jehovah and that you can in this way secure his forgiveness and blessing? Far better would it be to shut up the temple and make an end altogether of the sacrificial service, than to keep up this disgraceful mockery. It only arouses Jehovah's displeasure. He accepts none of your polluted offerings. The heathen serve him far more acceptably. Throughout the entire world he is honored, and in every holy spot, where men worship, incense rises and sacrifices are presented to him. These are far purer than your polluted offerings, for they are given in the true spirit of worship, while you regard the temple service as merely a wearisome, meaningless form. Let no one expect to win Jehovah's favor by offering to him animals unfit for private use. Rather a curse upon the man who tries to cheat God by bringing to him a despicable beast in payment of a vow. Jehovah is not, as you seem to think, the petty god of an insignificant people, but an omnipotent, exalted King, before whom the great heathen nations bow in humble reverence.

The sad degeneracy of the priesthood (2 : 1-9)

Hear, O priests, the solemn charge which Jehovah gives you: " If you do not worthily represent me, as you have solemnly covenanted to do, I will send disaster upon you, and you shall be deprived of the special prerogatives which you now enjoy. Indeed, the judgment has already begun, for you give no evidence of repentance. You shall suffer the consequences of your neglect to observe the laws of cleanliness in performing my sacrifices. Know that I have sent you this solemn warning, because of my ancient covenant with your tribe. According to that sacred contract, I agreed to give you life, peace, and prosperity. In turn I commanded you as a class to reverence me; your ancestors did so, humbly and wholeheartedly. Truthfully they revealed my will to the people without deceit or selfish intention to mislead. In complete harmony with my divine purpose and faithfully, they discharged their duties; and in so doing they saved many from committing acts of sin. The priests should be educated, enlightened teachers, for to them the people turn for instruction and to ascertain my will, since they are recognized as my inspired interpreters. You, alas, have utterly failed to realize the ideal of the priesthood. Instead of doing as you solemnly covenanted, you have led the people into rather than from evil doing. When they came to you for an inspired decision in regard to a doubtful question, not answered in the written law, you misused the authority of your high office to mislead and deceive them. Thus you have forfeited your commission. You have yourselves broken the covenant between us, so that it only remains for me to punish you like common criminals. Your crimes shall prove your undoing. Instead of enjoying the honor of the people, you shall be the objects of their contempt. In proportion as you have failed to perform your duties and have been influenced by

Malachi 2 : 10 — *Messages of the*

personal motives in giving official decision, shall you be publicly humiliated.

<small>The cruel consequences of disregarding the marriage bonds (2 : 10-16)</small>

Since we are sons of a common Father and Creator, and therefore all brothers, why do we disregard the ties of blood, so that we deceive and wrong one another in order to gratify our own selfish desires? [The members of this community have proved traitors to each other and have acted disgracefully and have polluted the holiness of Jehovah's sanctuary by marrying women from the heathen nations about. May Jehovah drive from the community and from participation in his worship any one who is guilty of this sin, and may no one be found to plead the cause of the offender].[1] You cause Jehovah's altar to be wet with tears of supplicants demanding vengeance, so that all of your religious service is hateful—mere hypocrisy—in his eyes. Do you ask "How?" and "Why?" It is because, in order to gratify your base ambitions and passions, you divorce without cause your rightful wives, with whom you have solemnly covenanted and with whom you have since childhood lived in the closest relations, that

---

[1] Verses 11 and 12 break the logical connection between verses 10 and 13b. Their language and thought are entirely different from those of the rest of the section. The thought in verse 10 is somewhat indefinite. Verses 11 and 12 may well have been originally an explanatory note, added by the prophet or by a later editor who lived after the radical reformation of Nehemiah and Ezra, which was in time introduced into the text. As it suggests, the practice of divorcing native wives was probably the result of marrying heathen women.

Malachi 3 : 3

you may introduce into the sanctity of your home women of alien faith and alien blood. Did not the same God create and care for both you and the wife who has journeyed with you from your youth? And to what end? It was that through you he might rear up a godlike race, uncontaminated with degenerate blood—a race which would perform his will.[1] As you value your very life be not faithless to the wife who has the first claim to your fidelity. Divorce, and the cruelty to the wife which is its inevitable consequence, are most heinous crimes in the eyes of Jehovah. As you value your very life be not faithless.

3. *The Judgment which Jehovah will Speedily Institute* (2 : 17 to 4 : 6)

Jehovah is tired of hearing you complain that he shows especial favor to evil-doers, and that he never punishes vice nor rewards virtue. He declares that he will speedily send his messenger to prepare for the great judgment, and then he himself, the great judge for whom you are longing, will suddenly appear in your midst to set up his divine tribunal. How many of you will then be found free from sin? For Jehovah's judgment is like fire, and nothing but absolute purity will endure it. All that is impure must be burned out. These corrupt priests and

The cry of the doubters will be answered by the appearance of Jehovah to judge his people (2 : 17 to 3 : 5)

[1] The text of the first part of verse 15 is uncertain. The paraphrase is based upon the most probable reading.

Levites must first be cleansed, and then they will be fitted to minister at his holy altar. Then will the offerings of his people again as of old be acceptable to Jehovah. In his time of judgment he will also condemn the representatives in your midst of the old heathen cults, those who sin against the laws of social morality, those who pervert the truth and defraud others dependent upon them, those who wrong the helpless, and those who defy God himself.

Pardon to those who show their repentance by deeds (3 : 6-12)

This judgment is necessary, not because Jehovah's character or laws have changed, but because from the earliest days of your history you have failed to obey his commands. Come back to him in the attitude of true repentance, ready to do his will, and he will grant you full forgiveness. Do you ask how you are to show your repentance? Cease robbing Jehovah and forthwith bring in the tithes and offerings for the support of his temple and its ministers. Since your crops are smaller than usual, do not make the mistake of withholding from Jehovah. Bring all his just dues into the temple-treasury and see whether he will not make your fields and vines richly fruitful and stay the destructive advance of the locusts. Then, instead of living under the shadow of suspicion, engendered by misfortune, you will be the envy of all peoples, because of the peace and prosperity which shall be yours.

You are unjust to Jehovah when you declare that there is no advantage in serving him and that all your fidelity in keeping his commands has been in vain. "We are

forced to bow down before the arrogant sinners, who, for- The vindica-
tified with their wealth and influence, defy Jehovah with faithful in
impunity," is the secret wail of the faithful. But the the coming
Lord has heeded their cry and has caused a record to be (3 : 13 to
made of their fidelity. He also proclaims that in the day 4 : 3)
when he arises to judge mankind, he will guard and preserve them as his own peculiar treasure, and will show them special favor, as a father to a devoted son. Then, O doubting ones, you will plainly recognize the advantage of doing what is right and of serving Jehovah, though no immediate rewards appear. Indeed, the great day of Jehovah's judgment is coming. Then shall these arrogant, seemingly prosperous sinners be consumed completely, like straw in a huge furnace. Then to you, who have been faithful to Jehovah through this long night of discouragement and affliction, release and vindication shall come like the rising sun which brings light and freedom and new life to the awakened world. Then joy inexpressible shall fill your hearts. Then, instead of being obliged to congratulate the wicked over their prosperity, you shall find that they are but as dust beneath your feet.

If you desire to be reckoned with the faithful in Jeho- A funda-
vah's great judgment, carefully observe the laws which he form will
gave through his servant Moses to his people. To pre- alone deliver the
pare you for that supreme moment of testing, the Lord is community
about to send to you a prophet with the uncompromising struction
zeal and courage of Elijah, the first great prophet of re- (4 : 4-6)

form. He will bring harmony and unity into your family and civil life, where now there is only wrangling and division and treachery. Thus he will deliver you from another overwhelming destruction at the hand of Jehovah.

III

MESSAGES OF DENUNCIATION AND EXHORTATION (ISAIAH 56 TO 59)

1. *The Date and Authorship of Isaiah 56 to 59*

When we pass from the fifty-fifth to the fifty-sixth chapters of Isaiah we are at once reminded by a change of style and theme that we have before us the product of a different hand and age from those which produced the glowing prophecy preserved in Isaiah 40 to 55. Many echoes of the language and thought of the exilic chapters are found in the closing sections of the book and probably explain why later editors appended them to the writings of the great prophet of the exile. They certainly were written by men who had studied his prophecies and caught his spirit. Like the author of the Book of Malachi, they were in all probability educated in Babylonia. Their zeal for the strict observance of the Sabbath, and their uncompromising attitude toward the Samaritans and the other peoples of Palestine were characteristic, not of the Judean community itself, but of the pious Jews of the dispersion, who, like Nehemiah and Ezra, returned to Judah. Their indignation against the corrupt leaders of the Palestinian community was such as Nehemiah felt in the presence of the same evils.

A reading of chapters 56 to 59 suffices to show that they were primarily addressed to the Jews in Judah, and not to those in the exile, and that they were written some time after 520 B. C., for the temple evidently had long been standing. The conditions and evils with which the unknown prophet or prophets deal are precisely the same as those which aroused the invective of the authors of Malachi and of many of the post-exilic psalms. The same misfortunes are referred to as having already overtaken the community. The same peculiar hope that the divine judge will speedily come to Jerusalem to punish the wicked and vindicate the righteous is also expressed (59 : 15^b-20).

On the other hand, there is no evidence that the social evils, which seem to have been effectively eliminated by Nehemiah in 445 B. C. (Neh. 5), had yet been checked. Furthermore, the deep popular dejection, which is clearly the background of these sermons, belongs to the period before, rather than after, the rebuilding of the walls of Jerusalem. The people still look for those " who will build up the ancient ruins and rear again the long-deserted foundations " (58 : 12). Not only has the social and religious corruption of the community reached its height, but a spirit of expectancy is in the air which strongly suggests that they come from the years immediately preceding the first appearance of Nehemiah.

The atmosphere of 56 : 1-8 is more peaceful. The question whether or not eunuchs should be excluded from the assembly of the Lord, as the Book of Deuteronomy commanded, may well have been raised when Nehemiah and his associates, who were probably eunuchs, returned from the court of Artaxerxes, and performed for the Judean community a service which richly merited " an everlasting memorial and monument" (56 : 5).

As in the pre-exilic prophecies, short sections may also have been added by later editors. Thus the passages of promise in 57 : 13^b-21 and 58 : 13, 14, which interrupt the logical sequence of the thought, and which are characterized by a different style from that of the immediate context, may well come from a period subsequent to the reforms of Nehemiah and Ezra.

The question as to whether these four chapters represent the work of one or several prophets is really unimportant. Differences in style and point of view rather favor the latter conclusion. If it be true, it is interesting to note that Nehemiah and Ezra, like Josiah in 621 B. C., were by no means alone, but had the practical support of a group of able and fearless prophets to prepare the way and second them in the great reforms which otherwise

Isaiah 57 : 2

might never have been realized. It also emphasizes the fact, which is often overlooked, namely, that the forces which created Judaism were not merely legalistic and external, but also deeply spiritual, appealing to the hearts and consciences of the people. The great reformation which came in time affected their conduct as well as their forms of worship.

2. *The Selfishness and Incapacity of the Leaders of the Community* (56 : 9 to 57 : 2)

Alas! the people are the helpless prey of their cruel, pitiless foes, who attack them with impunity, for their leaders who should guard them are too lazy and too stupid even to raise the alarm when danger approaches. They who should protect prey upon the people, and their greed is insatiable. They are intent only upon increasing their own wealth and upon gratifying their own selfish, sensual appetites, and foolishly think that they can keep up their mad revels forever. The people the victims of the neglect and greed of their natural protectors (56 : 9-12)

Honest men, who faithfully discharge their duties to God and their fellow-men, die miserably because of the neglect and wrongs of those who should champion their cause, and yet, so corrupt are the times that no one pays any attention to these enormities. Fortunate are they who find in death that peace which is impossible in this wrangling community. The fate of those who strive to do right (57 : 1, 2)

3. The Shameful Heathen Practices of the Samaritans (57 : 3-13ᵃ)

<small>The scornful attitude of the Samaritans (57 : 3, 4)</small> Come and hear your condemnation, half-heathen, immoral people, scions of a mixed race! Do you, shameless apostates, presume to make sport and jeer at the weakness and misfortunes of the true servants of Jehovah?

<small>Their corrupt religion (57 : 5-13ᵃ)</small> Consider your own practices. [Beneath the sacred trees you observe the ancient heathen orgies which your fathers learned from the original inhabitants of the land, and keep alive the hideous rite of sacrificing helpless children in order to win the favor of the old deities of popular superstitions.] Down in the deep valleys you have venerated sacred stones and presented to them your offerings as though they were divine. On the sacred heights, like the Canaanites of old, you have committed deeds of lewdness under the name of religion. Forsaking Jehovah, you have shown great zeal in courting the favor of heathen deities.[1] Hopeless though your quest was, your energy did not relax. Did you seek to appease those heathen gods because you were afraid of their baneful influence? Was it fear of them that made you desert

---

[1] The meaning of verse 9 is very obscure. If the translation "to the king" be adopted it would naturally refer to a political embassy to the Persian king. The Hebrew word for king is the same, however, as the name of the Ammonite god Molech. The above interpretation has been given because it agrees more perfectly with the thought of the context.

Jehovah and his service? Since he did not at once punish your infidelity, you cease to reverence him. Be not deluded. Jehovah will bring your acts to judgment. Your disgusting heathen rites will not be your salvation, but your destruction. Instead of delivering you, the false idols in whose worship you are so zealous will be among the first to be destroyed.

4. *False and True Worship* (58 : 1-12)

Let this erring people hear Jehovah's earnest message of warning. They observe all the forms of religion and appear eager to know the divine will and to do it. And now they complain because Jehovah has given them no material evidence that he appreciates the devotion to him which is shown by their many fasts and sacrifices. Would you know the real reason, O people? Your fast-days are a mere mockery, for while you are pretending to deny yourselves in the name of Jehovah, you are really intent on your own selfish interests; you extract the last penny due you from your poverty-stricken debtors; you quarrel with each other and do not hesitate to commit deeds of violence. Think not that fasting will secure Jehovah's favor. Do not call the mere formal bowing of yourselves to earth in prayer, and the wearing of the symbols of enduring self-denial, a genuine fast, acceptable to God. The form of fasting which alone is effective with him consists in championing the cause of the oppressed, in

Jehovah desires mercy, not sacrifice (58 : 1-7)

securing justice and liberty for every man, in sharing what you have with those who need, in giving homes to the homeless, and in never refusing those who demand your help.

<small>The rewards of true service (58:8-12)</small>
When you observe your fasts by such acts as these you will speedily have evidence of Jehovah's pleasure. Prosperity will come to you instead of your present misfortunes. Then will your real moral worth be known both to yourselves and to the world; and Jehovah will give you the honor which you will thereby richly merit. Then will he quickly respond to your petitions. If you will cease to oppress and despise and malign each other, and devote yourselves to relieving want and affliction, Jehovah will grant you the realization of your fondest hopes. Strength and prosperity shall take the place of your present weakness and distress; for he will bestow upon you his tenderest care. Then these ruins and walls, long deserted, will be repaired, and Judah shall no longer be famous for its desolation, but for its prosperous cities and villages, rebuilt and restored by its faithful and loyal inhabitants.

5. *The Social Crimes of the Community its Undoing* (59:1-15ᵃ)

<small>The deep depravity of the leaders of the community (59:1-8)</small>
Think not for a moment that Jehovah's power is not sufficient to deliver you, nor that he cannot hear your petitions. The fault is not with him, but with you. Your sins make it impossible for him to answer your prayers.

Later Prophets Isaiah 59 : 12

You sin not against the ceremonial law, but against each other. By unjust decisions and legalized oppression you shed the blood of your brothers. In your dealing the one with the other you lie and deceive and trust to falsehood to win your selfish ends. You prey upon society. Your craftily devised plans are only for the destruction of your neighbors. He who opposes you will fall a victim to your treachery and desire for revenge. You who are the recognized leaders of the community contribute nothing to the welfare of society. All your energy and intellect are devoted to entrapping and destroying your fellows. The ways that make for peace and which promote the cause of right are unknown to you. Injustice and anarchy are the fruits of your life-work.

Let us be frank and confess our guilt. We have been the prey of our wicked neighbors and have not been vindicated before Jehovah's tribunal simply because our sins rise up to condemn us. While we hope for deliverance, our misfortunes only increase. Instead of attaining independence and a nobler national life, we are groping along under an ever-darkening cloud of calamity. We do nothing but loudly lament our hard fate, and look in vain to Jehovah to deliver us from all our woes. The cause of all our trouble is our own heinous guilt. We cannot shut our eyes to our many transgressions. We, who had made a solemn covenant with Jehovah, have proved traitors, and have failed to fulfil his just demands. We

An appropriate confession on the lips of the community (59 : 9-15ᵃ)

have perverted the truth, we have defeated the cause of justice in our public tribunals, and we have banished the principles of right so completely from our social life that an honest and upright man cannot live in our midst without being the constant victim of shameful wrongs.

6. *Jehovah's Impending Judgment* (59 : 15ᵇ-21)

Jehovah to champion the oppressed (59 : 15ᵇ-21) Jehovah has seen the gross injustice which has flourished unrebuked, and it has aroused his righteous indignation. With surprise he has noted that no human champion has arisen to espouse the cause of the innocent against their cruel oppressors. Therefore he himself will right the great wrong. Like an invincible warrior he will come to execute vengeance upon those who are hostile to him and upon all who thwart his righteous purpose. Throughout the entire habitable earth his name will be known and honored. Those of his people who have proved faithful to him through this time of adversity and general corruption, he will deliver and vindicate in the eyes of the world. Jehovah also declares that then he will make a new covenant with his faithful people, and that they and their descendants shall become for all time the repositories and guardians of his personal revelation to mankind.

7. *Promises to the Faithful* (57 : 13ᵇ-21 ; 58 : 13, 14)

They who trust Jehovah and are faithful to him will yet again possess as their own the land of their forefathers.

/ *Later Prophets* Isaiah 58 : 14

Let all barriers be removed which now stand in the way of their occupation. Jehovah the omnipotent, holy Ruler of the universe espouses the cause of the meek and oppressed. He himself will personally comfort and inspire them with new hope and joy. Upon those who have sinned he will not always send adversity in punishment, for, if he did, frail humanity would not survive the judgment. For a brief period he will punish his guilty people in order to turn them from their wicked, defiant course. Then, when they show signs of true repentance, he will give them peace and prosperity, instead of affliction. Expressions of joy, instead of lamentation, shall be on their lips. Peace shall they proclaim to all members of the race, whether in Judah or in the distant lands of the dispersion. The wicked, however, who persist in their evil course, like the ever-heaving sea, shall know no restful peace, for their vile deeds put them out of all harmony with God, with their fellow-beings, and with themselves.

_{Peace and prosperity from Jehovah awaits all who genuinely turn to him (57: 13b-21)}

[They who regard the sanctity of the Sabbath, who do not pursue their ordinary business occupations on that day, making it a holy day in fact, and who restrain their speech, finding joy in the observance of the law, shall be richly blessed by Jehovah and shall be given the land of Judah as their abode and possession.]

_{The reward for faithfully observing the Sabbath (58: 13, 14)}

Isaiah 56 : 1

8. *Promises to Proselytes and Eunuchs* (56 : 1-8)

Right doing impartially rewarded (56 : 1, 2)

This is Jehovah's message to you : Faithfully follow the injunctions of the priestly law and do what is right, for he will ere long deliver and reward according to their deserts all who prove true. Blessings are in store for the man who walks uprightly according to his light, carefully preserving the sanctity of the Sabbath and abstaining from wrong-doing.

Jehovah's religion for all who accept it (56 : 3-8)

Let not the foreigners who have joined the Judean community and adopted the religion of Jehovah fear that they will be excluded from the ranks of his chosen people; nor let the eunuchs complain that there is no hope of their name being perpetuated, since they can have no offspring. If they will faithfully observe the Sabbath and discharge all the obligations laid upon Jehovah's people in the law, God will give them in the temple itself a memorial, better and more enduring than offspring. The foreigners also who unite with the people of Jehovah, and who truly love him and faithfully serve him and keep his law, observing the Sabbath, shall be allowed to worship in the temple, and their sacrifices shall be as acceptable as those of native-born Jews. This is in accord with Jehovah's will, for it is his intention that his temple shall be a common sanctuary for all peoples, and that not only the scattered Jewish exiles, but also the Gentiles, shall be gathered to Jerusalem, there to worship him.

PROPHETIC MESSAGES OF EN-
COURAGEMENT IN CONNEC-
TION WITH THE WORK
OF NEHEMIAH AND
EZRA

PROPHETIC MESSAGES OF ENCOURAGEMENT IN CONNECTION WITH THE WORK OF NEHEMIAH AND EZRA

I

THE HISTORICAL BACKGROUND OF ISAIAH 34; 35; 60 : 1 to 63 : 6; 65; 66

1. *The Rebuilding of the Walls of Jerusalem and the Institution of the Priestly Law*

The earnest reform sermons of the unknown prophets who attacked so strongly the sins of the community, and who proclaimed that a messenger of the Lord would soon appear in Zion, seem to have aroused some of the Palestinian Jews to action. Weak and surrounded by foes, they could expect no help from their neighbors. Naturally they turned to the source of all authority in that age, the great king who ruled the Persian empire.

Fortunately for them there was at the court at Susa one of their race who was cup-bearer to the reigning Artaxerxes, and so had constant access to the royal presence. Fortunately also the youthful cup-bearer, Nehemiah, was loyal to his race and religion, and gifted with both tact and determination.

Upon him the deputation from Judah, headed by his kinsman Hanani (Neh. 1 : 2 ; 7 : 2), waited, and poured into his sympathetic ear their account of the pitiable conditions existing among "the remnant who are left of the captivity there in the province," and of the defenceless state of Jerusalem, with its ruined walls and gates. Nehemiah, who was deeply moved by the recital, resolved to improve the opportunity which his position gave him to appeal to the king for the necessary authority and to devote himself to re-establishing his race securely in the city and land of his fathers.

Presented on a favorable occasion, his request met with the favor of the kind-hearted Artaxerxes, so that the royal cup-bearer was immediately granted a limited leave of absence, with a commission as governor of Judah, and was provided with a military escort. Thus were procured the royal permission and concessions without which any attempt to rebuild the city of Jerusalem would have been both impossible and suicidal.

Although accompanied by certain other loyal Jews of the dispersion (Neh. 5 : 8, 14), and possessed of great personal wealth, which he devoted to the cause, he found the task which he had essayed far from easy. Almost insurmountable obstacles confronted him both within and without the community. As the sermons of contemporary

Later Prophets Isaiah

prophets indicate, its leaders were supremely selfish, holding the lands and possessions of the poorer classes under mortgages, and their children as slaves (Neh. 5 : 1-12). They had also allied themselves by marriage to the leading families in the surrounding nations—the Samaritans, Ammonites, Philistines, and Arabians. In this practice the high-priestly family had set the example (Neh. 6 : 17-19; 13 : 4, 28).

Nehemiah, being one of the Jews of the dispersion, among whom at this period marriage with a foreigner was regarded with much greater horror than among the Jews in Palestine, could not look with favor on any such alliance. Although up to the time of his arrival the neighboring peoples, and especially the Samaritans, appear to have enjoyed the right of worshipping at Jerusalem whenever they wished, he at once incurred their bitter hostility and that of their influential sympathizers within the community by declaring that they should " have no portion, nor right, nor memorial in Jerusalem " (Neh. 2 : 20^b).

In the face, however, of violent opposition from without and of treachery within, Nehemiah, by good generalship, and by his own personal courage and energy, in a surprisingly short time pushed the repair of the walls through to completion.

To the poor, discouraged Jews of Judah the rapid rebuilding of the walls of Jerusalem must have seemed a miracle. In the time of their greatest distress a powerful champion had appeared from the distant east, gifted with wealth and influence, to do for them that for which they had long prayed, but which they could never have accomplished alone. It was perfectly natural that they should regard these achievements as only the beginning of a new and glorious era of prosperity.

In this expectation they were not destined to be entirely disappointed. The rebuilding of the walls accomplished three things very essential to the restoration of the Jewish race in Palestine. It made Jerusalem, for the first time since its destruction in 586 B. C., a safe place of abode, and therefore attractive to returning exiles. Furthermore, Nehemiah's work aroused the gratitude of the Palestinian Jews toward their kinsmen in the east and so prepared the way for the fundamental work of reformation which must be carried through before the two sections of the race could again unite and live in harmony. Finally, it revealed to the more enlightened and more orthodox Jews in the east the needs of their brothers, who lived under the shadow of the temple; while Nehemiah's example inspired some of the more zealous with a genuine patriotic and missionary spirit, which led them to leave their homes and to return to Judah as apostles of the expanded law of Moses.

During his second visit to Jerusalem, in 432 B. C., Nehemiah himself carried on still further the sweeping social and religious reforms which he had begun in 445 B. C.

Later Prophets   Isaiah

(Neh. 5 ; 13), and which were the necessary preliminaries to the action of the Great Assembly recorded in Nehemiah 10. He made provision for the adequate and regular support of the Levites and temple ministers, and by the efficient use of his authority enforced the observance of the Sabbath, respecting which the Jews in the east were far more strict than those in Judah. Whereas in 445 B.C. he had tolerated the custom of intermarrying with foreigners, he now set to work energetically to remove the evil. There is no evidence that he demanded, as did the later reformers, that all who had married foreign wives put them away. In the case of the masses he appears to have contented himself with impressing them with the enormity of their action and with extracting a solemn promise that they would not countenance the practice in the future. Tobiah, the Ammonite, who had married into the family of the high-priest, was excluded from the special privileges which had been given him in connection with the temple, and one of the grandsons of Eliashib, the high-priest, was driven from Jerusalem, because he had married a daughter of Sanballat.

In all probability the excluded priest was the one for whom, according to Josephus, Sanballat built the rival temple on Mount Gerizim. Obviously, to Nehemiah was largely due the schism between the descendants of the northern and southern Israelites. Since the reformation of Josiah they had worshipped together at Jerusalem, but henceforth the Samaritans had " no part and portion " in the service of the Jewish temple. The fact that they had formerly been united only intensified the bitterness of the division. It is not strange that this feeling found expression in certain of the contemporary prophecies.

The late editor of the Book of Ezra-Nehemiah, or else a later copyist, by mistake placed the account of the expedition and reform work of Ezra before that of Nehemiah. The evidence, however, is practically conclusive that it should follow rather than precede. Nehemiah's reforms, for example, are clearly those of a pioneer, and without them Ezra's success in persuading or compelling all who had married foreign wives to put them away (Ezra 10) would have been impossible. In the prayer attributed to Ezra he also seems to refer directly to the service of Nehemiah in repairing the ruined city (Ezra 9 : 9). The account of the Great Assembly in Nehemiah 9 and 10, which the editor of Ezra-Nehemiah places after the report of Nehemiah's work, also presupposes (9 : 2) that the "separation from strangers" recorded in Ezra 9 and 10 had just taken place. Their language and thought confirm the conclusion that Ezra 7 to 10 and Nehemiah 7 : 70 to 10 : 39 originally formed part of the same narrative. (For further consideration of the evidence compare Kent, " History of the Jewish People," pp. 106-110, 192-199.)

A restoration of the activity of Ezra to its original historical position after the work of Nehemiah enables us to appreciate in their true relation the forces which moulded Judaism and which led to the restoration of the "true Israel" to Palestine. While Nehemiah's reform measures established precedents, the principles which prompted them had to be embodied in a law and adopted before their permanence could be assured. This fact explains the significance of Ezra's expedition and the promulgation of the Priestly Law at the Great Assembly. When the Judean community accepted the new code in place of the simpler law of Deuteronomy, which had governed them hitherto, the Judaism which figures so prominently in the New Testament narrative was born.

The late editor of Ezra-Nehemiah states that the expedition of Ezra was in the seventh year of Artaxerxes (Ezra 7 : 7, 8), but does not indicate which one it was of the three Persian monarchs who bore that name. Like the rest of the later Jewish historians, he did not distinguish between the three. It may in all probability have been because he did not know that there was more than one Artaxerxes that he placed the account of Ezra's expedition (in the seventh year) before that of Nehemiah's work (in the twentieth year of Artaxerxes). The Artaxerxes under whom Ezra lived was probably the second ruler of that name, who reigned between 404 and 358 B. C., so that the birth of the "true Israel" may with reasonable certainty be dated 398-397.

The formal acceptance of the Priestly Law, with its

stern prohibitions against affiliation with aliens who might contaminate, confirmed the schism between the Jews and Samaritans. This act in turn attracted to the Judean community thousands of loyal Jews, so that there was a genuine basis of fact in the declaration of the prophet that " a nation was born in a day." In the years immediately following the Great Assembly the restoration of the Jewish race was partially realized. Ezra's expedition was but one of several which are recorded in Ezra 2 (Neh. 7). For a brief period the Jews witnessed the fulfilment of many of their fondest hopes, so that joy and expectation took the place of lamentation.

2. *The Date of the Individual Prophecies*

In the light of these historical facts, the sermons preserved in chapters 34 ; 35 ; 60 : 1 to 63 : 6 ; 65 ; 66 of the Book of Isaiah find their true setting and interpretation. The language is so general and the historical references so few and indefinite that, like the psalms of the period, which they resemble very closely both in vocabulary and in thought, it is impossible to assign them with certainty to a definite year. Their indefiniteness and broad outlook are characteristic of the prophecies of the latter half of the Persian period. Their intense love for the temple and its service, their equally strong hatred of the hostile heathen world, and their expectation that Jehovah will

Later Prophets Isaiah

soon appear to exalt his people, are all marked characteristics of Judaism.

The references to the temple and the character of the social evils which are denounced indicate that the prophets who wrote these sermons had primarily in mind the post-exilic Judean community. Their frequent reflections of the thought and form of expression of the earlier prophets, and especially of the author of Isaiah 40 to 55, stamp them at once as post-exilic. The conspicuous absence of exhortations to reform suggests that at least the worst evils within the community had been eliminated. A decided turn in their fortunes evidently is the basis of their new sense of Jehovah's favor.

In chapters 60 to 62 we recognize the impression which Nehemiah's mission made upon the minds of the faithful in the community. Already its "light is come." To Jerusalem the prophet declares: "Strangers will build your walls, and their kings will minister to you." The gifts which faithful Jews have brought from distant lands are an earnest that "men will bring to you the riches of the nations." These glowing prophecies may have been issued either on the arrival of Nehemiah or of Ezra's expedition bringing rich gifts for the temple. The rebuilding of the walls of Jerusalem is still put in the future, and the remembrance of the misfortunes of the community is so fresh that the earlier date is on the whole the more probable.

The tangible evidence that Jehovah was reviving the fortunes of his people led them to believe that he would soon deliver them from their hereditary foes, those enemies of progress who had opposed so bitterly the rebuilding of the walls of Jerusalem. From their point of view they regarded the destruction of these malignant foes to be absolutely essential to the vindication of Jehovah's justice and to the establishment of his kingdom. As in the prophecies of the exile and in the Book of Malachi, the Edomites figure as the type of Israel's enemies. While the language and thought of chapters 63 : 1-6; 34; and its complement, 35, indicate that they belong to the era introduced by the work of Nehemiah, there are no definite data from which to determine the exact date.

The half-heathen people to whom Jehovah had called through his prophets, whose idolatrous practices are condemned in chapters 65 and 66, are without much doubt the Samaritans. The alien temple referred to must be the one on Mount Gerizim, and hence the prophecy must be dated subsequently to 432 B. C. The statement that the new nation has been born, the expectation that Jehovah will soon establish his universal kingdom, since his people are at last doing his will, and the strongly ritualistic tone of the closing verses of chapter 66, all suggest that the Priestly Law has been instituted in Judah and that they come, therefore, from the bright, hopeful years immediately following the Great Assembly.

II

THE GOSPEL PROCLAMATION TO THE JEWISH RACE
(Isa. 60 to 62)

1. *The Song of Glorified Zion* (60)

At last, after long years of discouragement and waiting, O Judean community, the deliverance and prosperity promised by Jehovah is at hand. Like the first rays of the rising sun, his glory is bursting upon you, while the heathen world is enveloped in deep darkness. Foreign peoples and rulers will soon come to profit by the glorious revelation of Jehovah's might, which has been vouchsafed to you. If you could but see, they are already on the way. From the distant lands of the dispersion the scattered remnants of your race are returning, and the weak ones are being borne back, as children are carried by their mothers. Soon you will be filled with joy unutterable, for, like a great flood-tide, the wealth of the world shall come pouring in upon you. From every quarter the rich trading nations shall come, bringing offerings for Jehovah's sanctuary, and praising him because of the great deeds which he has done. *The exaltation and restoration of Jehovah's people (60 : 1-9)*

Foreigners, instead of attacking you, will rebuild your fallen walls, and the kings who now rule over you will serve you, for Jehovah's indignation against you has given *The rebuilding of Jerusalem (60 : 10-13)* place to compassion. Then it will not be necessary to close your gates against foreign foes, for all the nations shall bring to you their richest products. Then, as in the days of Solomon, shall the valuable woods of Mount Lebanon be brought to rebuild and beautify the temple.

<small>The prosperity which Jehovah will bring to his people (60 : 14-22)</small> The descendants of those who now despise and attack you will come to you as suppliants. Jerusalem, instead of being a desolate city, aside from the great currents of the world's life, shall be known to all as the city blessed by the presence of the great and righteous Ruler of the universe. When the best of the world is placed at your disposal, you will appreciate the power and love of the God who is your deliverer. Instead of your present poverty, Jehovah will give you unbounded prosperity. The principles of peace and justice shall dominate your political life, and deeds of violence and destruction shall be unknown. Jerusalem shall be far famed as a haven of refuge from wrong and oppression. No longer will you be subject to the changing fortunes of this cruel, selfish land, for Jehovah himself will ever be present to protect and supply your every need. Then will all of his people conform to the just demands of his law, so that it will never again be necessary to drive them into exile. Thus this remnant of a people, under Jehovah's nurturing care, shall again become a powerful nation. Speedily will he bring about the realization of these promises.

Later Prophets Isaiah 61 : 9

2. *Jehovah's Promise of Salvation and Restoration* (61 : 62)

The spirit of the Highest has touched my spirit, prepar- The mission
ing and commissioning me to announce in his name a and message
message of comfort to those crushed by affliction, to pro- of the proph-
claim release for the distant exiles, and the approach of et-servant of
Jehovah's judgment day, in which he will graciously re- Jehovah
store his chosen people and punish transgressors, and to (61 : 1-3)
declare to the sad and scattered remnants of the Jewish
race that their present doubts and lamentations shall
speedily give place to joy, for Jehovah is about to re-establish them gloriously in the land of their fathers, so that
they shall be an honor to his name.

The reunited people will rebuild the ruined cities which The re-
have lain desolate since the days of the old Hebrew king- established
doms. The menial tasks of caring for the flocks and tilling nation
the soil will then be performed by foreigners, so that all of (61 : 4-11)
the chosen race will be free to act as the consecrated priests
of Jehovah. The best products of the world will be brought
to them for food and clothing. In return for the wrongs
and affronts which they have suffered, they shall be alloted
double portions of earthly possessions, and their joy shall
be unending; for injustice is an abomination to Jehovah,
and by him fidelity is always rewarded. In the coming
days all mankind will realize that the Jews are the especial
objects of his favor. Then will they exult because he has

Isaiah 61 : 10   *Messages of the*

delivered and vindicated them; rejoicing shall take the place of the present lamentations. In his own good time, as surely as spring follows winter, the Lord will give to his people victory over their foes and honor in the eyes of all the nations.

The exaltation of Jerusalem (62 : 1-7)
I will not cease to prophesy until Jerusalem's exaltation and restoration is complete. Forsaken, desolate city and land, you will yet be the admiration of the world, an honor to Jehovah, who will declare his favor by restoring you. His affection and regard for you are like those of a bridegroom toward his bride. Over his holy city he has set prophetic watchmen, whose duty it is unceasingly to raise the warning cry, and unremittingly to remind him of his gracious promises, until he fulfils them in the exaltation of Jerusalem to a position of surpassing honor among the cities of the world.

The deliverance of Jehovah's afflicted people (62 : 8-12)
By his omnipotence Jehovah has solemnly promised that their foes shall no longer despoil his people of the products of their toil; but unmolested shall they enjoy them within the sacred precincts of his sanctuary. All obstacles in the way of their glorious restoration shall be removed. The divine proclamation has gone forth; Jehovah is about to redeem and reward his faithful ones; quickly all the world shall know it. The disgrace of the past shall be removed. Soon they shall be recognized as the peculiar objects of his mercy and tender care.

III

VENGEANCE UPON THEIR GUILTY FOES AND DE-
LIVERANCE AND HONOR FOR JEHOVAH'S
PEOPLE (Isa. 34 ; 35 ; 65 ; 66)

1. *The Opposite Fates Awaiting the Samaritans and Jews* (65 : 1 to 66 : 5, 17, 18ª)

Jehovah declares that, although they have never genuinely sought him, he has freely offered to that half-Israelitish, half-heathen people who dwell on the borders of Judah the privilege of participating in his worship. Through his prophets he has urged them to acknowledge him as their God, and to abandon their wicked practices, but in vain. They constantly arouse his indignation by their shameful heathen rites, and by their defiance of the sacred ceremonial law. At the same time they lay claims to superior sanctity. Jehovah will not tolerate such brazen apostasy. Their heinous crimes and the idolatrous practices of their fathers will receive at his hands their just recompense. ^{The obduracy and vile practices of the Samaritans (65 : 1-7)}

He will not, however, destroy all of the remnants of the Hebrew race. The fidelity of the few Jews who serve him will influence him, not only to preserve them, but also from them to rear up a people who will again, as of old, occupy the entire land of Canaan from east to west. ^{The preservation of the faithful few (65 : 8-10)}

They who spurn the worship of Jehovah, and, intent

Isaiah 65 : 11

The want and sorrow in store for the traitors to Jehovah (65 : 11-15) only on attaining their selfish ends, pay homage to the heathen gods of fortune and destiny, will be destined to destruction. Since they have disregarded his gracious invitations and done only evil, they shall experience the horrors of starvation, thirst, disgrace, and inexpressible anguish; while those who are true to him shall have their every need satisfied. The name of the Samaritans will be preserved only on the lips of those who curse; while to his loyal followers, the Jews, he will give a new name, expressive of their nobler character.

The glories of the new era about to dawn for the Jewish race (65 : 16-25) Henceforth in this land of sacred memories Jehovah will be the only God whom men will worship. Him will they trust and praise, because he will deliver them from all their present woes. He declares that he will institute a new era, in which the imperfections and troubles of the past will be forgotten. Instead of the present poor, half-populated Jerusalem, he will rear a new city which will be a constant source of pride and joy to him and to its inhabitants. No more will wails of lamentation rise from their lips. No longer will the weak ones—children and old men—perish from exposure and privation. All shall enjoy peace and prosperity and die in a ripe old age. Then will Jehovah anticipate all their wants, even before they feel them. Then will be realized the earlier prophetic ideal of perfect peace and harmony throughout all creation; and wrong and violence will be unknown within the precincts of the sacred city.

Later Prophets Isaiah 66 : 18a

Do you ask which sanctuary—the one at Jerusalem or the one on Mount Gerizim—is acceptable to Jehovah? Know that he needs no sanctuary, for heaven is his place of abode and the earth only his footstool. Everything was created by him. He needs no temple built with hands. He ever looks, not upon the structures which men raise for his worship nor upon the forms of ritual, but upon the attitude of the worshipper. They who humbly, reverentially, and obediently do his will are assured of his blessing. {Faith and obedience the only essentials in Jehovah's worship (66 : 1, 2)}

Let not those who worship him in their own selfish way, combining with their offering of oxen and sheep the sacrifice of human beings and of unclean beasts, who pay homage to idols, as well as to Jehovah, think that they will thereby secure his blessing. Because of their defiant, wicked course, he will send dread calamities upon them. Their awful fate shall bring encouragement to the objects of their hatred, the faithful members of the Hebrew race, who are now serving Jehovah according to their light. Although they who mistrust his power to deliver them, and who revive the ancient forms of nature worship, seem to prosper, their destruction Jehovah declares is certain. {They who worship him half-heartedly, introducing vile heathen rites into their service, only incur his wrath (66 : 3-5, 17, 18a)}

2. *Jehovah's Judgment upon the Hostile Nations and Especially upon Edom* (63 : 1-6 ; 34)

Do you feel, O Jews, that you are the helpless victims of your foes, and especially of the cruel, treacherous Edom- {The divine warrior (63 : 1-6)}

Isaiah 63 : 1

ites, who in the time of your distress seized and still hold a large portion of the territory of Judah? Look up and with the eye of faith behold your invincible champion returning from executing bloody vengeance upon your enemies. It is Jehovah who, finding that there was no one else to deliver his people, has come, as the upholder of justice, by his own omnipotent power, to vindicate them and to destroy completely the hostile heathen nations.

The sentence upon the hostile nations (34 : 1-4)

Let all the peoples of the earth know the fate which awaits them at the hand of Jehovah. His fierce wrath is aroused against them and he has condemned them to death. When he executes his sentence upon them they shall die by thousands. Their corpses shall lie rotting upon every mountain and hill-top—all nature shall be affected by Jehovah's judgment upon man's sin.

The awful fate awaiting the Edomites and their land (34 : 5-17)

The Edomites shall be the especial objects of his destructive wrath. Their many flocks shall be slain in the great sacrificial feast which Jehovah is about to institute in their proud capital. In that day of his vengeance their entire land shall be soaked in blood. To complete the destruction, it shall be inundated by floods of bitumen, which shall go on burning unceasingly, so that the land shall be impassable. It shall become a lone desolation, inhabited only by the unclean birds and beasts that frequent ruins. Thus Edom's rulers shall perish. Its palaces shall become the abode of wild animals and foul spirits. Vile serpents and vultures shall haunt the

Isaiah 66 : 7

desolate wastes where now stand the proud cities of your foes. The judgment is certain, for Jehovah has determined to execute it, and its effects shall last, not for one short moment, but forever.

3. *The Glorious Era to Follow Jehovah's Judgment* (35)

For Jehovah's people, however, the desert places and pastures shall be clad with a brilliance of bloom. The rich fertility of Mount Carmel and the plain of Sharon shall extend over the entire land. Let those who have lost hope and courage be strengthened and fear not, for Jehovah will surely come to deliver his people, and to punish their foes. Those who are now afflicted shall be relieved and filled with joy. Parched Judah shall be supplied with flowing springs and streams. These desolate ruins shall be reclaimed. The good shall be separated from the wicked. Violence and wrong shall cease. The exiles of the Jewish race shall return with songs of joy on their lips, and sadness shall be only a memory of the past.

<small>The blessings in store for the faithful Jews (35)</small>

4. *The Establishment of Jehovah's Universal Kingdom* (66 : 6-16, 18ᵇ-24)

If you will observe closely you will note the indications that Jehovah is about to complete his work of judgment, and visit upon those who defy him their just deserts. See how this struggling community almost in a moment, without any effort on its part, has through the return of loyal

<small>The restoration of the Jewish nation and the rebuilding of Jerusalem (66 : 6-11)</small>

Isaiah 66 : 8 — *Messages of the*

exiles grown into a nation. Such a marvel is unprecedented in human history. No sooner did the Jews in Palestine truly exert themselves to rebuild Jerusalem than her sons came streaming back. Surely Jehovah will not begin this glorious task of restoring and vindicating his chosen people and then fail to bring it to completion. Let all who love the holy city, who have mourned over her desolation in the past, rejoice over her exaltation, and the still greater glories in store for her.

<small>Jehovah's protecting care over his restored city and people (66 : 12-16)</small> Jehovah declares that to his city and nation, so long the prey of powerful foes, he will give peace unceasing, and the heathen peoples, instead of attacking, shall bring to you their richest products in overflowing profusion. They shall devote their best energies to restoring you to your land, and to supplying your every need. Jehovah's care for you will be like that of a tender, loving mother. When you appreciate it, your hearts will be filled with joy, and you will regain your courage and enthusiasm. The whole world shall then know that Jehovah at last has shown his love toward his servants. By fire and the sword will he execute vengeance upon all who are hostile to him.

<small>At last all people will recognize and worship Jehovah (66 : 18ᵇ-24)</small> The time is coming when Jehovah will lead all men to appreciate his power and glory. Convinced by the wonders which he will perform, they shall become apostles to the distant nations, who have not heard of his marvellous character and acts. The heathen world shall be so thoroughly

impressed with his might and holiness that they will bring your exiled kinsmen from the distant lands where they have been scattered to Jerusalem as an offering to Jehovah. Of these he will appoint some to serve as priests in his temple. In this new order of things, which he is soon to institute, you and your race will be perpetuated through your descendants, who will unceasingly succeed each other. [On the appointed days all mankind will join with you in the worship of Jehovah, having learned from the awful fate that has overtaken those who rebelled against him, the lesson of reverential and faithful obedience.]

THE MESSAGE OF JOEL

THE MESSAGE OF JOEL

I

THE DATE AND THEME OF JOEL'S PROPHECY

The half century succeeding the solemn adoption of the Law by the people of Judah was in many respects the most hopeful and encouraging of any which had followed the nation's downfall. Under the potent influence of a common system of laws which minutely regulated the life of each individual, the population of the province became united, and therefore increased in strength. Many Jews, moreover, attracted by the congenial atmosphere of the reformed community must have come back from distant lands to settle in Judah. By their aid, and through the renewed enterprise of the inhabitants, considerable territory was added to the effective domain of Judah, especially toward the west and northwest. The community increased, not in numbers and strength alone but in prestige and influence in comparison with the other petty surrounding states. Once more it became a potent factor in the affairs of Palestine. This advance in material prosperity, rendered far easier by the weakness of the central government under Artaxerxes II. (404-358 B. C.), was paralleled by a gradual revival of the old aspirations after independence and of an eager expectation that at last Jehovah's promises were about to be fulfilled in the overturning of the foes of the nation and the exaltation of Judah to a world-wide rule.

There are many indications which converge to prove that the prophecy of Joel comes from this period of peace and growth. The bitter days of exile are past (3 : 1, 2, 17); the community is no longer threatened by some great world-power, like Assyria or Babylonia, but has to deal with Phœnicia, Philistia, and Edom (3 : 4-6, 19) and their petty enmities. These political conditions suit well the era when Assyria and Babylonia were no longer in existence and when Persia, the nominal ruler of southwestern Asia, was comparatively inert. These conditions, however, came to an abrupt end with the accession of Artaxerxes Ochus, whose powerful and cruel reign aroused the hatred and fear of his subjects throughout the Asiatic world.

Still more decisive are the references to the religious life. The sin which stirs the heart of the prophet is neither idolatry nor civic unrighteousness, but an undefined failure to render to Jehovah his utmost claims. The community is a unit. Its leaders are priests and elders, who can gather all the people to a "solemn assembly" (2 : 16). The calamity which presses upon them is the

Later Prophets   Joel

danger, not of political overthrow, but of the cessation of the daily temple offerings. Without question the prophecy was put forth at a time when religious interests dominated all others and appealed to the community as a whole ; when the temple at Jerusalem was the only recognized sanctuary (1 : 9), and the natural centre of civic activity (2 : 1, 15 ; 3 : 17) ; when the word " Israel " had become synonymous with Judah.

Opposed to these indications of a date for Joel in the first half of the fourth century B. C. is the place of the book in the canon. The editors who arranged the twelve Minor Prophets into a book apparently supposed that Joel, like Hosea and Amos, was a pre-exilic work, for their arrangement of the order of the books is in general chronological. Influenced by this judgment, not a few scholars have sought to date the prophecy in the earlier part of the reign of Joash, before Hazael invaded Judah, about 825 B. C. (2 Kings 12). At no other pre-exilic date would it be possible to account for its peculiarities. These scholars have also been influenced by the opinion that Amos 1 : 2[a] is a quotation from Joel 4 : 16[a], and Amos 9 : 13 from Joel 4 : 18.

The arguments advanced to prove that Joel is the earliest prophetic book in the Old Testament create at the best no more than a possibility for the early date and are opposed by cogent and important considerations. The book of Joel has some twenty literary parallels to a dozen different biblical books. A minute examination of these (compare G. B. Gray, *Expositor*, September, 1893) seems to prove that Joel was the one who quoted. References to the Greeks as slave-traders and the absence of references to the northern kingdom or to Moab, Ammon, or Aram are not easy to explain at 800 B. C. Moreover the allusions of Joel to the "northerner" (2 : 20), to the river flowing from the temple (3 : 18) and to the "day of Jehovah," while perfectly natural to one who followed Zephaniah, Jeremiah, and Ezekiel, are obscure and less effective as original expressions. If uttered before 800 B. C. prophecy overlooked them for more than two centuries. Strangest of all would be the expectation of the prophet that the heathen nations would be completely destroyed (3 : 2, 9-14). This hope is in line with the vision of Ezekiel (38, 39) and well expresses the desire of the later post-exilic, but is quite out of harmony with the ideas of the earlier prophets. They predicted severe judgments on the guilty nations, but did not anticipate their extirpation.

The theme of the Book of Joel is one familiar to the reader of prophecy. A great calamity is interpreted morally by the prophet as a call to repentance. The ensuing reformation affords a basis for the promise of great blessings, expressed in part apocalyptically under the form of a gathering of all hostile nations for judgment and extermination.

Later Prophets Joel 1 : 3

Attention has often been called to the structure of the book. It is carefully balanced, the enumeration of the woes of the people contrasting with the detail of their promised blessings. It abounds in rhetorical passages and striking figures, indicating the greatest care in elaboration.

II

THE COMING OF THE LOCUSTS AND JEHOVAH'S JUDGMENT (1 : 1 to 2 : 17)

1. *The Locust Devastation a Summons to National Repentance* (1)

During the half century following the adoption of the Law, after a series of unexampled calamities brought on by drought, by fire, and finally by locusts, the prophet Joel was impelled to deliver a warning message to his people. <small>The occasion of the prophecy (1 : 1)</small>

" O people of Judah, old and young alike, give strict attention to the message which Jehovah has put into my heart. What an unprecedented series of calamities has fallen to our lot in these days! For generations to come they will be told and retold as examples of unparalleled disaster. The land is bare. Swarm after swarm of destructive locusts have devoured the crops and the <small>The destructive locust visitation (1 : 2-4)</small>

Joel 1 : 4   *Messages of the*

foliage. The vegetation which the gnawer[1] spared, the swarmer has discovered and consumed; what the swarmer failed to find, the licker has searched out; what the licker overlooked, alas! the finisher has destroyed. Every chance of vintage or harvest is gone.

The universal lament (1 : 5)

"Let all classes join in lamenting the awful disaster. Awake from your drunken sleep, ye revellers, who love to quaff huge measures of sweet wine, cry aloud in your vexation, for the beverage you long for can no longer be obtained. Like a well-organized army these locusts have invaded our beautiful land. They are eager to devour, untiring, innumerable, as irresistible and destructive as lions. Not content with devouring plants and vegetables they have attacked the fruit-trees, consuming the leaves and finally stripping off the bark, leaving them ghastly and bare in the burning sun.

The locust army (1 : 6-7)

The bereaved land (1 : 8-10)

"Like a young wife mourning for her husband, the devastated land lies desolate. No longer can the stated services of the temple be continued. The daily vegetable offering and libation of wine cannot be provided in glad acknowledgment of Jehovah's presence and favor. The priests who stand in the holy sanctuary and minister before him are heart-broken. Even the land itself and its produce seem to join in the chorus of grief.

"Manifest freely your disappointment, you that culti-

---

[1] These four terms for the locust represent vividly its powers of destruction. Probably only one kind of locust is designated.

vate the soil and keep the vineyards, for not only the wheat and barley and the highly prized fruit-trees, but all the trees alike are rendered useless to promote the joy or well-being of mankind.

<small>The despair of the land-owners (1: 11, 12)</small>

"O priests of Jehovah, spend not your strength in useless grief, but put on sackcloth in token of your penitence and proclaim a day of public fasting and prayer. This calamity is a harbinger of what will be far harder to bear, namely, Jehovah's day of retribution. That day will reveal the might of the Almighty.[1] Beware lest he find it necessary to manifest himself against us.

<small>The call to a public fast (1: 13-15)</small>

"Need I point out the providential character of this misfortune? See how wide-spread it has been. Do we not look helplessly on while the means of expressing our joyful service of thanks to God are taken away, not only by the greedy locusts, but by this extreme drought. The seed grain is shrivelled up with the heat, the granaries are allowed to fall into disrepair. Cattle wander here and there in great distress in search of pasturage; even the sheep are unable to find subsistence. O Jehovah, we can but appeal to thee. Locusts, droughts, and fire have utterly swept away our resources. Even the dumb beasts are turning toward thee their longing eyes, pleading in agony that this dearth of water and of pasturage may have an end."

<small>The added effects of drought and fire (1: 16-20)</small>

[1] The Hebrew contains a clever assonance in the words "devastation" (shōd) and "Almighty" (shaddai).

2. Only Repentance will Avert the Terrors of Jehovah's Day (2 : 1-11)

The day of Jehovah at hand (2 : 1-2ᵃ)
"Sound the sacred trumpets from the temple mount that the people may awake to a sense of their danger. The day of Jehovah is very near, a day when the sun will be obscured and the whole sky be darkened, save where a few beams of the sun gleam through the enshadowing cloud, as at sunrise on the mountains. But the clouds will be made up of swarms of locusts approaching in resistless hordes without number. The sight will transcend all experience or expectation. To the one

The march of the locust army (2 : 2ᵇ-5)
watching their advance the country before them seems fair as the garden of Eden, but behind them it resembles a fire-swept wilderness. Like a mighty host of cavalry they approach; the noise of their wings in flight is like the noise of chariots rumbling over the hills; the sound of their browsing is like the crackling of a fire driven through dry stubble; they are as eager as a phalanx panoplied for war.

Their attack (2 : 6-9)
"At the sight of them whole nations are seized with panic; all countenances are livid with fear. In unbroken ranks they advance steadily to the charge, marching straight ahead, no one hindering his neighbor. No expedient serves to stop their onset. They swarm over the walls, enter the houses through the lattice-work, and take

possession of the city in spite of all the exertions of its inhabitants.

"At their approach even earth and heaven tremble and the sun, moon, and stars withdraw their light. Jehovah, too, at their head, manifests his presence in loud thunderings, befitting the huge and powerful instrument of his will, and heralding the advent of his awe-inspiring day. The accompanying phenomena (2 : 10, 11)

"Yet, O Judah, it is not too late to avert this crowning calamity. Manifest by grief and fasting your sincere repentance, for Jehovah is gracious and compassionate, ready to forgive and bless. There is yet time for him to turn aside from his course of judgment and permit the earth once more to bring forth the fruits which we rejoice to offer to him The need of repentance (2 : 12-14)

"Sound the trumpets, therefore, for a great religious assembly of all the people, small and great, young and old. Let none be excepted. Acting for all the people, who are assembled in the outer court, let the priests, standing between the entrance of the sanctuary and the great altar of burnt offering, offer public supplication to Jehovah, saying, 'O Jehovah, forgive and spare thy people and this holy land lest the heathen nations, noting how we suffer, may make a mock of us, declaring that thou hast cast us off.'" The call to a solemn assembly (2 : 15-17)

III

THE PROSPERITY, INSPIRATION AND DELIVERANCE FROM ENEMIES IN STORE FOR JEHOVAH'S PEOPLE (2 : 18 to 3 : 21)

1. *The Return of Prosperity* (2 : 18-27)

The results of penitence (2 : 18)
    Stirred by the exhortations of the prophet, the people assembled together at a solemn fast to express their penitence; the priests interceded for them, and Jehovah, moved by a desire to sustain the dignity of his name among the nations and filled with pity and love for his people, gave them through his prophet a gracious answer to their plea.

The renewal of prosperity and removal of the locusts (2 : 19, 20)
    "In the days to come, O repentant servants of mine, I will grant you again in great abundance the products of the earth and will show my favor so openly that all the world will recognize that I am protecting and blessing you. Moreover, this plague of locusts—fit emblem of the hordes from the north who seek to crush out your national life—I will destroy. With a strong wind will I blow them into the desert or into the two seas to miserably perish in such quantities that their carcases, cast up by the waves, will exhale pestilential odors, for they have over-done their deputed work."

    "O land, cease from all grief and fear, for Jehovah is

mightier than his instrument and is about to bless us. Promise of
O beasts of the field, be afraid no longer, for the pastures abundant
will soon be green and the ravaged trees will bear their harvest
fruit abundantly. Rejoice, O children of Zion, give praise (2 : 21-27)
to Jehovah, for he will regularly send down the early rain
to soften the earth, the winter rain to stimulate the crops,
and the late rain to ripen them. In the abundant harvests
which will result, Jehovah will repay the losses of these
years of repeated devastation by locusts and drought.
When you are enjoying the resulting ease and plenty, you
will in happy contentment acknowledge your indebtedness
to Jehovah and be proud that you are his people. Thereafter your faith in his care will never weaken."

2. *The Inspiration and Deliverance of all true Israelites*
(2 : 28-32)

Having thus proven by these signs that he has forgiven Promise of
his erring people Jehovah will do greater things. He (2 : 28, 29)
promises to pour out abundantly his spirit upon all Israelites, young men and maidens, the feeble and the
strong, upon every class, even the very humblest. Not
prophets nor priests alone, but everyone shall then have
insight into the will of Jehovah.

Then will be seen signs of the day of Jehovah, his Deliverance
day of judgment. There will be extraordinary portents hovah's day
in earth and air, arresting attention and presaging mis- for true Is-
fortune. Those, however, who publicly acknowledge (2 : 30-32)

Joel 2 : 32

with heartfelt earnestness their trust in Jehovah will be absolutely secure from danger. Many of these will be in Jerusalem, but some will even be found among the Jews dispersed far and wide.

3. *The Judgment of the Heathen Nations* (3)

Nations to be summoned for judgment (3 : 1-3)

"In the day when my people find deliverance, safety, and restoration," Jehovah declares, "I will reckon with the nations which have taken advantage of their weakness. I will bring them together at the valley called 'Jehovah judges,' and will contend in judgment with them there. Much have I to charge against them—the wide dispersion of my people, the seizure of the soil, their sale as prisoners of war into slavery at a low price. I will demand a full accounting.

The special punishment of Phœnicia and Philistia (3 : 4-8)

"In that day, inhabitants of Phœnicia and Philistia, what will be your answer to my charge? Has there been any justification for your cruel treatment of Israel? Were you executing vengeance? Nay, it is vengeance that you deserve, and speedily shall it come upon you. Not only did you enrich your palaces with the plunder of Judah, but you sold Jewish captives into distant slavery among the Greeks. Behold I am about to incite these very victims to return, make captives of your children, and sell them into slavery to the distant nation of Sheba. This is Jehovah's proclamation."

Later Prophets   Joel 3 : 16

Let heralds declare to all the nations that Jehovah invites them to combat. Let them equip and send forth their veteran warriors. Let them make every effort, transforming the implements of peace into weapons of war, and arousing such a martial spirit that even the weak will declare themselves willing and able to fight. Let all these hosts assemble for the strife in the valley "Jehovah judges." There, O Jehovah, cause the angelic hosts to come to meet them. The summons of the nations (3 : 9-11)

"Let the nations advance," proclaims Jehovah, "I will be ready to meet them. No longer will I argue the case with them, but I will be seated on my throne of judgment, prepared to pronounce their well-deserved doom. Great has been their wickedness and certain shall be their fate. They are like a harvest ready for the sickle or a vat laden with grapes for pressing. The time has come for decisive action." Jehovah's word (3 : 12-13)

Hear the distant hum of the throngs in the valley, awaiting Jehovah's rapidly approaching judgment. The signs of his day will soon appear. The sun and moon will be eclipsed and the stars will cease to shine. Mighty storms will herald Jehovah's approach. Heaven and earth will quake before him. His judgment, however, is for his foes alone; to his own people he will be a stronghold and defence. When he has delivered them, his people will know that he is their only God, dwelling on Mount Zion, able and ready to protect and bless. He will de- The awful judgment (3 : 14-17)

301

Joel 3 : 17

<small>The subsequent prosperity and safety of Judah (3 : 18-21)</small>

fend it from all foes and prevent it from being defiled again by the foot of strangers.

Then at last will he abundantly bless his people. The land of Judah shall become astonishingly fertile and attractive. Never again shall there be a lack of water, nay, from the temple itself a stream shall issue which will turn the arid ravine of the Acacias into a beautiful valley. Egypt, however, so certain of her fertility, and Edom, our exultant foe, shall become barren and desolate, because of the unprovoked massacres of Jews which they have abetted. Their innocent blood shall be avenged and remembered that all may know that Jehovah cares for his own. Judah shall ever be prosperous and full of people. Never again shall Jerusalem be destroyed.

MESSAGES OF DOUBT AND HOPE
FROM THE CLOSE OF THE
PERSIAN PERIOD

MESSAGES OF DOUBT AND HOPE FROM THE CLOSE OF THE PERSIAN PERIOD

I

THE LAST HALF-CENTURY OF PERSIAN RULE

The analogies between the reformations of Josiah and Ezra are many and do not cease with the institution of the respective codes. Not only were both followed by a seemingly idyllic period of peace and prosperity, but each also begat in the minds of leaders and people a false conception of their relation to Jehovah which led them into overwhelming political disasters. Reasoning that after such devotion as he had shown, Jehovah must grant success to his every act, Josiah attacked the powerful army of Necho, to learn only too late his fatal mistake. The same false, presumptuous faith finds expression in the corresponding later period. Now that they were faithfully observing the dictates of the law, they felt invincible and looked expectantly for the speedy overthrow of the hostile nations which opposed and oppressed them (Joel 3 : 9-21).

During their declining years, the Persians, by their corruption and cruelty, completely forfeited the esteem with which they had earlier been regarded by the Jews. After the long, supine rule of Artaxerxes II. came to an end in 358 B. C., Artaxerxes III., better known by his private name, Ochus, came to the throne. He proved one of the cruelest and at the same time one of the most energetic princes which the ancient Orient produced. His ability, however, was not at first manifest. Egypt under native kings had for a long time defied the authority of Persia. Early in his reign Ochus invaded the land of the Nile with a huge army, there to meet with an overwhelming defeat. The states of Palestine, encouraged by the Egyptians, were influenced by this disaster to revolt about 350 B. C. The Phœnicians, led by the town of Sidon, headed the rebellion. Persian soldiers and officials were murdered and the rebels for several years carried all before them, since Ochus, engaged in putting down insurrections in other parts of his empire, was unable to send an army against them.

In view of these conditions it is exceedingly probable that the Jewish community in Palestine eagerly joined the general rebellion. If not voluntarily, they were led by force to unite with the rebels. The biblical narrative stops with the reformation of Ezra, and Josephus has handed down only one or two imperfect traditions, so that few details have been preserved respecting this critical epoch in Jewish history.

Later Prophets Isaiah

Combining, however, the testimony of a variety of sources (see Kent, " History of the Jewish People," 230-232), it appears that the Jews seriously compromised themselves, so that when Ochus was finally at liberty, about 346 B.C., to execute a bloody vengeance upon the rebels in Palestine, they were among the victims of his wrath. Their cities were captured and doubtless given over for pillage to his brutal soldiers. Not content with slaughter, the conqueror deported large numbers of the Jews to the province of Hyrcania, south of the Caspian Sea. Thus by sword, by fire and captivity, the strength of the revived and reformed Judean community was again shattered. Out of a seemingly clear sky a thunderbolt had suddenly fallen. When they had looked expectantly to Jehovah for vindication and exaltation, their merciless foes had been allowed to trample them and their sacred institutions in the mire. Their faith suffered even more than their body politic from the shock. The crisis was all the more intense because they firmly believed, as earlier prophets and sages had taught, that righteousness was always rewarded by Jehovah with prosperity, and conversely that misfortune was a certain index of divine displeasure; and yet they were conscious of having, as never before in the history of their race, carefully carried out the demands of their God as revealed in the Law. Through the calamities which had overtaken them, not only did they stand condemned in the eyes of the world, but also Jehovah's power and justice were fundamentally questioned.

II

THE LITERATURE OF THE PERIOD

It would have been strange indeed if Israel's inspired teachers had remained silent at this great crisis in the history of their race. From this otherwise little known quarter of a century probably comes an interesting section of the literature contained in the Old Testament. The problem so graphically and fully presented in the Book of Job is exactly that of the Jewish community at this time. The situation after the hordes of Ochus had devastated the land and temple furnishes an entirely satisfactory historical background for certain psalms like the seventy-fourth and seventy-ninth.

The same is true of the remarkable section contained in Isaiah 63 : 7 to 64 : 12. An appalling national catastrophe wrings from the prophet a wild cry almost of despair. In its language and spirit the section is closely related to the other post-exilic chapters of the Book of Isaiah; but in its theme and teaching it stands unique. Its historical allusions and thought find their most perfect historical setting in the reign of Ochus. It is not so much a prophecy as a psalm of mingled thanksgiving and

Later Prophets Isaiah

lamentation. It voices the feelings of the best elements of the community as they gazed upon the ruins which the brutal Persian soldiery left behind them. It may therefore be dated about 346 B. C. The author clearly writes from the point of view of Palestine.

The vagueness of the references and the obscurity of the thought of Isaiah 24 to 27 make it impossible to determine with absolute certainty its date. A profusion of evidence, however, indicates that these chapters are not from the prophet Isaiah, but from a much later period. They bear most of the characteristic marks of late post-exilic prophecy: indefiniteness, absence of distinct historical allusions, and many lyrical and apocalyptic elements. Their affinities are all with the prophecies of Joel and the closing chapters of the Book of Zechariah.

The same is true of their thought. There are none of the calls to repentance which characterize the earlier prophecies. Their tone is strongly legalistic. The idea of a universal world-judgment is exceedingly prominent. The author or authors live chiefly in the future rather than in the present, although the meagre evidence is sufficient to indicate that their home is in Palestine. The peculiar angelology is that of the Books of Enoch and Daniel.

These chapters were evidently written in the shadow of a great calamity. The Jews are victims of merciless foes. Jerusalem not long before has been devastated. Robbers still rob. Great cities have been laid low. These references find their exact counterpart in the destruction of Sidon and the ravaging of Palestine and Egypt by Ochus.

At the same time there is a basis for hope. The world is being "turned upside down." Existing conditions are being reversed. From the "far countries of the sea" Jehovah's avengers are advancing. The end of the old order is near, and a new era is dawning. Again, the years immediately following the death of Ochus, in 337 B. C., which witnessed the sudden and complete collapse of the great Persian empire and the marvellous series of victories which made Alexander master of the East, constitute the most satisfactory background.

Sudden transitions in thought and literary form suggest that the chapters were not originally a literary unit, but that they represent two or more independent compositions, coming, however, from the same general period and possibly from the same author.

III

THE WAILS AND PETITIONS OF THE DISTRESSED JUDEAN COMMUNITY (ISA. 63 : 7 TO 64 : 12)

1. Jehovah's Past Acts of Deliverance (63 : 7-14)

In the past experiences of our race Jehovah has revealed himself as a God omnipotent, kind, and merciful.

Later Prophets Isaiah 63 : 17

In our moments of distress and danger he has delivered us, because we were his people. In every hour of trial he was present in person to uphold and save us. Only when our fathers refused to follow his divine guidance did he turn against and discipline them, that they might recall and appreciate all that he had been and done to them. Then they remembered how he delivered their leader Moses, while yet a helpless child, from the waters of the Nile (Ex. 2 : 3-10), how he revealed his will to the hearts of his people and how he exercised his miraculous power through Moses so that the waters of the Red Sea were driven back and they went forth from the land of Egypt into safety and freedom. Thus, O Jehovah, in the past didst thou gain great renown in the eyes of mankind as a God able and eager to deliver thy people. Israel led by Jehovah in the past (63 : 7-14)

2. *A Cry for Deliverance from Present Calamities* (63 : 15 *to* 64 : 12)

Again from thy heavenly abode take pity upon thy afflicted people. Reveal by an act of deliverance thy might, thy deep interest, and thy divine compassion. Do not long delay, for we stand towards thee in the most intimate relationship of love and dependence. Our venerated ancestors are powerless to help us. Thou alone art eternal and able to redeem in the present as in the past. Do not drive us into rebellion by the extreme severity of the judgment which thou art sending upon us. For the sake of Save, al-mighty to deliver (63 : 15 to 64 : 5a)

Isaiah 63 : 17

those who faithfully serve thee, restore thy people. For a brief period we possessed in security our land and sacred city, but now our enemies have again defiled and destroyed thy holy temple. We are as helpless in the hands of our cruel foes as though we had no God like thee to claim and champion us. Oh, that thou wouldst reveal thy almighty power by some signal act of deliverance, so that thy true character might be made known to those who now defy thee and that all nations might revere thee. Surpass our fondest hopes and surpass thy acts in the past, for the human mind has not yet conceived of what thou art able and willing to do for those who put their trust in thee. Oh, that thou wouldst speedily thus reveal thyself to those who are earnestly striving to follow thy commands.

The pitiable fate of city and people (64 : 5b-12)
Alas, the sad reality! Driven into doubt and defiance because of the misfortunes which thou hast sent, we have sinned against thee. Notwithstanding our strenuous efforts to keep thy law and do what is right, we are like one defiled and ceremonially unclean. All our strength and prosperity are gone and we are crushed under the overpowering sense of guilt which results from our calamities. Every one of us has ceased to look to thee for deliverance and vindication, for thou hast given no evidence that thou hast heard our petitions or forgiven the guilt of the past. But to thee alone can we look for help, for thou art our creator and natural protector. Without thee we are pow-

erless. Do not cherish forever thy righteous indignation because of our sins. Be merciful and deliver, for the eternal, intimate relation between thee and us still exists. Take pity upon the cities of thy land, upon Jerusalem, ravaged and desolate. Our sacred temple, the object of our reverence and joy, where our fathers have worshipped thee, is burned with fire, and all that we cherished is in ruin. Wilt thou, O Jehovah, continue without interfering, to tolerate these things, and wilt thou continue to send these woes upon us?

IV

THE FINAL JUDGMENT AND THE ESTABLISHMENT OF JEHOVAH'S KINGDOM (ISA. 24 : 1-23 ; 25 : 6-8 ; 26 : 20 TO 27 : 13)

1. *The Overthrow of Existing Conditions* (24 : 1-23)

Jehovah has laid waste the whole earth, reversed existing conditions, and scattered nations far and wide. All social distinctions are ignored. Those in authority experience the same fate as the governed, for Jehovah has determined to make the earth a universal desolation. [The universality of the judgment (24 : 1-3)]

Earth and heaven are fading away, because they have been rendered unclean by the touch of men who have broken the divine commands and proved faithless to the [Man's guilt the cause (24 : 4-6)]

Isaiah 24 : 6

eternal covenant established after the flood (Gen. 9 : 1-17). As a result of Jehovah's condemnation, the earth is consumed and its guilty inhabitants, so that only a few survive.

The universal sadness (24 : 7-12) The land, devasted by the armies of Ochus, fails to yield its ordinary fruitage. The most hopeful lose heart. All expressions of joy cease. Cities[1] like Jerusalem and Sidon are shapeless ruins. Houses are deserted. Proud capitals are left desolate and defenceless.

The overthrow of the present worldpowers (24 : 13-20) Throughout the whole earth shall this judgment extend. Only a small remnant shall survive. Distant nations on the border of the great sea are arising to proclaim Jehovah's might and glory. His faithful people shall in time be recognized and honored. But for us the present brings only misery. We are the victims of shameless robbers. Terrors, toils, and traps[2] await mankind at every turn, and there is no escape. One catastrophe follows another in quick succession. The present order of things is being overturned. The Persian empire is going to pieces and new world-powers are arising on the distant horizon. Already the general dissolution has begun.[3] The quiet of mankind leaves no hope that the present conditions will survive or be restored.

[1] The Septuagint reads for "city of chaos," "every city."
[2] Hebrew, *pákhad wa-pákhath wa-pákh.*
[3] The language of verse 20 represents onomatopoetically the breaking and cracking of the earth.

Isaiah 25 : 8

In the coming day of judgment Jehovah will take Jehovah's
vengeance upon the celestial patrons of the nations and overthrow of present
upon the earthly potentates who rule over them. To- rulers and his assump-
gether shall they be cast into a dungeon,[1] where they shall tion of di-
be confined until Jehovah shall execute still further ven- rect government
geance upon them. Marvellous changes shall also take (24 : 21-23)
place in heaven and on earth, for then Jehovah himself will
set up his kingdom with his capital at Jerusalem and rule
directly over his people, introducing the old simple tribal
organization.

2. *The Nature of Jehovah's Universal Rule* (25 : 6-8)

In that coming day, when he assumes his earthly rule, The joy
and on this sacred site, Jehovah, the supreme Lord of all, which Jehovah's rule
will as host give to all mankind the highest temporal and will bring to all mankind
spiritual blessings. Then will he remove the causes of (25 : 6-8)
grief from all peoples and wipe away from every face the
tears which symbolize inward sorrow. Even death, the
most fertile source of grief, shall cease to be. Then will
he also remove completely the ignominy which has so
long bowed down his chosen people. This new and
glorious *régime* shall surely be a reality, because Jehovah
has decreed it.

[1] Compare Enoch 18 : 13-16; 2 Peter 2 : 4; Jude 6; Rev. 20 : 2, 3.

3. *Jehovah's Unceasing Care for His People* (26 : 20 to 27 : 13)

<small>The present a period of judgment (26 : 20, 21)</small>

Painful are the woes and carnage of the present, but they will continue only for a brief period. Endure them as best you can, O chosen people, for in this way Jehovah is executing judgment upon the guilty world. Soon the crimes and bloodshed of the present will be revealed in the sight of all and will be avenged by Jehovah.

<small>Jehovah will protect his people from their powerful assailants (27 : 1-6)</small>

Like the god Marduk in the old Babylonian myth, Jehovah will slay with his invincible sword the evil monsters, the terrible, bloodthirsty nations—Egypt, Persia, and Greece—which attack his people. He declares that he will unremittingly watch over them as over a highly valued vineyard.[1] Carefully will he supply their every need. Hostile foes in their midst will he destroy, or if they turn to him in faith they will find him ready to receive and protect and eager to be reconciled to them. Under his benign care the remnant of his people shall grow again into a strong and prosperous nation which shall confer rich blessings upon all mankind.

Terrible as have been the misfortunes which have overtaken them, Jehovah has not punished his people as severely as he has their conquerors and oppressors. If

---

[1] Evidently the prophet purposely draws a contrast to the parable of the vineyard in Isaiah 5.

Later Prophets Isaiah 25 : 4

they would expiate their guilt so as to secure his forgive- His con-
ness, let them destroy completely the last vestiges of the siderate
old idolatry. True, their fortified cities are now destroyed his people in
and the inhabitants scattered in exile, but it is because (27 : 7-11)
their folly has made it impossible for their Creator and
Lord to show his mercy.

In the coming day, however, Jehovah will carefully Re-estab-
separate his people from the mixed population, now the Jews in
found in the territory which once belonged to Israel, and Palestine
will preserve his own, eliminating all foreign elements. (27 : 12-13)
He will also summon all Jewish exiles in the east and
west and they will return to worship him in his sacred city
Jerusalem.

V

SONGS OF THANKSGIVING TO JEHOVAH (ISA.
25 : 1-5 ; 25 : 9 TO 26 : 19)

Worthy of highest praise art thou, O Jehovah, be- His omnip-
cause of thy marvellous acts and because of the certainty justice
with which thou dost fulfil thy prophetic word. Mighty (25 : 1-5)
cities (like Tyre and Sidon) protected by frowning battle-
ments, hast thou made barren wastes. Even the heathen,
beholding, are impressed and honor and praise thy name.
Tyrants tremble before thee. To the weak and oppressed
thou hast always shown thyself a champion in the time

Isaiah 25 : 5 — *Messages of the*

of direst need; but insolent tyrants have received their just retribution from thy hand.

A champion of his people (25 : 9-11) — In the coming days we will exult as we look back upon the deliverance from our enemies which Jehovah is about to effect. He will protect and strengthen Jerusalem, but her old foes shall be overthrown and humiliated, and no art or effort will save them.

He saves those who trust in him (26 : 1-6) — Then will we praise Jehovah because he has given us an impregnable city, protected by his divine might, as our abode. Its gates shall be opened for his upright, redeemed people. Therein will he preserve in safety everyone who steadfastly trusts in him. Therefore let not your faith in him waver. If you desire evidence of his might, consider how he has thrown down that proud and powerful city Tyre, so that the humblest man can trample upon the dust of its ruins.

He will yet deliver his people from their oppressors (26 : 7-14) — Prosperity and peace thou givest, O Lord, to those who do right. Thy commandments we have kept and to thee we have given our adoration and praise. Thou art the object of our heart's deepest love. To thee we have looked for vindication. Only by the execution of thy righteous judgments canst thou teach the wicked inhabitants of the earth what is right, for, if thou in mercy sparest them, they continue in their evil course, ignorant of thy omnipotent rule. Therefore let the thunderbolts of thy wrath descend upon thy enemies who destroy thy people. Thus deliver and give us prosperity, for we are weak and dependent upon thee alone. Hostile earthly rulers have usurped thy authority and dominate us. We have no saviour beside thee. To thee we look for deliverance. Surely thou wilt save us. Already the work has begun. Egypt, Assyria, and Babylonia are dead and will never rise again from the land of shades to oppress us. Persia is tottering to its ruin. Soon thou wilt have completely destroyed all those mighty nations which rule over us so that there will not even be a remembrance of them.

Thou didst for a brief period revive our nation and swell its numbers through the return of many of its loyal sons. Thou didst extend our narrow boundaries. In our time of trouble when thou didst in thy wisdom discipline us we still looked to thee for help. Mortal agony, like the pangs of a woman in childbirth, came upon us when we strove but in vain to deliver our land from the cruel oppressor (Ochus?) and to institute thy righteous kingdom on earth. Alas! our efforts were futile. Before the cruel tyrant thousands of loyal patriots fell; but these martyrs shall rise again from the dead to participate in the glories of Jehovah's Messianic kingdom and to receive their rewards. Their immortal souls shall be like seed sown in the earth which shall germinate and spring into new life under the influence of the dew from Jehovah. Thus the spirits of the faithful dead shall rise from the land of shades to enjoy life on earth.

He will completely revive the Jewish nation (26 : 15-19)

MESSAGES OF PROMISE TO THE
JEWS IN THE GREEK PERIOD

MESSAGES OF PROMISE TO THE JEWS IN THE GREEK PERIOD

I

THE AUTHORSHIP AND HISTORICAL BACKGROUND OF ZECHARIAH 9–14

The transition from the eighth to the ninth chapter of the book of Zechariah is very abrupt and marked. No longer does the prophet at specified times speak in the first person to a clearly defined audience. The author's name is not mentioned and the circumstances under which he speaks are obscure. So wholly different are the tone, style, allusions, and theme of the later chapters from those of the first eight that there would probably be no thought of identifying their authors if all had not been combined into one book.

These differences raise one of the most perplexing questions in biblical criticism. The great majority of scholars hold that they indicate that chapters 1-8 and chapters 9–14 are from different hands, but there exists a wide difference of opinion regarding the date of the later section and its unity. Some think that chapters 9-14 are pre-exilic, chiefly on the ground of the allusions to Damascus, Ephraim, Philistia, Assyria, and Egypt.

Such a question as this must be answered by studying the general character and force of the prophecies under consideration. Thus regarded it seems most probable that Zechariah 9-14 is of post-exilic origin, not from the Babylonian or Persian, but from the Greek period. After Alexander the Great had made his rapid conquest of Asia and closed his career, his great empire was divided, after much conflict, among his generals. Judah for more than a century became a bone of contention between the descendants of Ptolemy, who founded a kingdom in Egypt in 322, and the Seleucids, who a little later established their capital at Antioch and acquired the control of all Syria. In these circumstances the historical allusions to Damascus, Hamath, Phœnicia, and Philistia become once more perfectly natural; while the general apocalyptic character of the utterances accounts for the symbolic use of the terms Egypt and Assyria to denote the two nations who were fiercely struggling to establish a control over hapless Judah, and for the use of the words Ephraim and Israel to indicate Judah. Almost every argument for a pre-exilic date (700–600) applies quite as well to this Greek period.

Three reasons in particular confirm the general conclusion that these chapters as a whole—with possibly slight exceptions—belong to a time subsequent to Alexander's conquests, not far from the first half of the third century B. C. The Greeks are referred to, not as in Joel as a distant nation of slave-buyers, but as a leading heathen power, already in conflict with the Jews (9 : 13). Again the general theme of the chapters is a bloody conflict between Judah and her oppressors, terminating in a destructive judgment from Jehovah upon all of Judah's foes. Such a theme connects these chapters with Ezekiel, Isaiah 24-27 and Joel, rather than with pre-exilic prophecy. Finally the oracles of the chapters are not the practical, personal predictions and exhortations of the earlier prophets, intended to encourage, comfort, or rebuke contemporaries, but the fervid apocalypses of the latest period which turned all eyes toward a certain future and assured aching hearts of the final triumph of Jehovah's kingdom.

It is not possible to furnish an exact setting for each prophetic oracle. The coming of the Prince of Peace in chapter 9 seems clearly to have been the correlate of the victorious march from upper Syria southward of some conqueror, probably of Alexander the Great. The next four chapters, with their story of oppressive foreign rulers on north and south, of a people forgetful of Jehovah and unresponsive, of a disunited Judah, but of a repentant and earnest future, find a satisfying background in the struggles of the Ptolemies and Seleucids over the hapless Jews during the years following 300 B. C. Some few

Zechariah 9 : 1

scholars have argued that an equally satisfactory historical setting would be found still later in the Maccabean age, but the fact that these chapters are found in the prophetic canon argues for a date prior to 200 B. C.

Whether the utterances of chapters 9–14 came from one writer or from more than one is uncertain. The general trend of scholarly opinion may be said to be in favor of the unity of the section.

II

THE COMING OF ALEXANDER AND THE PRINCE OF PEACE (9)

1. *The Advance of the Conqueror* (9 : 1-8)

Jehovah's judgment on Syria (9 : 1-2a)

Have confidence, O Judah, in view of the approaching danger, remembering that Jehovah, our God, rules over the universe. It is he who guides the destinies of mankind, of the heathen and of his people alike. He has pronounced judgment against the inhabitants of the Orontes Valley and of Damascus. His conquering army shall destroy them and advance to further conquest.

Phœnicia helpless (9 : 2b-4)

Neither Tyre's ample resources nor her fancied strength nor Sidon's cleverness and skill will avail to save Phœnicia from its fate. The huge walls of Tyre shall be toppled into the sea and her palaces be consumed by fire.

Later Prophets   Zechariah 9 : 14

Onward will the victors march, to the terror and dismay of the cities of Philistia. Ekron will be humiliated, Gaza will lose her independence, and Ashkelon will be laid waste. In place of the haughty and proud inhabitants of Philistia, an ignoble half-breed race, delighting in idolatrous sacrificial feasts, shall possess the land. In time they will be cleansed from these pollutions and prepared for incorporation within the commonwealth of Israel. They will become a recognized part[1] of Judah, and gradually, like the Jebusites of old, they will be merged into the nation. *(Philistia to be ravaged (9 : 5))* *(The converted heathen will become a part of Israel (9 : 6-9))*

Then will Jehovah himself guard his people from all future attack; no conqueror shall again pass to and fro, for the land is under his special care. *(Jerusalem shall be safe forever (9 : 8))*

2. *The Conflict with the Greeks* (9 : 13-17)

Before the days of perfect peace can come Jehovah will use Israel as his instrument of vengeance upon the Greeks. As a well-appointed warrior will Judah enter upon the task. Jehovah himself will lead his hosts to victory, manifesting his presence by the destructive phenomena of nature. With his aid they will make a wholesale destruction of their enemies, slaughtering them without mercy until each warrior is red with blood, like the corners of the great altar of sacrifice. Re-established in their own land, Jehovah will give them great plenty and prosperity. *(Judah to be Jehovah's weapon against his enemies (9 : 13))* *(Their terrible slaughter (9 : 14-15))*

[1] By a slight change of vowels "chieftain" may be read as "thousand" or clan.

<small>Judah's peace and plenty (9:16, 17)</small> Happy will the people then be. Their young men will be strong and their maidens beautiful.

3. *The Promised Prince of Peace* (9 : 9-12)

<small>The coming of the Messianic King (9:9)</small> Therefore, O Zion, prepare to welcome your long expected king. After these enemies have been disposed of, he will enter the holy city, vindicated and victorious, yet lowly as becomes the servant of Jehovah, riding not upon a war-horse as if in triumph, but upon an ass in token of <small>His peaceful sway (9:10)</small> his peaceful sway. The implements of warfare—chariots, chargers, weapons, no longer needed, he will destroy. He will proclaim a universal peace to all the world, and be accepted as its Lord. "From the cheerless dungeons of <small>His deliverance of Jewish captives (9:11, 12)</small> exile," says Jehovah, "I will set free, O Zion, the captives, because of the offering of their blood so freely made by the people in this conflict. You who are still in prison, forego not hope. Jehovah will recompense you twofold for your sufferings."

III

THE FORTUNES OF THE JEWS UNDER THEIR GREEK MASTERS (10-13)

1. *Jehovah's Indignation against Their Tyrants and His Restoration of His People* (10)

O my people, never fail to seek Jehovah as the source of every needed blessing. He is willing and able to grant unto men the rain in its season and the produce of the field. Neither household images nor doers of enchantment nor interpreters of dreams are of any real help. Because you have had recourse to them, you are now like sheep without a shepherd, scattered, disorganized, and helpless, the prey of those who should care for you. *Jehovah, not idols, the source of prosperity (10: 1, 2)*

" My wrath is kindled," saith Jehovah, "against these false leaders, these foreign rulers, who have so misused you. I will display my power in behalf of Judah, transforming my poor, timid, leaderless sheep into bold and valiant war-horses and equipping them with reliable leaders, skilled in warfare and resolute to gain every advantage. Then will they overcome the proud warriors with ease and put to rout the dreaded cavalry. *His wrath against Judah's foreign oppressors (10: 3-5)*

" Then will I strengthen and redeem my people, restoring those carried off to captivity into Egypt and Syria. I will bring them back home, forgive all their transgressions, and establish with them a close relationship of confidence and affection. With courage and hope the hearts of my people shall be thrilled. From every quarter will I summon them, for I have prepared the way for their national reinstatement and for an increase in numbers as remarkable as that of old. However distant may have been their place of captivity they have never ceased to remember and honor my name and to wait for the day of deliverance and restoration. From south and north will I gather them and settle them in the places dear *By his power his people will be restored and blessed (10: 6-12)* from old association, crowded though these may become. Like Israel of old they shall pass under my guidance and protection through the Egyptian[1] sea. All that opposes their departure, whether it be the river of Egypt or its ruler or the indomitable will of their former masters, shall be swept aside. I will be their rock and fortress; in my name shall they openly exult."

2. *The Rejection and Murder of the Good Shepherd* (11 : 1-17 ; 13 : 7-9)

The successful war against Syria (11 : 1-3)

Alas, what sorrow awaits the Syrian kingdom. Over its bulwark, lofty Lebanon, shall sweep a destructive fire ; the famous oaks of Bashan will be felled by the foe. Hear the lamentations of its rulers whose resources are cut off, as lions roar whose lairs have been destroyed by fire, the nobles shall bewail their demolished fortresses.

Jehovah's command to properly shepherd Judah (11 : 4-6)

To me Jehovah gave an important commission. "Be a true shepherd," he commanded, "to my poor sheep, so abused by those who have ruled over them. Their foreign masters have treated them as brute beasts without remorse or mercy, exulting in their value as property. [I am about to visit mankind in judgment and to abandon the nations to the will of their arbitrary and cruel rulers.]"

So I entered on the task assigned me and became

---

[1] Following a plausible conjecture by Wellhausen, adopted by Nowack and G. A. Smith.

the shepherd of the maltreated flock in place of their mercenary owners.[1] As symbols of my office I took two staves, naming them, respectively, Grace and Union, to betoken God's loving care for Israel and the spirit of concord which I hoped to establish. I quickly dealt with the evil shepherds whom I displaced, but the fickle people grew weary of my just rule and our connection came to an end. Announcing to them that they must henceforth suffer the legitimate consequences of their deeds, I openly broke the staff Grace in token that Jehovah's protection was at an end. For my hire they gave me contemptuously the wages of a common slave, thirty silver pieces. This money, at Jehovah's direction, I cast into the temple treasury[2] to indicate that my service was wholly as his representative, and that they had rejected him, not me. I then broke the staff Union also in token of the failure to reunite the people.

The failure of the prophet's attempt (11:7-14)

Jehovah then commanded me to assume the insignia of a shepherd, but this time of one who would destroy his flock instead of ministering to it. "I am about to appoint a cruel ruler," he said, "who will neglect them and pursue his own advantage. Then indeed they will appreciate what I was willing and eager to do in their behalf.

Jehovah's punishment of the rebels (11:15-17)

[1] Following the Septuagint, "therefore the poor of the flock" (v. 7) should be read "for the Canaanites (*i.e.*, merchant-owners) of the flock." So in v. 11.
[2] By the change of a letter the word "potter" becomes "treasury." The last clause of v. 13 seems to justify this change.

Zechariah 11 : 17

Nevertheless I will in due time punish for his wickedness the worthless ruler, to whom I shall abandon them."

The murder of the good shepherd and its consequences (13 : 7-9)
"Arise, O sword, and slay my true shepherd and fellow-worker," Jehovah will say, "that the ungrateful people may realize what they have done to their own despite. Without protectors they will be scattered and broken, both old and young. Two-thirds of the people will perish, but the remainder by these terrible trials will be purged of guilt and will gladly acknowledge me as their God."

3. *The Certain Deliverance of Imperilled Jerusalem* (12 : 1 *to* 13 : 6)

Jerusalem besieged but delivered by Jehovah (12 : 1-7)
Jehovah of hosts, the creator of the universe and of man, the one whose promise is very sure, gives this message of comfort to you, O beloved city! "I am about to expose you to a determined assault from enemies among whom even the people of Judah will be numbered. But those who eagerly gather to consume your treasures, as revellers quaff huge bowls of wine, will find the draught overpowering. Jerusalem shall be like a bowlder deeply set in the earth. Those who try to move her will only wound themselves in vain. I will smite with a panic the armies which gather against her, but I will show my favor unto Judah and lead her chieftains to acknowledge that I am protecting Jerusalem, so that they will turn against their former allies and destroy them. Jerusalem shall remain unharmed, but Judah shall be allowed to

gain the victory in order that the inhabitants of Jerusalem may have no occasion to boast of their prowess."

As one result of this deliverance, Jehovah will transform feeble Jerusalem into a formidable fortress. Even the lame and feeble folk shall be as valiant as King David, while their leaders shall be like the angel of Jehovah in might. Although Jehovah will aim to destroy the hostile nations, he will endue his own people with a spirit of deep and sincere penitence. Instead of giving way to wild rejoicings at their deliverance, they will mourn bitterly for the good shepherd, whom they brutally murdered, giving unrestrained expression to their grief as on great national mourning days. Every member of every family in all the land will join in this heartfelt repentance.

The various results of this deliverance (12 : 8 to 13 : 6)

A third result of Jerusalem's deliverance shall be the opening of a fountain of purification, at which all her sin and filth may be removed. But above all, Jehovah promises to abolish the very names and memory of the idols which once were revered, and to remove from their position of influence the base prophets and all who are given over to evil. Since the prophets as a class have become mere mercenary, untruthful professionals, whose nearest relatives feel compelled to silence or slay them, they are no longer worth maintaining. So completely will they be under the ban that they shall cease to boast of their visions and to wear rough cloaks of skin, like Elijah, and will claim instead that they are farmers. When one of these is asked concerning his wounded hands, he will reply, evasively, "I received these wounds from my friends."

IV

THE JUDGMENT OF THE HEATHEN AND EXALTATION OF JERUSALEM (14)

The capture of Jerusalem by the heathen severely requited (14 : 1-7)
Behold a day is approaching, O Jerusalem, when Jehovah will manifest himself in judgment against the nations and in redemption for his own people. He will first cause the pagan peoples to assemble before the city for war. They shall be successful, spoiling the city, doing their will upon the inhabitants, carrying half of them into captivity. Then will Jehovah arise to protect the remainder. When he takes his stand on the Mount of Olives an earthquake shall split the mountain into halves, making a deep ravine between the sundered portions. The day shall be a day of gloom; panic will seize upon all hearts; but when Jehovah has manifested his prowess and accomplished his purpose, the gloom will be exchanged for light.

Jerusalem's prosperity and exaltation (14 : 8-11)
At that time a stream of pure and sparkling water shall flow forth without ceasing from Jerusalem, east and west, to fertilize the land. Jehovah will then be the undisputed

king of the earth; no deity shall be compared to him. The country round about Jerusalem shall be made into a vast plain, the city being exalted in its midst and rebuilt as before. The city shall be perfectly secure. Never again will there be need of a destructive divine judgment upon her.

Meanwhile those nations which dared to attack the city shall miserably perish in their very tracks, smitten with a loathsome plague. [Stimulated¹ by Jehovah they shall put each other to death. Judah shall fight against Jerusalem and much spoil shall be gathered from the nations.] Similarly it shall affect the animals which they possess. The awful judgment of the nations (14 : 12-15)

The survivors of these heathen nations will go up to Jerusalem each year to worship Jehovah and observe the feast of booths, when all are accustomed to return thanksgiving for bountiful harvests. Should any fail to do this, their punishment will be the withholding of rain. Even Egypt will suffer this penalty if she transgresses. The penalty of refusing to observe at Jerusalem the feast of Tabernacles (14 : 16-19)

At that time Jerusalem shall become truly a holy city. All that stands for display or power shall be consecrated publicly to Jehovah. So vast shall be the multitudes thronging to take part in the temple services that the pots used for ordinary purposes shall be as large as the great The perfect holiness of Jerusalem (14 : 20, 21)

---

¹ Verses 13 and 14 clearly break the connection between verses 12 and 15. Where to place them is not clear.

Zechariah 14 : 21

altar bowls, and every pot in Jerusalem and Judah shall be consecrated for use in the ritual. No person who is not in sympathy with the true purposes of the sanctuary shall ever again set foot therein.

THE MESSAGE OF THE BOOK OF JONAH

THE MESSAGE OF THE BOOK OF JONAH

I

THE DATE OF THE BOOK OF JONAH

Like most of the writings of the later prophets, the superscription of the little Book of Jonah says nothing respecting its date. Fortunately there are certain internal evidences which aid in answering this difficult and important question. The hero of the story is without much doubt to be identified with the Jonah, son of Amittai, the northern Israelitish prophet who, according to 2 Kings 14 : 25, lived during the reign of Jeroboam II. (780-741 B. C.). It is obvious, however, that neither Jonah nor one of his contemporaries is the author of the present book. This is indicated to the Hebrew student by the presence of certain peculiar words and constructions which are found only in the latest books of the Old Testament; but other and still more patent testimony is not wanting. Nineveh, which was not destroyed until 606-605 B. C., is spoken of as no longer existing (3 : 3). It is described in the general language of later tradition as " an exceedingly great city of three days' journey." The title "King of Nineveh" occurs in the sense in which it is here used nowhere in contemporary literature. Its use and the absence of the name of the king are in accord with the habits of post- rather than pre-exilic writers. The questions with which the book deals also first came into especial prominence during the latter part of the Persian and the opening years of the Greek period. The prayer in chapter 2 likewise reflects the strongly legalistic spirit of later Judaism, and is made up almost entirely of quotations from post-exilic psalms. On the other hand, the presence of the book in the canon of the prophets instead of among the "sacred writings," is reasonably conclusive evidence that it was written at the latest before 200 B. C., when that canon is referred to by the son of Sirach as definitely closed. To fix its date more exactly is impossible unless in the identification of Jonah with the Jewish race the destruction of the gourd in which the prophet took such delight is intended as a reference to the destruction of the temple by Ochus about 350 B. C. Certainly it was during the century following this event that the hatred of the heathen reached its height and found most open expression.

II

THE PURPOSE AND METHOD OF THE AUTHOR OF THE BOOK

The anonymous author of this unique book was unquestionably one of the greatest of the later prophets. Unfortunately a failure to understand the method which he employed to present his inspired message has in recent ages done much to obscure its real sublimity. As in the case of not a few of the books of the Bible, claims have been made for it of which the original author never dreamed, while its true character has been overlooked.

Thus the same Bible students who recognize that prophets like Isaiah and Ezekiel and the greatest of teachers frequently used the parable as a means of enforcing their lessons, maintain that the Book of Jonah is literal history, although it bears on its face the characteristic marks of the allegory or parable. The conspicuous absence of the usual historical details has already been noted. A host of questions which the historian could not have left unanswered are ignored, as, for example, the name of the king of Nineveh, the nature of the sins of the Ninevites, the details of the prophet's preaching, and his earlier and later history.

The occurrence of the conventional number three in describing both the time spent by the prophet within the great fish and the extent of the city of Nineveh is also suggestive of the parable. The freedom and *naïveté* with which grotesquely supernatural elements are introduced find no parallel in the historical writings of the Old Testament: the sudden appearance and equally sudden disappearance of the tempest, the choice of Jonah by the lot, his preservation within the great fish, his being cast ashore on a friendly coast, the marvellous effect of his reluctant preaching upon the Ninevites, and the sudden growth and end of the gourd. The actors in the story belong to the realm of parable rather than of real history, as is illustrated by Jonah's prompt flight, his frank profession of his guilt, his readiness to give his life to save even the heathen, the surpassing generosity and justice of the ignorant sailors, their sudden conversion, the wholesale repentance of the Ninevites, and the superlative obduracy and meanness of the prophet. Throughout the entire story the object is plainly not to record facts but to enforce essential truths. The kinship with the parables of the Old and New Testament is perfect.

The reason why the true character of the story has been overlooked by many—although by no means all—Bible students is probably because it is associated with the name of Jonah the son of Amittai. Neither the name of the prophet nor that of his father occur elsewhere in the Old Testament, except in the passage in 2 Kings to which reference has already been made. Possibly "the son of Amittai" was added by some later scribe who naturally identified the Jonah of the book with the prophet who prophesied in the days of Jeroboam II. If so, "Jonah" may have originally been used allegorically because of its meaning "dove." It is more probable, however, that with the name of Jonah the son of Amittai was associated a tradition concerning a miraculous deliverance and a mission to the heathen which the author freely adapted to his purpose.

An appreciation of the didactic, allegorical character of the book prepares the way for the appreciation of its real purpose and teaching. The author lived in an age when the prevailing tendency of his race was toward an attitude of extreme exclusiveness and hostility toward the heathen. Nehemiah excluded the half-Israelitish Samaritans from participation in the service of the temple at Jerusalem. The wall of separation was built high and strong by the reformers who framed and instituted the Levitical law. Only those foreigners who left their land and people and identified themselves completely with the Jewish community were allowed to share its religious privileges, and then at first with certain restrictions.

Instead of the fervent missionary zeal which finds noble expression in Isaiah 40 to 55 and Zechariah 8, certain of the later prophets—especially the prophet Joel, and the authors of Isaiah 25 to 27, 64 to 66, and Zechariah 9 to

14—voiced the prevailing desire of the Jews to see their heathen foes punished by the avenging hand of Jehovah. They regarded their overthrow as the necessary premise to the institution of the kingdom of God on earth. Notwithstanding the earnest protests of the prophets, the majority of the Jewish race regarded themselves as the chief, if not the sole, objects of Jehovah's favor, and viewed with extreme impatience and indignation the success and prosperity of their heathen masters.

There was undoubtedly great provocation for the hatred and jealousy with which the Jews viewed the heathen. The century following 350 B. C. was filled with shameful acts of cruelty and wrong, and the Jews were the victims of the most shocking indignities. There was little in the character of the peoples with whom they came in painful contact to arouse their affection or to kindle their missionary enthusiasm. It was a crisis in which the very life of Judaism was in jeopardy. It is not strange that they forgot their high calling to be Jehovah's witnesses to the world and that curses were oftener on their lips than blessings. All the more wonderful, therefore, are the exalted messages of tolerance, charity, and pity which the author of the Book of Jonah endeavored so tactfully and vividly to impress upon his unreceptive race.

The portrait of Jonah is not so much that of a single prophet as of the Jewish race, which like the son of

Later Prophets
Jonah

Amittai was called to be Jehovah's prophet to the nations, and whose experiences and motives were those of the rebellious messenger of the Lord. Its consciousness that it was called to proclaim Jehovah's message to the heathen, of whom the Ninevites were typical representatives, came to it through the enlightened souls of its inspired teachers even as it did to the Jonah of the parable. It refused to do the will of Jehovah and, as a punishment and discipline, storms from the east—Assyrian and Babylonian invasion —swept over it, until the Hebrew kingdoms were engulfed. Then came, in 586 B. C. and the years which followed, one of the most remarkable miracles of history: the Jewish race politically dead, lost in the seething waves of tempestuous oriental politics, survived in the person of the exiles carried by Nebuchadrezzar to Babylon.

In likening the experience of his race at this time to that of a man swallowed by a great fish, the author of the Book of Jonah was not drawing upon the storehouse of Semitic mythology, as some have urged, nor introducing a new idea into Jewish thought, for the figure was already familiar to his readers through the writings of his predecessors, and especially in the words of the author of Jeremiah 51. In referring to the fate of the exiled people he declared: " Nebuchadrezzar the king of Babylon has devoured me and crushed me . . . he has swallowed me up like a great sea-monster, filling his maw from my delights, he has cast me out" (verse 34). The same prophet anticipated the manner of Jonah's deliverance in referring to the restoration of the Jewish race in which he predicts, in the name of Jehovah: "I will punish Bel in Babylon, and I will bring out of his mouth that which he has swallowed" (verse 44).

In the exile the Jews, like their representative Jonah, learned that the heathen possessed many qualities worthy of admiration. The justice and moderation of the rude heathen sailors in a situation whose peril tended to bring out only the brute instincts of man, were well represented historically by the highly developed judicial system of the Babylonians. Their conquerors also served their gods with as much devotion as the Jewish exiles did Jehovah, and in their ethical standards there was much to admire.

In the Babylonian exile, also, the Jews, through their most inspired prophet, formulated, and we may believe partially accepted, the great thought that they were Jehovah's witnesses to heathendom. Partial success seems to have greeted their efforts to perform their duty as preachers of repentance (compare, for example, Isa. 56 : 6-8). Contrary as it was to their selfish instincts, the conviction forced itself upon them that the heathen were worthy and capable like themselves of receiving blessings of Jehovah. Their subsequent painful contact with the peoples of Palestine and with the powers which ruled over them embittered them and turned their missionary zeal to hate, so that, like Jonah, they were angry with Jehovah because he did not at once destroy their heathen foes. When the brief period of prosperity which followed the rebuilding of the walls of Jerusalem by Nehemiah, and the institution of the Levitical law was suddenly changed to disaster by the brutal vengeance of Ochus, the Jews were again, as we have seen, "angry even unto death" with their God who thus allowed them to fall a prey to their enemies, forgetting, as did Jonah when he mourned the death of the gourd, that those foes possessed an importance of their own in the eyes of Jehovah.

In presenting in the portrait of Jonah the history and characteristics of his race, the prophet aimed not merely to show his countrymen their petty meanness and how far they were falling short of realizing the divine ideal; he also had a positive message. The book bristles with great prophetic truths. Nowhere is the infinite love of God for the ignorant, the sinful, and even for those who defy him, more beautifully and simply presented in the Old Testament. The fact that the fulfilment of every prophecy, however detailed and emphatic, depends upon certain conditions determinate upon human action is forcibly taught. The book also emphasizes the universality of Jehovah's rule, and indicates clearly the true place and rôle of the Jewish race in his creation. Above all, it set before the Jews their supreme opportunity and duty as Jehovah's enlightened messenger to proclaim his truth to mankind. It gave them encouragement that if they were faithful their labors would be crowned with success; it plainly stated that if they proved faithless they would be the objects of Jehovah's righteous wrath. Nowhere in the Old Testament are the fundamental principles of Christianity more simply and forcibly laid down than in this little gospel.

III

THE STORY OF JONAH AND ITS MORAL

1. *The Prophet's Refusal to Proclaim Jehovah's Message to the Heathen* (1 : 1-3)

Jonah's commission to warn the Ninevites (1: 1, 2) Listen, O members of the Jewish race and learn from this story the solemn lessons which Jehovah would teach you by the testimony of history and by the mouth of his inspired prophets. In the days of northern Israel's prosperity, when the cruel Assyrians were rapidly moving westward, but had not yet conquered and laid waste this land of Palestine, the divine command to undertake a strange mission came to Jonah the son of Amittai. He was ordered to go to the then great city of Nineveh, the capital of the hostile Assyrians who were already on the point of invading Israel, and in the name of Jehovah to denounce its crimes and to point out the sure consequences of their continuance.

The prophet, however, recognizing how great was Jehovah's mercy, and fearing lest the enemies of his race might heed his words, put away their sins, and obtain pardon, deliberately defied Jehovah and sought by flight to escape the task so abhorrent to him. To this end he secured passage and embarked at Joppa on a Phœnician merchant-ship, bound for Tarshish, one of the most distant cities of the habitable world, possibly thinking that he might thereby get beyond the limits of Jehovah's rule. His refusal to save the foes of his race (1 : 3)

2. *The Discipline, Conversion, and Deliverance of Jehovah's Rebellious Messenger* (1 : 4 to 2 : 10)

Soon by an awful experience the prophet learned his fatal mistake. In his righteous wrath Jehovah caused a mighty tempest to break upon the sea. The fragile ship, propelled only by oars and sails, threatened every moment to go to pieces. Terror seized the sailors, who realized the peril of the situation. Unable to do anything to save themselves from the fury of the storm, they turned each in supplication to the idol which he blindly hoped might deliver him. Masts, spars—everything that could be torn loose—were thrown overboard in order to lighten the ship, so that perchance she might ride the gale. Meantime the prophet, exhausted by the struggle against the divine promptings to duty, was lying fast asleep in the hold of the ship. Astonished at this strange action, the captain aroused him and commanded him also to call His condemnation by the storm (1: 4-7)

Jonah 1 : 6

upon his God in the hope that perchance his deity might in mercy deliver them from the death which yawned before them. When their prayers brought no relief, they concluded, according to the prevalent thought of their age, that some one of their number had incurred the displeasure of his god. To ascertain who was the guilty man, they appealed to the gods for a decision by means of the lot, and Jonah was the one thus designated.

His confession (1 : 8-12) In reply to their inquiries as to his occupation and nationality, he declared that he was a Hebrew and a worshipper of the God who rules supreme over both sea and land. Knowing from his earlier confession that he was a fugitive from his God and yet hesitating to execute the death-sentence upon him, they appealed to him to know what they were to do to deliver themselves from the consequences of his sin. Meanwhile the waves rolled higher and higher. Moved by their spirit of justice and reverence, the noble qualities in the prophet asserted themselves and he boldly acknowledged that he was the cause

His unintentional conversion of the heathen sailors (1 : 13-16) of their misfortunes. Although he counselled them to throw him overboard, they still struggled desperately to save the ship without sacrificing the prophet, whose courage they could not but admire; but their efforts were in vain, for the storm only increased and drove them farther and farther from the shore. Then, at last, with a prayer to Jonah's God for deliverance from bloodguiltiness and in recognition of his omnipotence, they cast the

350

rebellious prophet into the sea, and a sudden lull in the storm confirmed the rightness of their act. Reverence for the God who had thus marvellously revealed himself led them to offer to him appropriate sacrifices and vows.

In accordance with the divine purpose, the once rebellious but now converted prophet was swallowed by a great sea-monster, within which he was preserved alive for three days. *His preservation (1 : 17)*

As he meditated in his place of confinement, he prayed to Jehovah: " In my hour of anguish and mortal peril, I cried to thee for help and thou hast delivered me. Thou didst cast me into the bottomless sea and its waves closed over me. I felt that the joys of life, the privilege of worshipping thee, and of participating in the service of thy temple were for me forever at an end. In the dark depths of the sea I lay, enwrapped in the slimy seaweeds, far removed from the busy life of earth. Then thou didst deliver me from the certain destruction which had overtaken me. In my despair I cried unto thee and thou didst answer. Apostates who worship dead idols turn from thee, the source of all life and love. With deep joy will I renew by sacrifice my fealty to thee and pay the vows which I have made in return for my deliverance, for thou alone canst save those who turn to thee." *His prayer of thanksgiving (2 : 1-9)*

At Jehovah's command the great sea-monster threw out the prophet unhurt upon the dry land. *His deliverance (2 : 10)*

3. *The Repentance and Pardon of the Ninevites* (3)

His message to the Ninevites (3:1-4)

Again the divine command came to Jonah, led by his experience into an attitude of obedience, to go and proclaim to the Ninevites the message which Jehovah would give him. At once he set out upon his mission to the vast city with its encircling villages. When he approached it, he proclaimed, as he passed through its miles of streets, the short but awful message: "Before many days have passed this city Nineveh shall be reduced to ruins."

The repentance of the Ninevites (3:5-9)

Then the inhabitants of Nineveh gave heed to the warnings of Jehovah's prophet and proclaimed a universal fast in order to avert the calamity which threatened. When the prophet's words were reported to the king he laid aside his royal attire and put on the garments of mourning. He also issued, in his own name and in that of his nobles, a decree that every living being, man or beast, within the city should join in the fast, and clothe themselves in the garb of sorrow and supplication. All his subjects were fervently to beseech God's pardon, and abstain from all wrong-doing, in the hope that he might relent and not execute upon them the destructive judgment which he had announced through his prophet.

Their pardon (3:10)

Perceiving these evidences that, in accordance with their light, they had repented of their deeds and were ready to reform, Jehovah, in keeping with his true character and purpose, did not execute his vengeance upon them, so that

Jonah 4 : 6

their city remained intact until the evils which the prophet condemned became prevalent again.

4. *The Contemptible Jealousy of his Prophet Contrasted with Jehovah's Infinite Compassion* (4)

That Jehovah should recognize the heathen as capable of repentance and as objects of mercy aroused the jealousy and anger of the prophet. In his vexation, he declared that his flight, when first commanded to go to Nineveh, was because he knew that Jehovah was merciful and tender, ready and eager to pardon those who showed the least evidence of true repentance, and because he feared that his words of warning would prove, as they had, the salvation of the enemies of his race. Petulantly he asserted that he had rather die than live to see the heathen the objects of Jehovah's compassion and favor. Jonah's anger because of God's mercy to the heathen (4 : 1-3)

With the same patient, compassionate love as he had shown toward the ignorant heathen, the Lord replied to the peevish, intolerant declaration of his enlightened prophet: "Are you really as angry as your intemperate words would suggest?" Without answering, Jonah went forth from the city and made for himself a temporary abode outside its walls, where he waited, still hoping that some disaster would overtake the foes of his race. Then Jehovah caused a green vine to grow and cover the booth which the prophet had made, thus protecting his head from the heat of the burning eastern sun. To the selfish His meanness and intolerance contrasted with God's infinite love (4 : 4-11)

Jonah 4:6

prophet it brought great delight; but to complete the lesson which he wished to teach, the Lord caused a worm to destroy the vine, so that when the sun arose and a sweltering east wind began to blow, Jonah was overcome by the heat and again prayed that he might die. To reveal to him his petty meanness, and how unreasonable was his indignation because of the deliverance of the Ninevites, Jehovah again inquired, with gentle irony: " Are you really as angry about the destruction of the vine as you protest?" "Yes, I am exceedingly angry—so angry that I am ready to die because of it," was the hot rejoinder. Then said Jehovah: "Consider the utter unreasonableness of your position. You are bitterly incensed against me because I in my infinite wisdom have seen fit to destroy a short-lived vine, with whose creation and growth you had nothing to do, while in the same moment you are equally exercised because I, the Creator and Ruler of the universe, saw fit to show mercy and not destroy, as you desired, the great city Nineveh, with its thousands and thousands of human beings, ignorant of the truth and of right, and with its many beasts, as innocent of evil as that vine over whose natural end you are so greatly enraged."

APPENDIX

APPENDIX

I

THE MESSIANIC ELEMENT IN PROPHECY

The term "Messiah" as a proper name designating Jesus of Nazareth has become a familiar Christian expression. Either it or its exact equivalent, "the Christ," occurs many times in the New Testament. It is unquestioned that the Jewish people of the first Christian century looked for the coming of a leader who would restore Israel to her ancient glory and that they spoke of him as "the Messiah." Nor can there be any doubt that Jesus identified himself as this leader, was accepted by his followers as such, and asserted that a true interpretation of Old Testament prophecy would justify his claims. By many students, therefore, the study of Messianic prophecy is considered to be the collection, arrangement, and interpretation of the passages which allude, directly or indirectly, to this personal Messiah.

The historical study of prophecy, however, is influenced by three considerations. One is that the use of the term

Appendix

"Messiah" (literally "the anointed one") as a proper name arose during the last few centuries before the birth of our Lord, after the age of prophecy had given way to the age of apocalypse. A perfectly definite reference to Jesus as the Messiah should not be expected in the prophetic writings. Again, the term "Messiah" is used very freely in the Old Testament writings to designate any person "anointed," that is, formally consecrated to execute Jehovah's will or to represent his majesty. It is thus used of priests (Lev. 8 : 12), of the king (1 Sam. 2 : 10, 35; Ps. 18 : 50; Lam. 4 : 20, etc.), and even of the chosen nation (Ps. 20 : 6; Hab. 3 : 13). Finally it has a very general application in the writings of the prophets. They use it sparingly, preferring to designate the representative of Jehovah as a king, or a shepherd, or, more generally, as the "servant of Jehovah." In the ode of Habakkuk (3 : 13) the people, Israel, is referred to as "thine anointed." The term is also applied to an outside political agent, such as Cyrus (Isa. 45 : 1). It is hardly ever used, even indirectly, to denote the one on whom the prophetic hopes were fixed.

The reason for this is clear when prophetic allusions are studied. The prophets had no definite programme of the future in mind, nor any absolutely specific instrumentality. What they definitely and repeatedly asserted was the fact that there was a sure future in store for the people of God, however distressing the existing circumstances. This

Appendix

assurance rested on a perception of the divine redemptive plan for the world, as well as a conviction that this plan was to be realized through the Israelitish nation, selected by God for the purpose, and made ready for its work by a leader of some sort, variously portrayed as warrior, sovereign, judge, or prophet. Every prophet had this ideal future in his mind. It was his certainty that God would bring it about and his thorough understanding of the reasons for its delay that made him a prophet. He proclaimed that Jehovah, the ruler of the universe, the wielder of infinite power, constantly making use of world-conquering nations as his agents to punish (Amos 6 : 14) or destroy (Ezek. 30 : 10), or deliver from bondage (Isa. 45 : 1), would at the time determined by his omniscience redeem mankind to himself through Israel, causing all nations to acknowledge and obey him. When and how this would be accomplished no prophet was able to declare; each described certain essential factors in the historic process.

A review of Messianic prophecy must, therefore, be a summary of each prophet's contribution to this broader theme. Were it to include only passages referring to the expected leader and teacher of Israel, there would be but few to consider, several of the prophetic books containing none at all. From the more comprehensive point of view every prophet is a contributor, his message being related in some way to this Messianic hope respecting Israel's future privilege.

Appendix

The broader Messianic idea did not originate with the prophets whose sermons we may study. It finds expression in the earliest historical writings of the Old Testament. Throughout the prophetic narratives of the Hexateuch run, like threads of gold, three wonderful ideas: that God is a Being confessedly all-powerful but distinctively ethical and spiritual; that, as the righteous ruler of the universe he desires to redeem the world from sin unto union with himself; and that Israel has been chosen as his human instrumentality. These ideas cannot have been formulated later than the ninth century B. C., at least a century prior to the prophet Amos. By many scholars they would be given a far earlier date. At any time after it was possible for any Israelite to think of himself as a member of a well-organized, progressive, influential nation and to think of Jehovah as being interested in the outside world as well as in the inhabitants of Canaan, such ideas might have arisen in the minds of Israel's inspired religious thinkers. They are not mentioned by the earliest prophets as novelties, but as recognized truths of which their hearers are to be reminded.

For the following outline sketch of the development of the Messianic ideal the prophetic writings may be advantageously arranged in four groups: those of the eighth century B. C.—Amos, Hosea, Isaiah and Micah; those of the latter part of the seventh century B. C.—Nahum, Zephaniah, Jeremiah and Habakkuk; those of the exile

Appendix

and those of the post-exilic age. For a careful allotment of prophetic passages to these four periods the reader may be referred to this volume and its predecessor. In what follows only distinctive ideas will be mentioned. It must be kept in mind by the student, moreover, that a prophet often anticipates an idea which is credited to his successor, or repeats an idea previously worked out. As a rule each prophet sees with especial clearness one or two aspects of the general theme. To all the keynote of their revelations is not a deliverance from the power of sin but rather the promise of useful service. The latter is the supreme opportunity of which the former is a condition.

The first group of prophetic writings date from about 750 B. C. to 700 B. C. Amos, the earliest, warns Israel that Jehovah, the righteous ruler of the universe, might be forced by the immorality and irreligion into which the nation had fallen to inflict, by means of Assyria, a merited punishment upon her. Hosea, his successor, confronting similar but aggravated conditions, is forced to concur in the prediction of immediate retribution, but is inspired to proclaim that Jehovah's righteousness is only a manifestation of his compassionate love, and that his purpose in punishing is redemptive. As a corollary to these noble definitions of Jehovah's character and power, Amos, perhaps, and Hosea certainly predict a return from captivity of the repentant people and their restoration to the old-time unity and an ideal prosperity. Beyond this they cast

Appendix

no light upon the future. Isaiah, their pupil, applies to conditions in Judah similar convictions of the certain judgment of the " Holy one of Israel " for unrighteousness to be executed by his tool, Assyria, but makes much clearer the thought that a repentant " remnant " would eventually perform the task allotted by Jehovah to his chosen nation.

Two ideas he emphasizes on which his predecessors laid no stress: that Jehovah's purpose of redemption includes the world (14: 24-27; 11: 10; 18: 7), and that the Messianic future would be realized by Israel through a divinely granted leader, portrayed as a wise and righteous king, but also as a successful warrior (11: 1-10; 9:1-7; 33: 17-24). Micah reinforces the conception of the " Prince of Peace," the matchless leader and ruler of the " remnant," who will enable them to turn the tables on their foes (5: 1-6). He probably quotes from some contemporary (4: 1-4) the beautiful thought that Israel is to be the religious teacher of the world. He reiterates the threats of merited punishment (1-3) and the promises of a restoration of the purified " remnant " (4: 6, 7). He originates the thought that this remnant will execute Jehovah's will toward mankind, blessing some nations, destroying others (5: 7-8). These four prophets introduce all the ideas fundamental to the Messianic hope. It may fairly be said, however, that while they insist upon Israel's repentance and righteousness, they look forward to a time when other nations, impelled, if need be, by force, will follow the au-

Appendix

thoritative instruction of dominant and prosperous Israel. So far, there is but a faint foreshadowing of the teaching and spirit of Jesus.

The second prophetic group dates within the half century following 627 B. C. Two of them, Nahum and Habakkuk, predict, on the basis of the divine character and purpose, the certain downfall of the two nations which before and after 600 B. C. held Judah in their grasp. Their contribution to the Messianic scheme was political rather than spiritual. They assert that no obstacle, however formidable, can withstand Jehovah's power or make void his promises. In Zephaniah the leading thought is the familiar one that Judah's indifference to God's requirements will provoke a merited retribution. Two other ideas are made prominent: this judgment is a universal one, affecting all nations (2: 4-15), and by it Judah will be purified and prepared for service to God (3: 1-13). In Jeremiah, however, is the most complete presentation of the Messianic thought of the period. It was his bitter duty to affirm the necessity of Judah's dissolution as a political unit; but he was granted the privilege of seeing the religious corollaries of this action. It was to be the culmination of Israel's long process of discipline, fitting her to offer an instructive example (4: 1, 2) to mankind, and thus to bring about Jehovah's long-cherished plan of redemption (3: 16-18; 12: 14-17). In place of the lapsed covenant with the nation, Jehovah would form one with each true

Appendix

son of Israel (31 : 31-34). Over the purified and redeemed community, into which non-Israelites might enter (12 : 15, 16), would be a king (30: 9; 23: 5), the promised "David" (33: 15), guiding it in ways of righteousness. These four prophets emphasize the redemptive and educational value of the nation's experience, her divinely appointed function as a model to the pagan world whose service God desires, and the personal relationship Jehovah is about to establish with each one of his loyal people.

The prophets of the exile round out these glorious themes. Obadiah merely expresses an assurance of an ultimate return of the nation from captivity to re-occupy the land of Judah. Isaiah 13-14 and Jeremiah 50-51 voice the certainty that Babylon will go down to ruin. In each case the circumstances of the prophet forbid a broader deliverance. The real thought of the period is found in Ezekiel and Isaiah 40-55. Ezekiel affirmed with unmistakable clearness the responsibility of every man for himself (18 : 20; 14 : 14), the certain restoration of the captive people, their nurture through a "shepherd" or "king" of the Davidic type (34; 37 : 24), the permanence of their righteousness through the observance of needful forms of worship (40-48), and the general recognition of Jehovah by the nations as well as by Israel, because they will see and rightly interpret his dealings with Israel. The great prophet of the exile says the final word on these various themes. He describes the exalted

Appendix

character of Jehovah, his power, resources, transcendence, tenderness, righteousness. Every attribute affirmed by earlier prophets finds its place in his wonderful portrayal. His philosophical mind reviews the divine plan which from the beginning had as its goal the salvation of the world (48; 49; 51), restates the glorious mission for the sake of which Israel was chosen and trained by Jehovah (41:8 ff.; 42:1 ff.), and urges that through his consecrated agent Cyrus (45:1) and his beloved servant Israel the consummation is at hand. The heathen nations will acknowledge Jehovah, influenced both by the triumphs of Cyrus (45:6, 14-17) and by the teaching (42:4; 49:2) and the exaltation (52:13-15) of the ideal Servant. His portraiture of the Servant of Jehovah is notable for stating, not the warlike or even the kingly attributes of the one who would perfectly embody the divine ideals, but his self-sacrifice, winsome gentleness, heroism, and spirit of service. He marvellously foreshadows the essential characteristics of the life of Jesus.

Subsequent prophecy could not improve upon the teaching of the exile. With some exceptions the Messianic hopes of the post-exilic age centred around the supremacy of Israel (Isa. 61:5, 6; Hag. 2:7). Nations were to share gladly in her religious privileges (Isa. 61:6, 9; 66:23). Those who opposed this consummation would be judged and annihilated by Jehovah himself (Zech. 14:12; Isa. 24:21-23; Joel 3). That the idea of win-

Appendix

ning the world to Jehovah by other means than that of force was not the last thought of Israel is fortunately made very clear in the beautiful parable of Jonah, with its matchless presentation of divine love and grace for all the world.

This sketch suggests the relation of these prophecies to the life and teachings of our Lord. No fair historical interpreter would say that each prophet had his life in mind and consciously sketched some portion of it; they rather portrayed an embodiment of the divine ideal as it presented itself to them in view of the needs of their age. On the other hand, no one would question that in the person and work of Jesus every distinctive feature of the ideal portrait found adequate and final expression. He was indeed the One for whom they were longingly waiting, " he which should redeem Israel."

It only remains to point out the fact that, if the fundamental Messianic thought was the plan of God for the redemption of the world to himself, we are still in the Messianic age. Even the sacrificial death of our Lord was only the greatest factor brought to bear upon the problem. The ideal of service which he illustrated he handed on to his followers (Luke 22 : 24-27 ; John 13 : 13-17). The mission given to Israel of preaching the good tidings to all men he reaffirmed. Not until the whole earth is Jehovah's will the expectations of the prophets be fulfilled.

Appendix

II

THE RELATION BETWEEN THE MESSAGES OF THE PROPHETS AND THAT OF JESUS

The faith of Judaism at the beginning of the first Christian century was a strange mixture of elements, old and new, prophetical and priestly, native and heathen, true and false. Contradictions and inconsistencies were inevitable. They were primarily the result of the fact that Judaism was not a dead but a living, progressive, growing religion. During its long centuries of development and change it had been influenced by many transforming forces from within and without.

The lack of unity in its faith was the more marked because of the extreme emphasis which was laid on the authority of the sacred writings of the past. As a matter of fact new beliefs constantly found acceptance, but nominally the "scriptures" were the constitution of Judaism and the one acknowledged source of revelation. An absolute unity in these sacred writings was incompatible with their origin, for they were the records of the unfolding life and thought of many different ages and of the various influences, native and foreign, which had moulded the Hebrew race. In the earlier prophets were found Jehovah's

Appendix

declaration: "I desire mercy and not sacrifice," while certain of the later prophets and the priests made the keeping of the law and the observing of its ceremonials the whole duty of men. On many fundamental questions even contemporary prophets did not entirely agree with each other, as is illustrated by a comparison of the teachings respecting the duties of the Jews to the heathen found in the Book of Jonah and the closing chapters of Zechariah.

The teachers of later Judaism, whose sole acknowledged function was to interpret the sacred writings of their race, made the fatal mistake of not recognizing that they contained the blade, the ear, and the full corn in the ear. The modern historical spirit which seeks to interpret the thought of each book in the light of its historical setting was unknown to them. Consequently they failed completely to distinguish between half and full truths, between the essential and the non-essential, between the spirit and the letter. Much of their time was spent in attempting to harmonize real inconsistencies by means of arbitrary and conflicting interpretations which only added to the general confusion.

Under the influence of party strife, hostile contact with the heathen, false systems of interpretation, and the tendency toward extreme ritualism the Jewish race was fast losing sight of its noblest spiritual heritage. The legal books were exalted to a position of commanding authority, while the prophecies were almost ignored. There was

Appendix

an imperative need of a reformer with authority to call back the Jewish people to their highest standards and ideals; but still greater was the demand for one divinely prepared and commissioned to sift out and unify that which was genuine and valuable in their faith and to give it back in living form to them and to humanity as a whole.

In God's providence, John the Baptist raised the cry of reform, reiterating forcibly and effectively the messages of Elijah, of Amos, of Isaiah, and of Jeremiah, while the one, the latchet of whose sandals he was not worthy to unloose, performed the incomparably greater service.

Naturally both were recognized as prophets by their contemporaries. Jesus openly proclaimed John to be a prophet—the most illustrious of that noble order. On no recorded occasion did the master repudiate the title of prophet when it was applied to himself. While it only partially described his real character and mission, it suggested his close and fundamental relationship to the inspired ambassadors of Jehovah. The tone of authority with which he spoke and the directness of his appeals at once distinguished him from the scribes and recalled the words of the Hebrew prophets. The same is true of the forms in which he presented his teachings. From his lips exhortations, warnings, and invective again fell as of old upon Jewish ears. Although the parable, the paradox, and apothegm were originally the product of the sages of ancient Israel, the prophets had often used them, as did Jesus, to impress

Appendix

their message upon the minds of their hearers. While the Master frequently gave to them a new and broader content, the figures of speech most commonly on his lips—the good shepherd, the vine, the light, the way and the divine Father—were those which had long been effectively employed by the prophets.

In the range of the subjects treated the same close kinship is apparent. Respecting the observation of the ceremonial law he had comparatively little to say, and when he spoke it was frequently to reject the teachings of the scribes. In common with the prophets, it was the character and demands of God, the normal development of man, and his duties to God and his fellow-men, which commanded the attention of Jesus. In his teachings, however, there are few references to the political and social questions of the hour. He preferred to lay down broad and general principles. As with the Hebrew sages, the individual, not the nation, was the object of his solicitude. The result is that, with a few exceptions which partake of the local coloring, his messages are of universal application, and do not require interpretation in the light of the age in which they were uttered in order to be understood and assimilated.

In the teachings themselves the relationship between Jesus and the prophets is equally close and the points of difference equally significant. It is the united testimony of the gospel writers and of his recorded words that he

Appendix

was a careful student of the sacred scriptures of his race. From each group of Old Testament teachers—prophets, priests, sages, and psalmists—he gleaned many truths, but naturally the most from the prophets. To the thoughtful student of the Old Testament it is obvious that their inspired messages are the source of most that is unique and eternal in that ancient library. The sages first sat at their feet, and then in their own peculiar way broke the truths thus acquired to the men and women with whom they came into intimate contact. Likewise the priests endeavored by symbol and forms to impress the same great prophetic principles upon the minds of the nation and individual. The psalmists also were disciples of the prophets or students of their written words, who voiced in prayer and song the same undying hopes and the same eternal truths; thus the Old Testament is transfused from beginning to end with the thoughts of the prophets.

It was inevitable that he who was the medium of a fuller and more perfect revelation of the same divine purpose, which had been made known in part to the prophets, should build largely upon the foundations laid by his inspired predecessors. Turning his back upon the traditionalism of the letter, which characterized contemporary Judaism, he exalted to their true position of pre-eminence the spiritual and ethical teachings of the prophets. Again the emphasis was placed not on the external act but upon

Appendix

the motive and the attitude toward God. In reality, Jeremiah and the authors of Isaiah 40 to 55 and the Book of Jonah stand much closer to Jesus than do the teachers of his day. Late Judaism had departed so widely from the way marked out by its earlier guides that bitter antagonism between him and its leaders was unavoidable.

Although we are filled with wonder and reverence because of the originality, the uniqueness, and the perfection of Jesus's teaching as a whole, so fundamental and close is the relationship between it and that of the prophets, that we find in the gospels very few individual truths the germ of which is not discernible in their writings. The relationship, however, is in most cases that of the germ or shoot to the fully developed flower.

Thus to the abstract conception of God as presented by the prophets, Jesus added nothing entirely new. Even his fundamental teaching of the divine fatherhood found frequent expression in the writings of his inspired forerunners. Hosea and Jeremiah proclaimed that Jehovah was the Father of his people Israel (Hos. 11 : 1, 3 ; Jer. 3 : 19; 31 : 9, 20). In a still more intimate sense he is spoken of as the Father of the righteous (Isa. 63 : 16), and of the individual (Mal. 2 : 10). Jesus, however, suffused this rather abstract conception with a wealth of personal meaning, thereby spanning the wide gulf which Judaism has established between God and man. In this way the conception of God was entirely changed ; instead of being

Appendix

regarded as a distant, almost impersonal Being, he was revealed as the affectionate, compassionate Father, whose heart was throbbing with inexpressible love even for his erring, prodigal sons. The truth half grasped by the prophets henceforth became the complete possession of mankind.

Similarly almost every one of the ancient ambassadors of Jehovah had spoken of the coming kingdom of God, but Jesus first clearly defined its nature, extent, and the conditions of entrance into it. Many and varied, and in details sometimes conflicting, were the pictures of that coming kingdom as presented by those inspired men of old, who under the influence of the divine spirit saw from their own individual points of view dimly the outlines of the great plan to be realized in human history. Some would almost limit its privileges to the chosen race; others pictured it as a temporal kingdom with its centre at Jerusalem; while others appreciated its spiritual and universal character.

Unlike the scribes, Jesus never attempted to reconcile the irreconcilable. Quietly but effectively he sifted out the eternal truth from that which was temporal. By emphasizing the essential he rejected by silence the false. Far different from the kingdom of God of popular expectation, which undoubtedly had a certain basis in the old prophecies, was that which Jesus pictured, and yet in the same old writings were to be found most of the elements which

Appendix

together made up the marvellous structure to which we are introduced in the gospels.

The same is true of his definition of the character and mission of the Messiah. It disappointed the fondest expectations of contemporary Judaism, and yet it was in perfect accord with the highest ideals of those prophets, who, like the author of Isaiah 40 to 55, saw most clearly the manner in which God's gracious purpose for mankind must be realized.

Thus the relationship between the teachings of Jesus and that of the prophets was most intimate and fundamental. In an age which was neglectful of their messages, he again gave them that position of transcendent prominence which they deserved. Sifting the gold from the dross, he unified their teachings, and in simplicity and with divine authority he gave them their perfect expression. Taking their truths, he brought them to full fruition in the message of the Gospel. Above all, in his own life he illustrated and made living and personal the abstract principles so nobly presented by the old champions of righteousness. Thus " the word became flesh and dwelt among us."

Appendix

III

BOOKS OF REFERENCE

As in the appendix to the former volume, the books which follow are mentioned for their usefulness to the non-professional student. No attempt is made to give a complete bibliography.

The contents of this volume span about four centuries. For the organized history of these centuries the student may be referred to Professor C. F. Kent's "History of the Jewish People," 1899 (Scribner's), or to the brief but complete sketch by Professor C. H. Cornill, "History of the People of Israel," 1898 (Open Court Publishing Co.). Two conservative surveys of the period up to the adoption of the Law are the excellent little primer by Rev. Professor A. B. Davidson, entitled "The Exile and the Restoration" (T. and T. Clark), and the vivid but judicious volumes of Rev. P. H. Hunter, "After the Exile" (imported by Scribners). An outline for the scientific study of the history and literature of the whole period by Professor F. K. Sanders will be published in 1899 (Scribners).

On the prophetic books it is always well worth while to consult the "Encyclopædia Britannica." The new Hastings "Bible Dictionary" (Scribners) contains the well-digested conclusions of our best scholarship. For a connected sketch of the

Appendix

prophets and their writings, Cornill's "Prophets of Israel," 1895 (Open Court Publishing Co.), is helpful. On the Minor Prophets, Farrar's little book, "The Minor Prophets," 1889, in the Men of the Bible series (Revell), is still useful. Professor Driver's "Introduction to the Literature of the Old Testament," sixth edition, 1897 (Scribners), is a mine of information. For the study of the teachings of each prophet, Professor Kirkpatrick's "The Doctrine of the Prophets," second edition, 1897 (Macmillan), is of great value, but for their interpretation in general no book is so helpful as Professor George Adam Smith's "The Book of the Twelve Prophets," Vol. II., 1898 (Armstrongs). The close student will highly appreciate Nowack's "Die Kleine Propheten," 1898 (untranslated).

For the study of Ezekiel there are four recent and first-class commentaries. That of Professor A. B. Davidson, in the Cambridge Bible series, 1892, is handy, reliable, and suited to the needs of the average student. Professor Skinner, in 1895, contributed to the Expositor's Bible series one of its most notable volumes on Ezekiel (Armstrongs). It is singularly clear and forceful. Bertholet's commentary in the "Kurtzer Hand Commentar" series, 1897 (untranslated), is of the first rank, a judgment also merited by Professor Toy's contribution to Haupt's Polychrome Bible, 1899 (Dodd, Mead & Co.), containing a choice translation and excellent notes.

On Isaiah 40 to 66 the most convenient and reliable commentary is Professor Skinner's volume in the Cambridge Bible series, "Isaiah XL.-LXVI.," 1898 (Cambridge University

Appendix

Press). Professor G. A. Smith's "The Book of Isaiah, XL.-LXVI.," in the Expositor's Bible series, is of standard value, 1890 (Armstrongs). Professor Cheyne's contribution to the Polychrome Bible on Isaiah, 1898 (Dodd, Mead & Co.), contains an independent arrangement, a beautiful translation and some valuable notes.

On Haggai, Zechariah and Malachi, Professor Marcus Dods has written an excellent little commentary for the "Hand-Book for Bible Classes" series. They are satisfactorily treated in the comprehensive works previously mentioned. The problems of Zechariah 9-14 are admirably set forth by Kirkpatrick, pp. 442 ff., and by Smith in the second volume of "The Book of the Twelve," pp. 449-62. The latter mentions the elaborated arguments of Stade and Eckardt in the "Zeitschrift für A. T. Wissenschaft" for 1881-82, 1893, of Robinson in the "American Journal of Semitic Languages," 1895, of Rubinkam and others. These detailed discussions will be of little interest to the average reader.

Joel is admirably treated by Professor Driver, in the Cambridge Bible series, "Joel and Amos" (1897). Articles by Davidson in the *Expositor*, March, 1888, and by Elmslie, somewhat later, are well worth reading. On Jonah there is no single commentary worth mentioning. Hunter, Vol. II., pp. 51-61, and the article by König in Vol. II. of the Hastings "Bible Dictionary," are very helpful studies. The article in the same volume of the Dictionary upon Joel makes a strong presentation of the argument for a pre-exilic date.

INDEX OF BIBLICAL PASSAGES

INDEX OF BIBLICAL PASSAGES

ISAIAH

CHAPTERS	PAGES
13 : 2 to 14 : 23	135, 136, 138–140
21 : 1–10	136–138
24	313–315
25 : 1–5	317, 318
25 : 6–8	315
25 : 9 to 26 : 19	318, 319
26 : 20 to 27 : 13	316, 317
34 and 35	282, 283
40 to 55	149–160
40 to 48	160–179
49 to 55	180–193
56 : 1–8	262
56 : 9 to 57 : 13ᵃ	255–257
57 : 13ᵇ–21	260, 261
58 : 1–12	257, 258
58 : 13, 14	261
59 : 1–21	258–260
60	275, 276
61 and 62	277, 278
63 : 1–6	281, 282
63 : 7 to 64 : 12	310–313
65 : 1 to 66 : 5	279
66 : 6–16	283, 284
66 : 17, 18ᵃ	233
66 : 18ᵇ–24	284, 285

JEREMIAH

40 to 43 : 7	87–91
43 : 8 to 44 : 30	91–94
50 : 1 to 51 : 58	134, 135, 140–145

EZEKIEL

CHAPTERS	PAGES
1 : 1 to 3 : 21	28–31
3 : 22 to 7 : 27	35–40
8 : 1 to 12 : 20	40–46
12 : 21 to 19 : 14	46–54
20 to 24	54–60
25 to 32	72–83
33 to 39	97–108
40 to 48	111–128

JOEL

1 : 1 to 2 : 17	293–297
2 : 18 to 3 : 21	298–302

OBADIAH

1 to 21	69–72

JONAH

1 : 1–3	348, 349
1 : 4 to 2 : 10	349–351
3	352, 353
4	353, 354

HAGGAI

1 : 1–15	206, 207
2 : 1–9	267, 208
2 : 10–23	210–212

Index of Biblical Passages

ZECHARIAH

CHAPTERS	PAGES
1 : 1-6	209
1 : 7 to 6 : 8	212-224
6 : 9-15	224-227
7 and 8	227-233
9	326-328
10	328-330
11	330-332

CHAPTERS	PAGES
12 : 1 to 13 : 6	332-334
13 : 7-9	332
14	334-336

MALACHI

1 : 2 to 2 : 16	244-249
2 : 17 to 4 : 6	249-252

www.ingramcontent.com/pod-product-compliance
Lightning Source LLC
Chambersburg PA
CBHW030425300426
44112CB00009B/856